The Tale Failed Nun

A memoir by Deborah C. Murphy

My fall from grace to madness.

Dedicated to my parent's and Andrew-
you are my rock,
without you I would not be alive.

To Rosaleen, Ita and Margaret -
you make me smile,
which is a miracle.

'Just living isn't enough,'
said the butterfly,
'one must have sunshine,
freedom,
and a little flower.'

(Hans Christian Anderson)

Preface

How did a thirty-eight year old woman, an ex-nun, with mental ill health and a problem walking come to write her memoir? I am not a writer, I am a reader. I have never been a diary keeper, a scribbler of poems, a blogger, nor have I ever desired to write a work of fiction. I read others, novels, mathematics, biographies, philosophy the yellow pages. I read others and bask in their genius, but I know I do not share that brilliance. So where has it come from? Well, I am a broken woman, with a broken mind and a breaking body. I was a nun for eleven years and I was a happy-chappy. Then I encountered a bitch that delighted in seeing my mind stumble and eventually fall over the cliff of madness. To get to the end, I now exist, a failed nun in a bedsit. It is a nice bedsit, with a large room containing my bed, settee, television, clothes and books and many, many pictures. There is a separate kitchen and a separate bathroom. I have nice, friendly, quiet neighbors and the only thing I lack is a dog.

But I am not like other 'normal' folk, I have mental illness. I do not object to the terms crazy, mad, disturbed, unbalanced, demented, loopy, barmy, bats, batty, bonkers, cracked, crackers, cracker-box, a few cards short of a deck, on another planet, insane, nuts, cuckoo, psycho, bonkers, deranged, dippy, flaky, mad as a hatter, mad as a March hare, nutty as a fruitcake, schizo, mentally incompetent, gaga, bananas, non comps mentis, imbecilic, weirdo, and so on, because these terms reflect the inner chaos of the mind. I have become the crazy cousin at family gatherings. As I sit in my bedsit night after night, I am lonely, confused, lost, anxious and unable to cope. I have to get out, I cannot sleep but I need to escape before I take too many tablets and say a final goodbye to this world. I walk the streets of Radcliffe, at midnight, three in the morning, when the stars are twinkling and I try and find some of that most elusive of possessions, peace. I cannot sleep. In the endless waking hours, I watch crap tv, with the subtitles on and the sound turned down real low, and I eat apples, vast amount of apples.

Walking the streets of my home town in the middle of the night is not safe. I come from a town where rough things happen. But, I want something dangerous to happen to me. I want someone to hit me with a joy-riding car. I want to be stabbed. I want my life to end, but I am afraid that if I commit suicide I will go to hell. If someone else takes my life then I have not committed the ultimate sin and yet this miserable existence of mine will be ended. Hallelujah.

So, I write. The pills do not help. Hospital does not help. Talking helps, but this relief does not endure. I keep coming across the advice to write. Get it out! Put your emotions on paper! You will feel better! Well, I will give anything a go. So I write, every day a bit more, tap, tap, tap. Does it help? I do not know really, but it is done now and here is my offering. So this is why I write, not because I take myself to be a gifted author, or I have had an unfulfilled desire to see my name in print, but because I want all the 'stuff' that has turned my brain to a soggy gray mess to be on the outside. Also, those nuns did a lot of damage and I want to warn others...the devil disguises himself as an angel of light.

A little word on failure. What does not kill you makes you stronger. Not true. Some things that does not actually kill you can leave one so broken that strength does not come into the equation. By failure, I do not mean taking up a musical instrument and after five years the violin still sets the local dogs howling. In a sense this is a failure, but it does not define one's life. By failure I mean total and utter failure, not an big red F in an exam, but a U, unclassified, not worthy of a grade. This is what I mean when I use failure plus nun plus me in the same equation. A total destruction of one's identity, one's existence, one's reason to get out of bed in the morning. Je suis une nonne. My deepest understanding of myself, and then I failed and now I am on a slippery slope to nowhere because I cannot see any way out of this mess of my life. This is what I mean by failure.

Contents

CHAPTER ONE

Childhood

Laughter and lollipops...

Happiness,
joy,
hope,
contentment,
these kind of poems -
are meaningless.
Only verse about misery
attracts me,
helps me,
soothes me,
has significance,
anything to say,
teach.
So I will shut up now
because I was a happy child
and poetry about happiness
is pukey.

Me, my brother Andrew and a donkey in Ireland

If we start at the very beginning, it's a very good place to start. In true Dickensian style, I will start by telling you what I am not going to tell you...confused? So was I aged fifteen trying to wade through Dickie's corpus. This is not a memoir of my childhood, but my convent reminiscences and my subsequent spiral into madness. A quick delve into my early years, just to join up some of the dots. Tip toe through the daffodils.

I was a September babe, born in Lancashire to Irish parents. I have three older brothers, and I was somewhat a surprise to my folks as there is a ten year gap between my nearest sibling and me. I grew up in a typical northern town, with rows of terrace houses and the odd mill. My childhood was as normal as can be, we did not change house, I went to the same school that my brother's attended, and I knew all my neighbors and we were the same as everyone else.

I love my working class roots, and have never desired to be 'upwardly mobile', the tory (not worthy of a capital letters) party never beckoned. I am a socialist at heart and I count it a privilege that I am a Manchester lass. When I graduated from Cambridge University, my darling Mum, Dad and eldest brother attended the ceremony and afterward we went to a pub for lunch.

I chose the pub because my parents like simple food, meat, potatoes, and all the restaurants in Cambridge are all fancy-smancy with garlic sauce over everything. I ordered chips, fish fingers, beans and a coke. My brother remarked 'you can take the girl out of Manchester but you cannot take Manchester out of the girl.' Thank goodness.

Note: I know grammatically Mum and Dad begin with lower case letters, but my parents are worthy of capitals, so all you grammarians, keep your hair on, don't get your knickers in a twist, and all those other delightful turn of phrases. I also think it is permissible to adapt words to our own specific usage.

Over the last eighteen years I have lived in some of the most beautiful towns this world has to offer, but nothing warms my cockles as much as my hallowed town and its people. Yesterday I was in a cafe in town and a bloke at the next table shouted over to me, 'Mrs., do you want half my breakfast, they have given me too much.' I declined the offer but it made me smile. I do not drive so I often get the bus and never have I been at the bus stop in Radcliffe when someone has not initiated a conversation. Once when I was in York I smiled at a lady on the street, for no particular reason (except in Radcliffe it is normal to smile at people as we go about our daily business), anyway, I displayed my white nuggets to this woman and she replied in (a very haughty manner) 'do I know you?' Her tone implied that I should not be smiling at strangers. How did the English ever get the reputation as being aloof? Non lo so.

Please excuse me because I go off at tangents all the time. I recall that when I first entered the convent aged eighteen I had to read the works of Teresa of Avila, many times, and she drove me mad, tangent, tangent, tangent. Stick to the bloody point woman. Now I am guilty of the same frustrating writing style, but I do as I do.

Back to my childhood. I was raised a Catholic, so I was baptized in the Church at the end of my street. My parents are the most wonderful people that have ever been put on this earth. As I have stated they are Irish and came to England for work, wed and set up home in Ealing, London. Dad had been in the Irish army and served in the Congo. They both worked bloody hard all their lives. Dad was a heavy goods driver and Mum did a number of jobs including a paper-round when my brothers were young; she would put the papers on top of the pram. I have learned everything from my parents. Dad left the house early and came home late and often worked seven days a week, all to make money for his family. He destroyed his health and now suffers a great deal from arthritis. There was a period as a teenager when I would not speak to Dad, he had not done anything wrong, I was just being a nasty bitch. How I regret that period – sorry Dad.

Then there was Mum. As a child I was Mum's shadow. She worked school hours in a D.I.Y shop. I would sit on the back of her push bike (on the bit where luggage goes) to and from school, and we were content together. I have many memories of my happy childhood, but one that stands out is Mum ironing in the dining room and on the record player was a sing-a-long record for children and I would be dancing about without a care in the world. They were halcyon days.

Me and Mum having fun in the sun

I also remember our coffee table. It was my play companion. My parent's still have this table in their living room and it is an object of beauty, not only aesthetically, but also because of the many happy hours we spent together. I would turn it upside down and pretend it was a boat. I would place a sheet over it and hide for hours. We did not have a garden and so my playtime was predominantly in our house and as I had no siblings of a similar age I often had to use my imagination to have companions to play with, playing school with my dolls was my number one game. I had a very innocent, protected puerility with no worries, truly golden days. I wish all children had such a carefree existence. When I think of the poor displaced children who are refuge camps; what are we doing to these poor critters? Or the desperate situation in Yemen. That we leave children who have no adult to care for them, starving, injured and afraid, prey to pedophiles and people traffickers...these are the children of the future and Tessa May and her cronies should hang their collective head in shame; they are more concerned with the next honors list.

First Holy Communion

Back home. Radcliffe is not the prettiest of towns and there are a number of social issues but this is my home and I love it. Our councilors have raped Radcliffe over the last eighteen years since I went and came back. When I was growing up we had two secondary schools, at one point we even had a further education college. We had a wide variety of shops including a few shoe shops, a sports shop and a thriving mini shopping center. These have all gone and now we have lots of beauty salons and take-away shops. The schools have gone, the shopping center is demolished and all the promises about building a new school have turned out to be as empty the councilor's brains.

We had the most wonderful swimming baths where I spent many happy an hour, now this is gone to be replaced with a shitty imitation...I hope that one of the Radcliffe councilor's reads this and blushes in shame and start thinking more about the good people of Radcliffe and not just their wage packet.

I want to interject here with a dream I had as a child. I have always had lots of nightmares, I am not sure why but that is the way the cookie crumbles. When I was about twelve years of age I had a particular nightmare that I have never forgotten and it frequently jumps into my line of vision. In the dream I was at home, upstairs in my bedroom, everything was normal and I was looking out of the window; this is where things get a little odd because I grew up in an end terrace and my window looked over the back of the house, but in the dream I could see the street adjacent to the gable-end. Sorry if this rather convoluted. On the street there was a creepy man, who was wearing black glasses and he was holding a white cane, but although he gave the impression of being blind I knew he was watching me. Then, as I was watching him, transfixed with fear, I could hear someone coming slowly up the stairs and I knew, without seeing that it was that man, even though I could still see him on the street. I was unable to move and I was consumed with dread that I can still feel this strong emotion as I write this recollection. I have absolutely no psychological training beyond reading *The Road Less Traveled*, but from my ruminations on this nightmare I think it refers to a teacher at my primary school who did not behave with due decorum; and that is all I want to say about this matter.

Yesterday I was sat in a cafe and outside there was a man who appeared to be blind, but when I saw him I freaked-out. I had to move away from the window so that he could no longer 'see' me.

Let's move on. I went to the local Catholic primary school. There is nothing about school that I disliked; I have always flourished better with a routine. I met and made some amazing friends. I was lucky that school work was never a challenge and although I was crap at spelling, for me, life at school was literally wonderful. There was just one shadow which I have referred to in the previous paragraph.

Onwards and upwards, to see what delights lay at the other side of the school gate. I moved, with a number of my friends to a Catholic secondary school and my felicitous life continued. I adored, and the superlative of adored that school. I had structure, friends, fun, challenges and all the other bundle of joys that should be the lot of every school child.

I will just give you a quick resume of my physical appearance. If I had to be summed up in one word it would be 'ugly'. I am the ugly duckling that never grew into a beautiful swan. From the top. I am short, not quite five feet. I have straight mousey brown hair. My face is pudgy, even though as a child and adolescent I was skinny (boney rather than slim). My eyes are tiny and are neither green nor blue but they change color according to the sun. My nose is too big and my lips are too slim. I have what in Jane Austin books would be called a weak chin, that in older women sort of joins with their neck (think Margaret Beckett). The top half of my body is tiny (flat chested and tiny shoulders), but I go wide at the hips; the traditional pear shape. It is practically impossible for me to get a dress as I need an eight on top and a fourteen down below. I have hideous legs. At school when I played sport I would don a gym skirt which would expose my stumpy legs to the world. I have the sort of knees that a maid would have if I went back to the Victorian era and I was employed in a stately home. Now I do wear skirts above my knee and I am under no illusion that this will not bring the boys running, but I do not care anymore. So I have no redeeming physical attributes, but I never, ever, ever minded because I believed that the body I have is the one God ordained for me; now I just think I must have slipped through the evolutionary net.

When I was a child I used to be in a dancing group. I never enjoyed this dancing, well the dancing was okay but I never made any friends and I just did not fit-in. I know that if I asked my parents if I could cease dancing they would have said yes, but I was an uncomplaining child and I went for years and my folks were never aware that I did not relish the whole experience. Anyway, once, when we went to a competition on the Isle of Man and one day a group of us were stood outside the hotel and an older girl said that we were going to have a mini beauty competition. In the end it was a beauty contest just between me and another girl. The older girl was the judge and she went through every part of our bodies, hair, face, body, legs and in every division I got zero and this other girl got full marks. I was mortified, it was the first time I realized I was an ugly duckling. I was only about seven or eight, but thirty years later it still impacts me every time I look into the mirror. Ugly. I have no mirror in my bedsit. I do not even like it when people look at me. Is that the real reason I hid in a monastery?

I have some beautiful friends, I mean physically stunning. My friend Nadia is not only a lovely character and a faithful buddy; she is also drop dead gorgeous. When she walks into a room she catches the gaze of men (and a few women). She has big beautiful eyes and a smile that is something out of a toothpaste ad. She can even play William Tell on her teeth; maybe she should go on BGT? Her body is perfectly proportioned and she has the knees of a lady. I have never, even for a micro-second been jealous of Nadia's good looks because as I mentioned before, God made me and who was I to argue? Also, it was my intellect that always caused me pride (Nadia is also super brainy but that is one of the things that enables us to enjoy each others company). I was able to hold my own in exams and it was my brain that caused me joy not by body. Now that my brain has turned to mush I have neither my body nor my brain to bring me any sort of pleasure. Tell me Pollyanna, what is a girl to do? How can I be glad about this?

Me and my beautiful friend

At this time in my life I was little Miss Positive, for me there was nothing I couldn't do (or at least try) and I smiled and laughed a lot. An incident that will corroborate this claim of my cheery disposition occurred when I was a tiny twelve year old and in my first year of secondary school. One day in February I got a really bad ache in my back. I have never suffered with back problems so it was an unusual occurrence. It was really terrible and no matter how I moved I could not find a position where I could find some comfort. It was difficult to walk and I struggled to make it home.

My Mum phoned the G.P and I went to see her (oh those days when you could actually phone the doc. and actually get to see them without a two week wait). The doc. was crap and just said it was growing pains and told me to take two paracetamol; she did not even examine me. So home I went with no relief. The next morning I could not move my legs at all. The pain had ceased but it left me numb. Mum called out the doc. who happened to be the same ray of sunshine as the day before; again she did not examine me and actually questioned Mum whether I was inventing the illness so I could avoid going to school. Inventing a stomach ache seems plausible, inventing paralysis seems somewhat extreme.

By Sunday morning I was unable to control my bodily functions (wee and poo) as I had no feeling below my waist. Again my parent's phoned the emergency doctor and after he had examined me he sent for an ambulance and I went to the local A&E. Then things flowed, I was admitted to the children's ward, underwent various examinations, moved to a children's hospital, and through all this time I was super positive. I never doubted that I would get better and I did not feel scared for even a nano second; the security I had experienced for the first twelve years of my life sustained me and gave me the courage I required to overcome and battle. Nothing bad had happened to me so I did not suspect that it would occur now. I was like an all-American cheerleader.

I was transferred to a children's hospital, Booth Hall which is now sadly closed. I really liked it. I had my own room with a television. I had numerous visitors, including teachers and friends from school. The food was nice, the nurses were nice, my physiotherapist was nice; all was well in my world. The nurses even nicknamed me 'Smiler' because I was always smiling. It never entered into my little noggin that I would be unable to walk again; all I had was a virus and they go with medicine, right? I was in no physical pain; I was numb from the waist down and went around in a wheelchair which did not seem a big deal to me.

My folks were, as usual, amazing. They both worked full time and every evening my Mum would get a train and a bus to come and visit me. My Dad would drive to the hospital after work and he and Mum would have their evening meal in the hospital restaurant because it was so late by the time they finally arrived home. Neither of them missed a single day. It was Lent and as Catholics my parent's always gave up alcohol, but Mum told me some years later that they were so stressed with my illness that they broke their Lenten fast that year. Every evening when they arrived home they would each have a brandy. I know how strictly my folks keep their Lenten fast that it meant a lot for them to break it. So it was serious stuff. They were stressed, but I had yet to experience that state of being.

The only time I was distressed was one weekend. I went home on the Friday evening and returned to the hospital on the Sunday. Leaving my family and returning to the hospital upset me as I have always been a home-bird. That was the only time I cried and that was the only weekend I went home.

I eventually began to act like a toddler and take a few hesitant steps. Learning to walk aged twelve is a very strange sensation, to take a step with only a minimum amount of control. The day I took my first steps the wonderful nurses gave me a gigantic ice-cream as a celebration. After a while I left the hospital and returned to normal life. I was still in a wheelchair but providentially my lovely school had a lift so I could return to my natural habitat. In the morning a specially adapted mini-bus would collect me from home and take me to school. At school I had a nurse who would wheel me around the school. The only worry I had at this stage is that I would not be walking in time for the rounders season. From a wheelchair I progressed to a Zimmer frame and then to crutches and eventually I was walking unaided but I was incredibly wobbly and the slightest bang would floor me; literally.

This period of illness, although not particularly significant for me at the time did have a major impact on me a few years later. Over the next few years I became physically stronger but it really, really hurt to stand for more than a few minutes and to walk caused pain to shoot up and down my legs. I remember exactly the moment when I was walking from the train station in Heaton Park to a residential home for the elderly where I did some voluntary work. It was a glorious summer day but I thought I was not going to make it to the home as the pain in my legs was too much. These were the days before teenagers had mobiles and I was not sure what to do. Do I just sit down on the pavement and ask a passer-by for help? No, it was one of those incredible eureka moments. I would not now or ever let this beat me into submission. I would endure the pain without medication and I would never limit myself because of this dark friend of mine. I would try, and if I failed and fall flat on my face (literally) so be it, but I would not sit around and use it as a poor excuse to opt out on life.

I can count on a thousand fingers how many times I have fallen. My body was more purple than pink. I call this illness my dark friend because although it has caused me a lot of pain, both physically and mentally (even now I hate people walking behind me because I have a limp and I do not like people to notice); it is also my friend because it formed my character for the good. I am very stubborn and tenacious. I prefer to do something by myself rather than ask for help, or rather I did before I had my break-down, now I would ask a duck for assistance if I thought it would avail me of some mental relief. Ignore the last few years for now; from my teenage years till age thirty five I was one tough cookie. I never told anyone of my physical discomfort. Occasionally I would bandage up my knees to make them stronger as they are wont to give way if I have done too much walking.

I did lots of sport at school but I was really crap. A few times I had to be carried off the hockey pitch as a blow would render my legs useless. Every time I tried to run I would fall so scabby knees were not a great look for a fifteen year old. I was not bothered.

The most embarrassing thing was and is my weak bladder (I blush even to write about it). Even now it is a problem. When a woman has to go a woman has to go; I simply cannot wait. So on days when I am not sure how long I will have to cross my legs before I reach a toilet I do not consume liquid. This was a real problem when I moved to Italy because in that heat it is necessary to rehydrate oneself, but if I was on a day trip to Roma and I had no idea how long I would have to wait for a 'rest room' then I would not drink anything which resulted in heat stroke and migraines. Holy joy!

Aged sixteen I sat my GCSE's and departed from my beloved St. Monica's. The girls of Malory Towers could not have been more distressed than I was to leave school. I went to Holy Cross Sixth Form College but I did not care for it at all. I found it cold and unfriendly. Granted, after St. Monica's anything was going to be a disappointment, but at that point Holy Cross had no community feel and I was more than content to leave it two years later.

Little Miss Positive

The summer I completed my A' Levels (with crap results) I entered a Carmelite Monastery. It was the eleventh of August, I chose that date because I had a devotion to Saint Clare of Assisi. Oh, roll back the years for a moment when I was eight. I watched *The Sound of Music*, with Saint Julie Andrews; undoubtedly the best sing along film of all time. Even though I was only a child at the time I was mesmerized by the habit clad nuns and the beauty of the abbey. I found it all inciting and I have watched that film numerous times over the years. Even though I enjoyed the entire film, when the credits started to roll at the end of the film I had the conviction that Maria was crazy to leave the abbey and marry her captain. How could she? The abbey and the nuns were perfect (or so I thought) and I longed to be there.

Thackeray states that every family has a secret. I think mine is madness. When I gaze at my family tree I see so many people who live on that liminal space between sanity and madness. Was my mind a ticking time-bomb that would eventually snap under pressure? I should have kept my mind wrapped in cotton wool, but I did not know. I felt so strong that it never occurred that the aneurism of madness was a danger. Would I rather have avoided university, avoided reading difficult books, avoided thinking about the 'big' questions? If it meant that I could have avoided depression I would have chosen to not study, have stuck to Enid Blyton, I would have got a job with no stress, I would have stayed at home and never had a relationship with anyone, because although that sounds like a life half-lived, I would have done anything, absolutely anything to avoid madness.

One strange thing I used to do as a child was that I had to count one to four, four times before I could do certain actions. I had to switch the light on and off four times. I had to put my socks on and then remove them and then put them on again. I never mentioned any of this counting to anyone because I intuitively knew that it was a strange thing to do and I did not want anyone to consider me odd. This counting has continued throughout my life and I still do this weird routine many times a day. However I got over the sock and light switch thingies as in the convent I did not have time to carry out these weird routines. I have no idea what this says about me and my mind.

So that is me, zero to eighteen.

How did this Manchester lass end up in a Carmelite monastery aged just eighteen? Well, I always wanted to be a nun. Other girls thought of wedding dresses and coordinating colors, not me, I wanted to be a nun, nothing more, nothing less.

So, when I was sixteen I went to York for a weekend, on a religious retreat. This was a retreat specifically for people thinking about entering religious life. I had seen the weekend advertised in a Catholic newspaper (the online revolution had not yet occurred) and it was with some Carmelite friars (men, not enclosed) at beautiful place named Hazelwood castle. The Carmelite friars sold this castle a few years later and it is now a hotel I believe. So off I tritt-trotted.

I did not tell them when I booked my place that I was only sixteen and when I arrived they were a little shocked that I was so young, but there I was and that was that. It was not a particularly memorable retreat but on the Sunday morning we went for Mass at a local Carmelite Monastery (nuns, enclosed) and this was my first encounter with the community that was going to be my home for six years.

After Mass, all the people on the retreat went to what is known as the parlor to meet the nuns. There they sat, all clad in a traditional religious habit, behind grills which was a tad freaky; I knew that I wanted to be a sister who worked in the community, a teacher, midwife or whatever. Not enclosed, no grills for me.

So the weekend drew to a close, I went home but these bleedin' nuns were in my mind. I visited a number of convents all over England at this time. I discovered many lovely communities of women, doing excellent work, but none of them had the home sign on the door mat, and so my odyssey to find my convent continued. These Carmelite nuns would not leave me alone (I do not mean that they actually hassled me, but they were there, in my consciousness), whenever I prayed about my vocation they came to mind and so I said 'okay God, enough. I will go and stay with them for a while and that will eliminate them as a prospective option.' I wanted to eliminate them from my soul, mind, body and future.

I kept putting this visit off, after my GCSE's, after the summer holiday, after Christmas, after Lent and so on and so forth. Then I took the bull by the horns, and after another year of procrastination, I went to stay with them (on the outside, in what is called the extern – for obvious reasons) for a few days and I found that untouchable thing; peace. That summer I went to stay on the inside for a few weeks and that was my vocation cemented. I had a year of college to complete and then I finally knew where I was going.

So, as my friends went off to university, as I broke my parent's hearts, I walked up the drive to the monastery door and that was that. My Father wanted to drive me to the monastery, but the journey would have been simply horrid, I opted for the train, bus and walk to begin my new life.

Note: I must interject with a note of pronouns and capital letters in connection with God. Now, I have four options when referring to God, firstly, he as is used in the Bible. Secondly, she and give a nod to the feminist community. Thirdly, it, but I find this term rather insulting. Lastly, they, and treat God as binary or as plural which raises a number of problems; is God one or plural? Then, do I use a capital G or go with the lower case? So, I am going to use the pronouns he and she interchangeably, not because God has a gender, but because that is the way English functions. I am going to stick to the capital G because it is a proper name. This use of the language does not represent my theology so please do not read to much into the whole linguistic thingie.

CHAPTER TWO

Carmelite Monastery

Alone with God alone.

How beautiful!

Back to eighteen. I loved my parent's and my family and my friends and my cat and my home and my books and my neighbors and my town and to leave them was like cutting my arms off. Therese of Lisiuex wrote in her autobiography that only those who have left everything and heard the monastery door slam behind them cutting one off from all that is familiar can know the strength of such emotions. I went because I am stubborn as a donkey and I believed that it is what God was asking of me.

Shush.
Silence, quiet, peace.
I sought; I am not sure which,
Communication with the divine
or escapism from people?
I went inside,
hidden and hiding.

I had a poster on my bedroom when I was growing up of Winnie the Pooh and Piglet; they have their backs to the viewer and are holding paws. Piglet is saying to Pooh Bear, 'I would follow you anywhere.' Every day I used to say that to Jesus, 'Jesus, I do not know where this path will lead, but I will follow you anywhere.' The anywhere led to a monastery gate. I would have gone to Mars if I believed that was my vocation...His child. Beloved.

So I rocked up to the monastery door, requested entrance and said 'Adios Mundo!'. I walked around my new home thinking 'what I have I done?' I hated it. It was cold and lonely and dark and quiet and I wanted to go home to where everything was familiar and soft and smelt of fabric softener.

Me as a postulant – aged eighteen

So the next stage of my life commenced. There I was, aged eighteen and alone. Recall, at this time, even though I was only eighteen, I was strong, mentally and emotionally I had the strength of Leviathan.

Oh, the six years I spent at Thicket had a huge wallop on my character formation, in that line of business only the strong survive. You may look at a picture of a contemplative nun and think 'ahh, she looks so lovely and peaceful,' and that may be true, but she is also a woman of steel (Maggie Thatcher has nothing on her) because without such a tough character she will crumble. The contemplative life is beautiful, but it is not easy to spend most of your life in silence and solitude; where every heartbreak is a secret between the nun, God and four cell walls.

I cannot say how home-sick I was; at every moment of every day I wanted to run as fast as my little, pudgy legs could take me back to Manchester. Even now I wonder how a mere eighteen year old stood at it, of course, as always God was the motivating factor for moi; I believed that God wanted me to dwell in those long, bare corridors and so I mopped up my tears, developed a strong backbone and a stiff upper lip and learned to obey. I used to take all the photos I had of my family, all the letters I received, all that connected me to my family and friends and placed them on my bed at night-time. I would lie in the middle of my mattress and place all these items around me. It meant I had to lie perfectly still or the things would have fallen off; I was like a corpse in a coffin with all the things I required to pass through death to the other side.

We could have as many blankets as we wanted and at one point I had fourteen blankets on my bed! It was so heavy that when I got in I could not turn over. Even without the blankets I had to lie still because I had a traditional monastery mattress that is it was stuffed with straw. Over the years the straw had moved which resulted in a ridge in the middle of the mattress, if I turned over then I fell out of bed. Eventually we got rid of these mattresses as mice had made a cozy home in them. These mattresses were so incredibly heavy and we had great fun sliding down the main staircase on them, we actually sat on these mattresses and slid down the shiny wooden stairs and I can confess that we did not keep holy silence that day. After that I got a regular mattress, but I still required all those blankets.

15

The magical mattress staircase. What fun...

I was born Deborah Catherine Murphy. When I was confirmed the name Josephine was adjunct. I have never cared for the name Deborah. A few people call me Deborah, the majority of people use Debbie, some very close friends use Debs (but you have to be of my inner circle to be this familiar) and my family have a number of pet names for me such as pain, gobbin. I like the name Catherine as this was my maternal grandmother's name. As for the name Murphy, well I think it is just stupendous. For as long as I can recall I have thought this name marvelous and I knew I would never change it; in fact I have never grasped why a woman would ever cast off her surname and assume that of her husband, as if she were an item of property.

When I became a nun, aged just eighteen, I was thrilled with the idea of changing my name. In Carmel, I chose my name (in some religious orders the superior chooses the name) and I selected Sister Joseph of the Cross. St. Joseph was my tip-top favorite male saint. I would spend a lot of time meditating on what it must have been like in the familial home of Jesus in Nazareth, with Mary and Joseph, the most perfect parents possible. How they must have loved each other, how calm and serene it must have been with no arguing or self-seeking, how joyous and flooded with laughter as they delighted to be together.

Also, I had assumed the female version of Joseph at my confirmation and so I had long pondered on this foster father of Jesus. Then I added of the Cross because there is a famous Carmelite saint named Saint John of the Cross and I wanted something of his spirit. All that suffering. Apparently, when Jesus appeared to John of the Cross, Jesus said to John something along the lines of, 'John, you have served me so well, what can I do to repay you?' John replied, 'I only want to suffer for you.' (That is the gist rather than the exact words). So six months after entering Carmel, I received a habit and my new name.

The heavy habit

The habit was the old-fashioned one, full wimple, to the floor and HEAVY. The veil was simply enormous; it was as big as a tablecloth and was made of linen. I first placed on my head a quaff which is like a big skull cap that Jewish men don. The purpose of this item was to stop the veil from sliding around the skull. Then on top was the toque (wimple) which covered all the head and neck and hung over the chest, shoulders and nape of the neck. Then came the under veil (yes, there were two) which I secured to the top of my head by way of a large pin. Then two large and sharp pins held everything in place on the shoulders and the veil hung all the way down my back. At first the pins I had were too large for my small frame and whenever I lifted my arm they dug right into the flesh at the top of my arm. I was not too enamored with pain at this point so I complained and I was given smaller pins. The veil however could not be changed for something smaller and it was just so bloody heavy. I only had to endure this veil for a year as I cast it aside when I made my first vows, but for that year I had a constant headache. Then over this, when I was at Mass or at prayer I wore a top veil. Thank-fully, this was a light piece of synthetic material that I again held in place by way of a pin.

I loved my habit, especially in Carmel as it is just beautiful. I also liked the habit in the Servidoras but in neither convent did I ever care for the veil. Priests do not have to wear a veil so why should nuns? They are really, really uncomfortable and I never saw the point of them. I like to feel the wind in my hair.

Let me explain how the parlor worked. It was a rectangle room with a wall down the middle, cutting the room in half. This wall had wooden grills in the middle that permitted the visitor to see the visited and vice versa. When close family or friends came to visit these grills could be removed so that a hug could be enacted. The nun still stayed on one side of the room as the wall was solid for about a meter at the bottom. In the parlor there were just a few chairs, a crucifix on the wall and that was it.

In some convents the separation in the parlor is far more dramatic. When I visited some Carmelites in Spain they had metal grills, horizontal and vertical, which could not be removed. Then on top of this there were spikes sticking out of the metal grills so that the visitor could not get too close without impaling themselves. Then on the nuns side there was a black curtain so there was absolutely no way Jose that anyone was going to gaze on these saintly faces.

It looks good but the sound was not easy on the ear

When I left Carmel, I was sad to also leave my religious name, but as my intention was to return to the religious life, I knew that one day I would assume a new name. So, in Italy what was it going to be? Now here is an odd name; Ransom. Yes, my name was Ransom, or rather Sister Mary, Our Lady of Ransom.

In the Servants of the Lord and the Virgin of Matara (the next religious Order I signed-up for) the tradition is to take a name that is an invocation of the Blessed Virgin Mary. There are literally thousands of these names and each country has their own specific title, for example, Mexico has, Maria de Guadalupe, Ireland has, Mary, Our Lady of Knock, France has Marie d'Lourdes and England has Mary, Our Lady of Ransom. This goes back to the fact that England is a Protestant country and Pope Leo XIII gave this title to England as a way of ransoming the country back to the Catholic faith. As the first woman from England there was never any doubt that this would be my name.

When the time is approaching to receive the habit (in the Servidoras), we all had to submit a list of names to our superior and she was the one who would chose the name and she might even choose a name that is not on the list. A week or so before we got the habit we would be informed of our new religious name. Sometimes there were smiles; often there were tears, and not always tears of joy. It was no surprise that I received Ransom, but sometimes, during the following four years when I was called Rrrrrrrransom a hundred times a day I wished I had gone for a Latino name, easier for the Spanish and Italian speakers to get their gobs around.

We were told that this is the name that God had wanted for us for all eternity, our true name. This leaves me with something of a conundrum. If there is a God, and for all eternity a particular name has been allotted to me; is this name, Deborah, Joseph, Ransom or again Deborah?

The nuns at Thicket Priory were as holy as you could find this side of the clouds and I have nothing negative to write about them. I wish each and every one of them peace, love and joy.

A rapid run through our horarium...I arose to the sound of a bell at five fifteen in the morning. This was always a shock to the system. It was cold in my cell and we each had a jug and a bowl that we filled with water the previous day and some days, splashing this water on my face took the strength of a competitor in the Highland Games. There were many days when I did not wash (gross I know but it was just freezing).

My cell was at the top of the house, it was originally the servant's quarters. The walls were painted an off green and the floor was lino. I had a desk and a hard-backed chair, one shelf for books, a bed, a stool, a wash-stand and a cupboard for my clothes. On the walls there was a holy water stoop and three black and white pictures (religious of course). That was it. No lampshade and wooden shutters instead of curtains. The windows were old and had developed gaps in them over the year, which I tried to fill in with blue-tac.

Sometimes, when I arose in the morning I would just stand in the middle of the cell for a few minutes, lacking the ability to move my limbs or spirit. Prayers were at five forty-five and I was frequently late, having just thrown my habit over my pj's (it was too cold to remove them) and I found myself entering the chapel half-way through the first psalm. Another sister said that she often viewed my tartan pj's...but I was not the only culprit, I often saw the night attire of other nuns poking out from below the habit line at Lauds (morning prayer).

I had four habits. One that I wore most of the year. A really old, tatty habit, with more patches than original material which I wore for really messy, dirty jobs such as painting a room. A very smart habit that was perfect which was reserved for when the bishop came to visit (a few times a year) or if a sister ever had to go to the dentist, hospital or what-not. Then there was my winter habit. Imagine a really heavy, brown blanket; this was the material for our winter habits. It could not be washed as the material would shrink. It was like walking around wrapped in a blanket, which when one is sat in a cold cell in February, is necessary.

So, I was not a natural early riser at that time and as I passed through the ante-choir and saw the dark blue sky and the twinkling stars the verse of St. Paul would pass through my mind, 'the day is at hand, the night is far gone', to which I would reply, when the stars are out, the night has not far gone my friend.

Prayer in the choir lasted fifteen minutes and then we had an hour of private meditation which could be done either in the chapel or in one's cell. Actually it is not correct to claim a cell as one's own. In Carmel, all things are held in common and to remind us of this we never referred to anything as one's own possession, rather we used 'our'. So, my cell was 'our cell'. My habit was 'our habit'. My pen was 'our pen' and so forth. Attachment to things of this world was an anathema.

After meditation at seven we all came back to the choir for certain set prayers to various saints, blah, blah, blah. Then it was breakfast which was a slice of bread, margarine and tea (no coffee). All meals were consumed in silence. On a Sunday or feast day there was either butter (a small cube) or marmalade. There was some cereal, but the milk was powdered and in my humble opinion, horrid.

Breakfast was in silence and usually taken standing up as it was a quick in and out. Then we popped off to our cells to make sure everything was spic and span, collected fresh water to wash with and disposed of the dirty water. Then work. We made altar breads and for the majority of my years in Carmel, it was my job to wrap the boxes of altar breads in brown paper and string and label them for postage. Most of the sisters were involved in the manufacture of altar breads in some way, from cooking to cutting, to sorting to counting and bagging. Each sister also had an area of the monastery that she had to keep clean. I had two corridors, the parlors and the community room. I like to clean.

In the middle of the morning we had prayers and Mass. Lunch was served at eleven thirty and consisted of boiled potatoes, veg and either fish or egg (we were vegetarians). There was always soup, but it was usually grim as it was just yesterday's tea liquidized. So if yesterday's tea was plain pasta (no sauce) then soup was liquidized pasta, which you would have to be very, very, very hungry to consume. I recall one evening I was on dish-washing duty and I saw some old toast in the dustbin, I was so hungry that I almost took the food from the bin to eat. I did not, because I would not eat anything without asking permission and so after I had finished the pans, I went and asked permission from my superior. She told me that I could not take food from the rubbish bin, but she did give me two digestive biscuits to keep me going till the next day.

After meal times, there was a rota for washing-up duty. If I was not on the rota that day I would go to mid-day recreation. This lasted for an hour, the first half was usually an activity such as apple picking, football, music, chopping wood or so forth, where we could chat. Now chat in Carmel is not like just having a good old catch-up with some buddies, we were religious sisters and always addressed each other as Sister X and we were careful about what we spoke about. We kept it all rather superficial, no discussion of spiritual reading or our meditations, no discussion of health issues or what we thought about the fare in the refectory. Careful thinking before speaking was the key. Engage brain before gob.

The second half of the recreation time was spent by oneself and in silence and if need be a sis could have a mini-snooze. At two we had another prayer time, just about ten minutes. After that we could go to the refectory and take a hot drink and with special permission, some bread and marge.

At half-past two the grown-up members of the community had spiritual reading time, but us baby nuns had class (novitiate). At three thirty I donned an apron and a pair of wellies and went to work in the veg. garden. I do not care for gardening. In the summer it was hard, sweaty work digging in a habit and we only had a shower once a week, so all in all I did not care for it. Then in the winter it was wet and cold. Yorkshire is a cold county and it was hard to warm-up for the rest of the day. Also, physically robust I am not, so all in all it was not the highlight of my day. I liked it on a Sunday when I did not have to venture forth to this wilderness.

When I got back into the building, roughly about half-past four, I went back to the packing office and continued playing with the brown paper and string. The evening prayer commenced at five-fifteen and another hour of private meditation finishing at half-past six. Then tea, which was a mini-meal. During meal times we sat in silence, but during one of the food intakes a sister would read out loud from the Bible and then a spiritual book, usually a biography of a saint.

At seven there was another period of recreation, this time we all came together in the community room. For the first thirty minutes we chatted whilst we knitted, sorted altar breads, pealed apples, worked on a jig-saw or whatever was compatible with sitting still and talking with one's neighbor. Now, again there were strict rules to be followed. We spoke quietly to our proximate neighbor, no raising of the voice to speak to a sis on the other side of the circle, there were the same rules about appropriate subject matter as was followed at lunch time. The last fifteen minutes we listened to our superior who would inform us of all sorts of juicy gossip (joke), no, she would tell us about anything in worldly affairs that we should pray about, such as a war. Or about people who had phoned the monastery asking for our prayers. We did not have a television or radio and only took a

Catholic newspaper. Our information mainly came via the priest who came daily to celebrate Mass.

Then more prayers. After this we had time to do our odd jobs, such as preparing the reading at meal times if it was your week on this duty, or catching up with last minute altar bread orders. Otherwise, one was free to write letters, pray or spiritual reading. I could write to my parent's once a month but I never got to phone them. They came to visit me twice a year, around Easter and September and those visits lasted for two hours (2.30pm-4.30pm). Four hours a year.

At nine the last prayer of the day was chanted and lights were extinguished at half-past ten. On a Sunday there was a slight variation on a theme, so instead of working in the packing room I worked in the kitchen, there was no gardening but had more time to read and do what we referred to as 'little crafts'. These were hand-made items such as knitting or painting that the superior could collect together at Christmas and give to the friends of the community. That's all folks!

11th of August 1997 - 11th of August 2003.

So, I stuck it in that place for six years to the day. It was hard, but because I believed it was my vocation then all the blows were prayers I could offer up for the conversion of sinners. I remember on a Friday evening we would spend longer in the chapel praying because of all the people out partying and consequently (in the minds of the nuns) sinning. As I knelt there I always wished that I was one of the party-goers and that the nuns would be praying for the salvation of my soul.

After five and a half years the question of final vows roused its head. I wanted to remain in the convent, but when I prayed about taking vows for life I had no sense of peace. I had to be honest to myself and admit that I was simply too immature to say 'yes' for the rest of my days. I renewed my vows for just six months to give myself more time to think and prayer about my vocation. Leaving Carmel aged twenty-four was painful, but a pain that was part of life, a pain that could be endured because I believed it was the will of God, a pain that was not the end, but merely a step on my journey to heaven via a monastery, a pain that would blossom as I tried to mature and re-enter a convent, a pain that was not depression because all was as it should be. It was not the pain, depression, hopelessness, that consumed my body and mind when I was cast out of the next convent I entered. To leave with one's hope and dignity intact is one thing; to be thrown out with no hope or dignity as if they were merely throwing out the week's rubbish is soul destroying. This is the subject of later chapter; I must try to keep some semblance of chronology.

Whilst I was in the novitiate I was accompanied by three fellow nuns in training, but at different times. When I entered another women joined just a few weeks after me. Now I was just eighteen and very innocent, I had not had much experience of people with 'problems'. At first we muddled along very well, both of us trying to find our feet. Then things got strange and I entered an episode of the twilight zone. She was clearly having some form of break-down but I was slow of the uptake (I tend to be slow on the uptake. Very slow).

This sister and I worked together in the same room, she packed boxes of altar breads and I wrapped and labeled the boxes for posting. It was winter and the room was freezing (no heating) but she kept opening the window next to my work-station and my hands became so cold that I was unable to wrap the boxes. The rule in the monastery was one of silence unless it was absolutely necessary to speak so I did not say anything to her and it never occurred to me to inform my novice mistress. Also, by this stage her behavior was somewhat erratic and I was ever so slightly afraid of her. One day she turned on me with a pair of scissors and boy was I out of my depth. I kept going to the bathroom to run my hands under hot water so that I could work. Then I simply had to shut the window. Naive!

The next day I received a right royal dressing down from my superior who informed me that this novice needed the window open because of her asthma and I was being selfish by shutting it, again I kept my lips tight shut.

We slept on the top floor of the house and her cell was next to mine and all night she would bang on my wall to try and keep me awake (which also meant that she was not sleeping). Then she stopped eating. It was all spiraling out of control. I was so worried about her and I was desperately sad that this woman who I once related to as a comrade in arms, with laughter and easy chatter had become an alien to me. Then one morning we were in the chapel for the first prayer of the day at five forty-five, and whilst we were chanting the psalms she fell to the floor and had an epileptic fit. I was so completely freaked out. Our superior told us to carry on praying whilst she went over to attend to the poor novice as she lay convulsing on the choir floor.

It all started to unravel. In Carmel the section of the Church where the nuns pray is called the Choir. We sat on stalls (individual wooded pews) in two rows, facing each other. The reason for this structure is because we chanted the psalms and therefore the prayer floated from side to side, first one side chanted a verse and then the other. Well, my poor fellow novice decided that one side of the Choir was good (hers) and working for God, whilst the other side (mine) was evil and working for Old Nick. So, as the cook sat on the 'evil' side, my companion believed that the food was poisoned and she started to refuse all food.

Now, eating problems are actually very common in religious life for a few reasons. The desire to control the flesh leads one to fast from food. In a life where every moment of one's day and night is ordained by another being, then food is one area of one's life that can be chosen and controlled. The female flesh in particular is deemed to be weak and evil and therefore women religious must work hard at controlling the baser desires and food plays a significant role in this battle.

After that I never saw her again whilst I was in the monastery. I was just informed that her parent's had come and taken her home. When I took my first vows (which should have been her profession day as well), she sent me a beautiful bunch of red roses. I missed her; not the latter her, but when we were first companions. We never mentioned her again in community. Only once did my novice mistress mention her to me in private; apparently this woman's psychiatrist wanted me to give my account of living with her so that he could understand her illness more, but my novice mistress made the decision for me and that was a no.

My side of the choir

After I left Carmel I met her only once at a party thrown by another woman who was also an ex-

22

nun. My fellow novice told me that she no longer went to Church and was struggling with psychological illness. That was the only time I have seen her post- Carmel as she said that she did not want to see me again; not because of anything that I had done, but because I reminded her of a really awful period of her life that she wanted to put behind her and hopefully forget.

Next novice. My next companion was such a great confrere and we got on so well. I had two novice mistresses whilst I was in Carmel. My first superior was gentle and I got on with her very much, but my second mistress was stern and she scared the whits out of me. I felt that she hated me and nothing I said or did was ever right. Every afternoon we novices had classes in various things such as scripture, Church teaching, and spirituality and so on. My first novice mistress would enter the novitiate and she would smile and say hello, then we would stand and say a prayer to begin the class and the class proceeded in a relaxed and cheerful manner; not so with number two. She would enter the room, no smile, no eye contact. We would stand and say our prayer and then we would proceed with us two novices reading from a book, taking it in turns. There was absolutely no interaction unless it was to be rebuked. This made my companion and I very close because that happens doesn't it? When two people are together in a conflict situation they often lean on each other for support.

Sometimes I heard the novice mistress shouting at my friend and I knew that she would eventually leave as she was a strong woman and would not endure such harsh treatment forever. I was so upset when she left and now I was on my own and had no cushion to ease the blows. One of the reasons I left Carmel was that I suspected that one day my novice mistress would become the mother superior and then she would be able to destroy me completely.

However, one very uncomfortable thing happened not long after this last novice left. My Mamma reads the sort of female-oriented magazine where people write a story about something dramatic that has happened to them, such as going to the toilet and having a baby pop out! Well, my ex-fellow novice wrote her tale about being in a monastery and she did not portray it in a good light; there were also photographs. Of course this worried my Mum because her daughter was still in the convent and she was disturbed about what was happening to me inside the high walls. Nothing I could say could allay her fears because the account in the magazine was all completely accurate, but I wish my Mum had bought another periodical that week.

Then we were one. It was like something from the pen of Agatha Christi, or perhaps more appropriately, Father Brown.

Actually, from my lay-person's psychological view, all the convents I have had dealings with, have had members of the community that had varying degrees of mental ill health. There was another nun in Carmel who had a massive and complete breakdown. She cried most of the time, her behavior was extremely erratic and in the end she was taken into a psychiatric hospital. In the way that we did not discuss personal issues in Carmel so I do not know the ins and outs of her poor situation. I do not recall exactly how long she remained in hospital, but it was quite a while, and even when she returned to the monastery she still appeared very ill to me.

The day she went into hospital my novice mistress (the second one) came to the novitiate to tell me. I was the lone novice at the time. Well, my novice mistress told me and I was duly shocked. My novice mistress actually came towards me to give me a hug, but the look of shock on my face must have made her change her mind, she stopped mid-step, turned on her heel and exited the novitiate. I do not know what shocked me the most, a sister going into hospital or my novice mistress trying to give me a hug!

In fact it was this nun (the one had suffered the major breakdown) who made me finally decide to leave Carmel. What happened was this. I was working in the kitchen one afternoon and one of my duties was to take the bin bags from the kitchen out to the large refuse containers outside. Now, in Carmel everything runs to clockwork, and I mean everything and always, never a deviation. Jobs were always done in the same way, at the same time and this resulted in sisters very rarely having to communicate with each other and silence reigned supreme.

This nun, who had returned from hospital, but was still very ill, was in the kitchen with me and she suddenly turned and asked me in a rather raised tone where I had put the bin bags. I was shocked, startled, for a sister to break the silence in such a manner, and at the question itself, because where would I put the bin bags except where I put them every day, for years and years? I was frightened and I tend to run from conflict so I just stumbled a reply and left the kitchen. Oh my giddy aunt, she followed me and in the corridor (where talking was NEVER permitted) she grabbed me by my arms and began a rant that made no sense, or at least I could make neither head nor tail of it all, gibberish. I managed to detach myself and I ran into a near-by toilet and locked the door till I knew she was gone (or at least I hoped she had).

Then I went to my novice mistress and informed her what had happened. Now, I know this poor sister had mental ill health, but I was informed that because I was younger than her in religious life, and I was just a novice and she was a sister in final vows, I had to apologize to her, even though I had not done anything wrong (and neither had she because of diminished responsibility) but I felt I had no reason to say sorry. I felt that to say sorry for the sake of peace would be a lie and of course I was not going to lie and so I refused to be penitent. A significant amount of pressure was put on me to say the magic word. Looking back, I should have seen the bigger picture, humbled myself and ask this mentally ill nun to make amends.

Even though, looking back this was not a particularly significant event, it was this that finally made me realize that I was not mature enough to stick at that vocation. Not my time of life as they say...

I then entangled myself in something that I regret. I was still very young and I had no one to lent on so I leant (wrongly) on another sister. Particular friendships were not permitted in Carmel as we were there to pray, suffer and live alone with God. Alone with God alone was the aim. This other sister was the second in command and she had been in the convent for over twenty years and therefore she should have know better.

On a purely natural level we got on very well, but we should never have become so close. When I look back with hindsight I understand that it was an inappropriate relationship, but I was alone, scared and trying to cope with the politics of a monastery that I was too immature and dull to grasp.

When I was at university this nun (whom I had got close to) told me that she was planning on leaving the monastery; I was horrified because although I had left, I had not taken my final vows and was free in the eyes of the Church to leave, and I was still at the time a hundred percent orthodox Catholic. But here was a nun in final vows and I was horror-stricken that she was going to leave and I told her that I thought she should honor the commitment she had made. However, left she did and came to live in Cambridge. She wanted us to have a closer relationship than I ever wanted and when I left university I also left her and our friendship died. For me it was always purely platonic, she wanted something sexual and that was never going to happen for me. At this stage I still wanted to return to religious life and she was set on a different tangent. I regret that we ever became such close friends, especially if this somehow contributed to her leaving religious life, but as Oscar Wilde claimed, 'experience is the name we give to our mistakes.'

Back to Carmel. Then a third novice came and I again had to play the bad cop to her good cop. In the eyes of my superior everything she did was amazing, and everything I did was about as welcome as a rotten egg for tea. There was no way I could be anything but in the wrong. Therese of Lisiuex wrote that if one if going to lose the battle it is best to run from the battle field. Carmel was a battle that I was never going to end in my victory, so I left. I had initially extended my vows for an extra six months, but I knew that just as I was right to enter Thicket aged eighteen, it was now right for me to leave those hallowed walls aged twenty-four. The idea was that I was just taking some time-out, but I knew I would not return and those first few weeks outside the monastery I experienced the same home-sickness that I had endured when I initially left my family. It had been my home for six years, a quarter of my life and how I struggled adjusting to the world I now re-entered.

Everything in Carmel is surrounded by silence, slippers instead of shoes, restricted speech, the way we shut doors, the way we placed a pair of scissors on a table and the world I was now thrown into was all topsy-turvy; noise, noise, noise, this seemed to be the idea, constant music, mobile phones, shouting, clip-clop high heels, talking ten to the dozen at meal times. It was as though I had entered *Orwell's 1984* and the talk was incessant. At meal times I had no idea what was going on as people spoke across each other, usually in a rather raised tone. However, when I left the monastery I went to live in a lay community and they held me secure whilst I adjusted to England 2003. I am very grateful for those beautiful souls that saved my sanity.

I have never returned to visit Carmel as I think it would be rather awkward and painful. In the Catholic world there is shame attached to leaving religious life, it is like a divorce even though I was not in final vows. That experience has taught me not to judge other people because we never know another person's life story. Also, I still wanted to be a nun, it was just a matter of where and when. In no way was my faith altered, I loved God as much as I ever had and I had hope in my heart and soul. I had expected to be miserable for a fairly long duration of time, but after a few weeks I felt really joyful. So I had faith, hope, joy, peace, love, charity, strength...what could hold me back?

Aren't smells are so evocative? As the great Victor Hugo claimed, 'nothing awakens a reminiscence like an odor.' Yesterday it was tipping it down here in Manchester and on the bus the windows were condensed. If you have never been on a public bus you will have no clue what I am talking about. The water runs down and if you have the joy of having a window seat the water will conclude its journey on your clothes. When I was smaller in stature my nose would be near this waterfall and there is such a horrid smell. Now that I have grown (4'11) my nose does not have to endure the window smell, but it got me thinking about the effect of smell.

When I was at primary school 'Margaret Thatcher the milk snatcher' had yet to wave her wicked wand and take away this source of nutrition. Yet, I detest milk. I could never drink a glass of milk, the smell of it I find revolting. This stems back to milk at school. The little milk bottles always smelt yucky and sometimes we would not be given the milk until the afternoon by which time the milk was warm. I can drink milk if it is heated and in things, like tea and coffee, but not by itself.

Now, I think our children should be given milk and orange juice at school, because I know many families where nutrition is not a key factor at meal times.. All you middle class, National Trust card bearing, yoga and Pilates folk who feed their offspring home-made bread and cucumber sticks with humus should come and hang out in the playing areas of Radcliffe and see kids who have shoes with the soles hanging off and with a face so pale that it makes you doubt they have any iron in their bodies. So the bloody tories think they are saving a pittance by not giving free milk and juice, but this is blinkered view, because these children will cost a fortune to the NHS as they develop without the necessary vitamins.

The Carmelite monastery had a particular smell which is unique to monasteries. It is a clean smell, but the clean that does not use contemporary cleaning products, but the old fashioned stuff of soap flakes and polish. I suppose this is what houses smelt like sixty years ago before all the sprays and fancy cleaning products appeared in our supermarkets. I love that smell. I have stayed in other monasteries and they all have the same smell. I have tried to recreate that lovely smell in my home but I have failed. I wonder what the secret is?

Now the convent in Italy did not have that smell even though it was a monastery because we were not enclosed and quite frankly it was not spotless, it was indeed far from spotless. We did clean every day but there were so many of us and we were young and spent a lot of time running around the place that dirt was not eliminated on a daily basis. The convent in Ireland also did not have a particular smell. I suppose this is a beneficial thing so that I cannot enter a building and be reminded of either Italy or Ireland.

When I was a kid, Good Friday was such a solemn day, kept with absolute rigidity. I recall one Good Friday, I was only about six or seven and my brother opened a tin of ravioli (the yummy Heinz one that I loved as a child but now appears not quite so appealing), put it in a pan and started to heat it. In walked my Father and picked up the pan and cast the contents into the bin. Now my Daddy is not one to waste ANYTHING. He could have told my brother to put the ravioli in the fridge till the following day, but such was the solemnity of the day that meat could not be consumed that it was thrown away never to serve human consumption.

We all 'gave up' something for Lent. For me it was sweets and the like, for my folks it was alcohol. As a good Irish family we could break this fast on St. Patrick's Day (but not for other major feasts such as the Annunciation), but I think my parent's went dry for the whole of Lent. My sweet deprivation was not actually a serious trial for me as I did not have a sweet tooth as a child (how things have changed, now I could keep Cadbury's in business if I were a millionaire). As I developed as a Christian I came to realize the role of the fast and I began to take it more seriously. I hated tea as a child and so one Lent I made a commitment to drink one cup of tea a week; but aren't we funny buggers, because by the end of Lent I actually liked tea so much that in consequent Lents I swung the other way and gave it up.

This was the time when all shops closed for Good Friday and no footie matches were played. When only the emergency services worked and there was no pleasure palaces open to pass the time. The only word for it is solemn. In the evening all the Christian Churches in my town congregated outside the Catholic Church and we walked in silence through the town with two strapping fellows carrying a stark wooden cross at the head. The roads were closed and the police gave us an escort. When we arrived at the center of the town, there were a few prayers and then we dispersed in a mood that cannot be described. It was not like a funeral where we would have a good catch-up afterward over tea and sandwiches. It was not like Christmas day because although no one was working, there were no presents, no feast, and no celebration. It was not like a national disaster because it was deeply personal, Jesus was dead because of MY sins and that made me hang my head in shame and sorrow. It was like holding your breath for twenty-four hours. Christ was hung on the rood but this was not the end; we still had the long waiting game of Holy Saturday and the joy of the resurrection on Easter Sunday, when the bells would peal with jubilation. In three days we went through every emotion.

Good Friday was not what I was expecting in Carmel. I thought it would be a day given to fasting and prayer; I got the first part correct but I was ever so wrong on the second. Now the monastery where I lived was one of the most beautiful building man has ever built in this green and pleasant land. It was big, really big, really, really big and it took a lot of cleaning. So early in the morning we arose to the sound of the matraca. Normally a bell was the waking call but the matraca sounded like a wooden box with bones in it and when it sounded it was an eerie noise that left one in no doubt that this day was unique in the year. Some sisters had been up all night praying but as a novice I was not permitted to stay awake and I was not so virtuous that I wanted to be.

In the dark before dawn we said our prayers in the chapel, but the morning meditation was skipped and replaced with cleaning. Needless to say that absolute silence was maintained to such an extent that one year I had to ask a sis a necessary question and she refused to answer me. Not a nook or cranny was left unattended. All the walls were swept and washed and sometimes painted. The numerous statues were examined more closely that a surgeon would probe a human body. The windows shone and the woodwork glistened and the sisters got sore knees and tired bones.

At lunch and tea we were served a homemade soup and bread. Even though this does not sound very much, it was a thick soup that was actually tastier that the food we consumed the other three hundred and sixty four days of the year. Then back to work, to make everything spic-and-span for the resurrection. I have never been a physically strong character and this day took its toll on my body. Please recall that all this was done in a thick habit and quite a few layers on the head.

As the monastery was built as a stately home it had a truly magnificent staircase; Downton Abbey eat your heart out! As the day drew to a close and all mops had been cleaned and returned to their appointed places the nuns returned to our cells and awaited the passage of time when we could rejoice in our spotless monastery. I dwelt up in the servant's quarters and so I had another set of stairs to climb before my bed welcomed me, but my body gave out at this point. I could not do it. I could not walk another twenty steps. However, it was a day of suffering and in Carmel one had to be seriously ill before one could seek any sort of relief, it never entered into my head to ask for help. I got on my hands and knees and crawled to my cell and even though I was thoroughly filthy I removed my habit, did not so much a splash a drop of water on my flesh and collapsed on the bed where slumber overcame me at once.

When I awoke in the night for the toilet I still had to crawl to the bathroom and pray that my strength would be restored by the following morning. We had a chamber pot in our cells to use in the middle of the night, but the walls were so thin that I was able to hear the sister in the adjoining cell which freaked me out so I never used mine and I always sneaked to the toilet. I am not so precious now and would not hesitate to use a pot in the wee (get it?) hours of the night.

This year, my first outside the convent, as an unbeliever I did not fast during Lent. It is not a time of dieting, but a time of denying the body for the sake of the soul, so what would be the point? I do miss the solemnity of Good Friday as now we no longer have the walk through the town (lack of police), shops and entertainments are open, even football matches are played. I miss the time of reflection, the wait before the dawn, the growth of hope and joy. All in all I miss Jesus but it is what it is; acceptance of the truth. I miss my faith – or what consisted of my faith. Maya is an Eastern word that refers to something as an illusion; that is what my faith was, an illusion and now I realize the joke is one me.

The situation of Carmelite monasteries in England (Wales, Scotland and Ireland) is sad. There is a gross lack of vocations to fill these beautiful buildings. I can look around me and philosophize about the decline in religious vocations in Europe, but I have no idea what the answer is. Nuns no longer seem relevant in a society that has free education, social care, the NHS, all the sex and abuse scandals have caused a twist in considering nuns and priests to be people of God to possible sadists

27

and pedophiles. Anyone who has watched *The Magdalene Laundries* cannot help but consider nuns in a new light, and not a positive one.

Logically, I think that most of these convents will follow the pattern of the seminaries and eventually close with maybe one Carmelite monastery in the north, one in the south and one each in Ireland, Scotland and Wales. In the past it was normal for Catholic girls to think about entering a convent, in today's contemporary society, a woman has so many options open to her, married, not married, living with a man, living with a woman, living with a dog, becoming an astronaut, doctor, journalist, nurse, waitress, land-lady, banker, prime-minister, no limits baby!. I remember visiting a convent when I was at university and one of the nun's was so surprised that I lived by myself and not with my folk's. Imagine, an unmarried woman living by herself! Also, another nun was discussing her niece and I asked her if her niece had any children and she replied, 'oh, no, she is not married yet'. How different she would find the world if she broke through the grills.

I have always found that God's mercy has manifested itself in practical ways in my vita. So, although I was sad to leave Carmel, I had no doubt that I was taking the right path. I loved my life in Carmel, but I found no pax when I thought about making final vows and so I had to leave. The choice was stay or leave, no other options were available. I was of course distressed to exit and leave behind my religious family of six long years, to leave behind the life I had formed, but my faith was strong and I knew that I would return to the religious life at some point. This was not forever, just for a while. Arevoir.

Before I entered Carmel I had made some friends who now worked voluntarily for a charity and so this is where I went on the eleventh of August 2003. This charity was a Catholic organization that went around England and Wales working in Catholic schools spreading the faith. So I joined a wonderful group of three women and four men, two mini-buses and a hectic schedule. It was the opposite of what I was used to, constant noise, chaos, travel, but it was a wonderful year and I am grateful that I was given this opportunity.

CHAPTER THREE

Youth 2000

So I took up my place in Leeds which was to be my base for the following year. We had two houses, one for men and the other for women. There was an office where all the practicalities of our life were sorted (well, sort of sorted) and a small chapel where we prayed. Ironically, when we were at home, we usually went to morning Mass at a local Carmelite monastery, which was a comfort for me, home from home. However, life was certainly topsy-turvy and it took a while for me to adjust.

When I left Carmel after six years there were mobile phones everywhere. On the bus or train I was unable to think because of the unremitting sound of chatter, chatter, chatter and most of it sounded rather banal, just an excuse to keep talking. The thing that shocked me the most were the incredibly personal details that people just gabbed into the ether; it was like watching a film with my Mum and Dad where some people take their clothes off, I did not know where to look! Once I was on a train and the young woman in front of me was having a phone conversation where she was giving rather a lot of intimate information and in a raised tone of voice so it was impossible not to hear. After about five minutes, and elderly woman stood up and said to this sex-charged female, 'I do not want to sit here learning all about your sex life.' The young woman instantly hung up her phone and the rest of the carriage clapped.

When I entered Carmel in the summer of 1997, only one person I knew had a mobile phone. This was a lad from school, who one day when we were in a meeting about something or other when this ringing came from his pocket. We were all so shocked when he whipped it out and had a mini conversation. When he told us that it was just his Mum asking him to bring home a loaf of bread we laughed, because the idea of using a mobile phone was a momentous thing and it stuck us as ridiculous that it would be used for such a banal subject as a loaf of bread.

Mobile phones disturb me. Not that people talk loudly about things best said in private, but the amount of time that people waste using them. I love philosophy, and I believe that every person has the capacity to be a philosopher, because we should all think about the meaning of life, where we have come from, where we are going, God, religion, ethics, war, peace, abortion, euthanasia, women's rights, men's rights, pig's rights, in short, everything. Aristotle (my favorite philosopher, if I was alive in ancient Athens I would have been a complete groupie), anyway he stated that *'All people by nature desire knowledge.'* It is innate to our nature to seek the truth and ponder on the profound meaning of life. However, everywhere I look people are agog with their phones. I am sat in a cafe at the moment and there is a couple near me, who are chatting amiably, but on another table there is another couple and both of them are just gazing silently at their phone. Perhaps they are texting each other?

So, when that year drew to a close I had to take another step on this crazy-pavement of my life. I wanted to go to university, but it had been a long time since my A 'levels and I thought it a wise idea to ease myself back into the academy. There was a Catholic college based in Oxford that offered a year of free study to women and men who for various reasons had stepped off the academic path and now wanted to resume this trajectory. I applied, got a place and hi, ho, hi, ho it's off to Oxford we go...

CHAPTER FOUR

Plater

Plater had been founded as a Catholic worker's college, in the early part of the twentieth century as a way for poor Catholic working men to study. As time progressed it was deemed surplus to requirements and so the college evolved as a place for women and men from any faith and none to return to education and possibly progress onto university.

We were a smallish community made up of people from every background imaginable, people who wanted to change careers and needed to retrain, those who had been in prison and were seeking a second chance, older folks who finally had the time to study, ex-addicts and ex-nuns (I was not alone), what a hotchpotch we were. It was a residential college and was free, tuition fees, room and board. All our housing and needs were provided and we lived on a really pretty little campus and myself and others flourished in that place.

We were like a cake,
take eggs, flour, butter and chocolate chips,
mix well, bake and serve.
Take some women and men,
ex-convicts and ex-nuns,

                    gay, straight,
                  Catholic, agnostics,
          clever, not so bight, and everything in between,
                black, milk and white choc-chips.
                   Mix well, bake and voila!

There were just three areas of study, law, psychology and theology. This resulted in us all becoming very close and friendly. I had a wonderful tutor and my classes were a complete joy, my brain was stretched and my heart flourished. It was still a Catholic college and therefore there was a chapel on the campus with daily Mass, although I preferred to go to a local Church just five minutes away as I enjoyed becoming part of the wider community.

That college was truly outstanding and gave so many people a second chance. The Catholic Church sold the college the year after I left which was just an act of money grabbing. It turned into a college for foreign (rich) students who want to study English. The Church tried to put a positive slant on this act of treachery and stated that they would use the money raised from the sale for bursaries, but when I ponder on all that was lost by the closer of Plater it makes me angry; money before people. Talk about selling your soul for ten pieces of silver.

As I have previously mentioned I had such a great tutor. He was very well educated (he was finishing his PhD whilst I was his student), interested in theology as a living subject (he is a vicar), interested in his students as mini-theologians, was able to actually teach and I am grateful to him for encouraging me, pushing me, nurturing my dormant intellect and challenging me to think outside the box. Thank-you Dr. Teal. I loved that year; I found the course material interesting but not particularly difficult so I had a lot of free time. I had a part-time job at the local petrol station so that gave me pin money and more importantly than anything I made a precious friend that year.

My friend Chris is the most generous person I have ever had the privilege to encounter, he helped those who were slightly mis-fits (including me!). We were about the same age; he was very good-looking and laughed with the innocence of a child. There was never anything romantic between us, even for a nano-second, we were just good friends. People sometimes thought that there was some romance but there was not. On a Sunday we would go to the hospital after Mass to take Holy Communion to those patient's too sick to go to the chapel. We often went around together and people would think we were a couple which made us laugh.

Now Chris is married and although I have never met his wife I know that she must be an incredibly special person to be worthy to have C. as a hubby. They have also been blessed with a nipper and with C. as his Daddy he is in safe hands.

At the end of my year at Plater I decided to go to uni. but I wanted to study to become a midwife. I had the idea that as a qualified midwife I could enter a missionary order and as a sister I could go to a developing country and make a difference, especially to the life of women. However, my tutor had different ideas. On my application form he wrote my reference and I can recall exactly what he penned about me; 'I think Deborah should study theology at a prestigious university'. So no surprise when I was rejected for a nursing course. At the same time my theology tutor strongly suggested that I apply to Cambridge, so I did and I got a place...so that was that. Oh, la, la. What a wonderful period of my life was just about to begin.

CHAPTER FIVE

University 2005-2008

There is no great genius without a mixture of madness.
(Aristotle)

In the summer of 2005 I headed off to Cambridge where I was to study for the next three years; they were glorious, happy, fulfilling, laughter-filled, friendship-filled, magical, challenging, stimulating days and I felt as though I had gone to an island where all I had to concern myself with was study (which as you might of gathered brings me joy – apart from Hebrew, but that is in year two so I will come back to that). Developing my brain and soul.

I realize that these next few pages are going to sound a tad nauseating, but I am sure that many people experience university as a charming period of their lives; so little responsibility and so many jollies.

I went to live in a gorgeous house that was originally set up by nuns as a hall of residence for Catholic women who were studying at the university. It is still a Catholic house of studies but the nuns are now a thing of the past. This house is the Catholic house of what is the Cambridge Theological Federation, which is made up of various colleges of differing Christian denominations who study together at Cambridge. The majority of the students at these colleges were training for ordained Christian ministry. Catholic priesthood is still a discriminatory affair with only those members of the population who have the privilege of a penis are deemed worthy of ordination. As the Nobel laureate Wangari Maathai stated, 'The higher you go, the fewer women there are.' How many women in the Vatican (apart from the cooks and cleaners)?

Let me explain the foundation for this discrimination...

The Catholic Church has what is known as Church law and Church discipline. Church law is fixed and cannot be changed, whereas Church discipline is able to be altered. The restriction of the ordained priesthood to men comes under Church law so that the Church claims that it can never be altered. Married priests are a matter of Church discipline and therefore it can be changed. In some Catholic rites such as the Byzantine rite married priests are permitted. So women, there is no way as a Catholic woman you are ever going to don an alb...just get out your duster and keep polishing those pews.

I have yet to hear a solid argument for the rule that Catholic priests must be men. Tell me, please tell me, what difference does having one penis and two balls make to a person's ability to be a holy priest? I think all the sex abuse that has riddled that Church shows that the answer is that it makes no difference. Why do Catholic women, who make up the majority of bums on pews put up with this terrible state of affairs? Why are women unworthy? Oh, because Jesus only chose men? So, he also chose fishermen therefore should all priests have spent time in a trailer boat? This is the twenty-first century and this is sexual discrimination, it is that simple. The law of the land should not permit such discrimination to continue. I do not understand why there is not more of a battle. That is not my club anymore, so it is also not my battle. I think the foundation of theology should be logical and this is just illogical.

So, this house in Cambridge was made up predominantly by Catholic women from all over the world. Some men were permitted to be residents, but only in one area of the house and they had to be over twenty-one, so it was just a few doctorate students. We also had a few Muslim women who lived on the female only corridor as this gave them the freedom to wander about without their veil.

It was incredibly interesting living there. One evening I went into the kitchen and one of the Muslim women was singing the Salve Regina which is a traditional Catholic hymn to Mary. I was so surprised to hear this devout Muslim singing a Catholic hymn, and in Latin no less. I asked her how she knew the prayer and she told me that before coming to Cambridge she had studied in Rome where she had lived with a group of Catholic nuns. Every evening after tea the nuns would sing the Salve Regina and she had just picked it up.

One evening this woman and a Catholic student gave a talk based on the role of Mary in the Koran and the role of Mary in the New Testament. It was one of those harmonious moments where all present came with a willingness to learn from the other. I have never believed that all people must become Christian in order to go to heaven, after all, why should a child born in Buddhist Tibet not be loved by God in the same manner as the child who lucky enough to be born in Catholic Spain? Anyway, as I sat there that evening, listening to these two intelligent women, I thought, 'if we were all like this, then we could live in peace.' No more wars now that is something that Church should be fighting for, not the subjugation of women.

I was often the only Catholic in my class and I had to fight a few battles, but it was exhilarating. I could feel my brain expanding as it absorbed new ideas. I loved all my classes and never has life been so good.

I made a good friend at university called Kate, she was studying to become a minister in the United Reformed Church (which she now is). We had a number of classes together and I really enjoyed her company. Sometimes I went early to class so that I could join in with morning prayer in their chapel. On a Thursday morning we had prayers in our own chapel with Adoration of the Blessed Sacrament. The Catholic Church teaches that the host at Mass is not just a mere symbolic sign of the presence of Jesus, but is ACTUALLY the presence of Jesus, body and soul, humanity and divinity, or so the story goes. I told this to my friend Kate one day, and her quick glib was, 'well, I can give you a piece of bread to look at.'

At the time I dismissed the comment, as the only Catholic in the class I was more than familiar with such remarks, and I was strong in my faith as so it was neither here nor there. In fact, I have also heard such comments from within the Catholic world; the Catholic seminarians at a northern college (now shut) the priest-students referred to Adoration of the Blessed Sacrament as 'wafer watching.' Now I look back on the hundreds, no thousands of hours I sat in a chapel and prayed to a piece of bread.

My Cambridge College was Robinson. I was not keen on dressing-up fancy for my evening meal, so I rarely went there for grub. Robinson is the youngest of the Cambridge Colleges and its architecture is rather contemporary. The gardens are stunning and the chapel had a famous Piper window.

The glorious Piper Window, Robinson College, Cambridge University

So goes my day. I arose early (after six years in Carmel, this was just habitual). Had a shower, breakfasted, prayed and went to the eight o'clock Mass at the local Church. I swanned around the streets of Cambridge on my bike. I got through three bikes in three years, as one was stolen and I was involved in two accidents. As I peddled my way around I often felt as though I was in a film. Here I was on my bike with my wicker basket, cycling along the tree lined streets with the lamp posts directly from Narnia and not a car in the world. I was not aiming to be Chancellor of the Exchequer; my aim was to be a nun so I did not burst a gut getting a first (I ended up with a 2:1). I was so happy with not a hint of depression. So happy. If only I had appreciated it more at the time.

Of course I had the normal ups and downs. In my third year my marvelous Mother got cancer which of course was horrific, but I was such a positive creature than it never occurred to me that she would not make a full recovery. She has made a full recovery.

After 8am Mass I went straight to my first lecture. In Cambridge the lectures tend to be in the morning with tutorials in the afternoon. All day I either attended classes or I studied. I often went to the Catholic chaplaincy for lunch but I did not stay long as I was keen to hit the books. I aimed to work for seven hours a day, Monday to Friday and five hours on a Saturday; Sunday I would leave free for frivolity. I eventually finished about six o'clock when I would have my tea. I am a truly terrible cook, I have no interest in it and I have no skill. I ate a lot of pizza. I could buy two pizzas for four pounds and I would eat half every evening with salad. I did eat a lot of salad and fruit which is my healthy bit but I also ate too much sugar and refined flour. I have not got a sweet tooth but I won't ever say no to a bar of chocolate.

After my evening meal, that I tended to eat whilst watching the news, I hit the theological tombs again. Then at nine I would check my emails, then head to the chapel to pray. My prayer at this point was influenced by a Dr. Thompson, an Anglican tutor from Ridley. He said that our prayer often takes the form of supplication, that is 'God please give me this, God please give me that, God please make me more intelligent/rich/attractive/holy.' Rather, Dr. T advised that we should spend more time thanking God for the graces in our life. So every evening I would kneel in the dark chapel, with the red light of the sanctuary candle burning to announce God's presence, and I would have a list of things to thank God for; I had so many blessings in my life at this point that it made me even more happy to thank God.

I am rubbish at learning new languages, not quite as bad as I am at cooking, but I could never claim to be a linguist. As a theology student I had to take a biblical language. I opted for Biblical Greek – it was a top choice. I had a tutor who was a saint. He was called John but we would call him Saint John behind his back. A thin humble man who spread peace and joy wherever he trod. He played the recorder and to begin his classes he would put Greek words to a well-known tune, then he would play the tune on the recorder and we would sing along in Greek. Then he would put a passage of scripture on the overhead projector and invite one us to stand up and translate it, explaining the grammar as we went along. In any other class this would have been rather intimidating, but with John it was (almost) a pleasure as he was a hero for us and therefore, just like primary school children, we longed to please our paladin. Also, he gave the brave soul a bar of chocolate! Imagine, we were all adults at university and our beloved teacher gave us a bar of chocolate to reward our bravery. At one point, he changed the chocolate to one of those health bars, but we stopped volunteering so he went back to Cadburys. How I loved that man. I thought that he must be like St. Joseph who is always portrayed as a humble, gentle being. I was incredibly jealous of his family as they got to live with him.

The class next door would hear us singing and we delighted in telling them about our chocolate treats. We had the best tutor and everyone knew it. There have been a few people I have encountered that have made a huge impact on me because of their holiness and John was one of them. It was actually a complex issue for me to accept because all I ever known were Catholics, I had not really had any contact with Christians of other denominations and so I had never considered that they too could be saints. Why does the Blessed Virgin Mary not appear to Protestants? How narrow-minded of me, I blush with shame at my bigotry and ignorance...I shout a big sorry to all non-Catholics. This is why I do not think that faith schools are a good idea; children should mix with children from different backgrounds or we can produce young people who have a skewed idea of what their neighbor's belief and this can lead to racism and xenophobia.

Back to Biblical languages. Due to the fact that Greek had gone so swimmingly, I decided to stay in the language pool and in my second year I signed up for Hebrew. It was not a mistake to take Hebrew because it was character forming, but I was most definitely the bottom of the class. Again, I actually enjoyed the classes as they were held in the most exquisite round room at Westminster College. It was a healing balm just to be that space. Also, I again had an amazing tutor, this time a woman, but like John also from the United Reformed Church. No singing or choc. this time but for me those were pleasant hours. I would let my imagination run riot and think that it was in such a room that C. S. Lewis would have held his tutorials.

In the end I was a desperate case when it came to Hebrew. On the morning of my exam it was raining so heavily that I decided to walk rather than take the bike. Cambridge is the driest city in England, with the same annual rain fall as Tel Aviv (stick with me sweetie, you will learn all sorts of useless trivia). It was unusual for it to be raining so heavily, and in the summer; maybe the gods were showing their sympathy to the miserable, exam ridden students. So there I was in my wellies and a rain coat and as I walked along I zipped up my coat. Now, I am clumsy, really, really clumsy; I have tripped over my own feet on numerous occasions. So to those who know me well, it will not be a surprise to hear that as I zipped up my rain coat, I caught my top lip in the zip and burst the skin. There was a lot of blood and I thought that perhaps it required stitches. At Cambridge there are no resists and one failed exam means adieu. There was no way Jose that I was not going to sit the exam, so I sat there for three hours with a cloth held to be bleeding, throbbing upper lip.

The exam went super-duper. Not because I have any real knowledge of Hebrew but because I had a wonderful capacity to memorize information and I knew what passages of scripture the questions would come from so with great effort, I memorized long passages of text by heart. Then when it came to a passage I had to translate, I would search for the words I recognized and then I could work out what passage it was and voila! I translated it into English and I passed the exam. I still recall some of my Greek but the only thing I can remember about Hebrew is that it has no vowels.

Cambridge, as you can imagine, was so snotty I am surprised it could actually breathe through its nostrils. It was snobby to a level that would not be out of place in Downton Abbey. I most definitely did not fit in. This is the crux of the matter; I did not fit in, I knew it and so did everyone else, but I really, truly, one hundred percent did not want to fit in with them, I was then, as I am now, a hard-core socialist who thinks that boarding schools are one of the cruelest institutions ever invented by humanity. Why, why, why, would you have kids just to send them off to a school for a large part of the year? Nothing can replace the warmth of a family. It is not a superior education because that can be obtained anywhere. Yes, they may be groomed for Oxbridge, but does this make them happy and well-rounded adults? No, of course not.

The question usually was 'what boarding school did you go to?' Although, as soon I said that I did not attend a boarding school and when I uttered that my Pater did not own an island then I became a leper and I went around with my bell shouting unclean. However, I was not an insecure eighteen year old desperate to be accepted, I was a self-contained entity who did not give a shit what world they came from. I was proud of my parent's because they had worked hard all their lives and they provided a warm and happy home for me to be raised in. I was so incredibly happy at school, and although I enjoyed reading Malory Towers, I never had any desire to swap places with Pat and her pals. I held out for buddies that were on my wave-length, and in time they came along, and they are like beautiful roses in the garden of my life. The others were just annoying, prickly thorns.

Many a time remarks were made to me about my working-class background. Rather than get upset at this scuttlebutt I dismissed them, and rather than the vulture making the waspy comments thinking less of me, in my mind I placed them on the level as dog poo on the pavement that gets on the bottom of your shoe and makes the whole room stink. For example, there was Hilary, a woman at the chaplaincy who was from Dublin. She was so full of herself. Sometimes she read at Mass and I had to put my head down and pretend to pray because I was trying to hide my laughter. Suddenly her accent went from Irish to the sort of fake aristocratic English uttered by bad, amateur productions of Lady Windermere's Fan. It was so fake and that is what so much of Cambridge was an act where Daddy's pay-packet somehow increases one's importance. Bullshit.

One day I asked Dublin's answer to Lady Windermere about a group that met at the chaplaincy on a Wednesday evening to discuss issues pertaining to faith. As I had a strong faith at this point I thought I would like to join. The stinging reply was truly worthy of Oscar Wilder, she looked down at me (metaphorically, as she actually only the same height as me) and said....wait for it....'it is not for the likes of you!' Very Christian. That was me put in my place; except I knew my place already and was content with my seat.

Another time we were at another group, (I forget what), there were those who were sat around the table and another row behind them. I was sat in the back row, keeping myself to myself, when suddenly this Banshee turned to me and said 'oh, this is just like the theater isn't it, where I guess you have never sat in the best seats?' I had done nothing to warrant this outburst apart from existing which some people seemed to have an issue with. Well, my dear, you can go and shove you pettiness where the sun don't shine.

In my final year at university my dear Mum got breast cancer. I remember clearly receiving the phone call. It was a Thursday evening. I cried and in shock but I knew I would cope. I was a strong lass who could face anything life had to throw at me and I liked being Miss Strong, I liked being Miss Independent and Miss Happy, this was my character that I had worked on for many years and here I was able to cope. I spoke to my youngest brother on the phone and he cried and I said that we will cope, Mum will recover and we will cope.

The following morning I caught the train home to Radcliffe and spent the weekend with my lovely Mum. Over the next few months I would make that journey many times, I studied on the train and in the hospital and late at night and early in the morning. Now my degree meant nada to me compared to my Mum, but I was fully confident that she would get better and therefore I had no reason to abandon my studies because come next September I needed to find a job.

My Harry Potter gown

Nietzsche observed that joy is the feeling of one's power increasing. My power and ability to cope brought me much joy and contentment. Now I cannot cope with any sort of problem and my power has been chopped from me like Samson and his hair and I do not know how to get it back, and I want it back because I do not know who I am.

I often went home during my three years at university and I frequently went to my local art gallery. There was a particular painting that fascinated me and I would sit and gaze at it, because it mirrored my soul. Here is a Carmelite novice, she is a plump, healthy looking critter and she holds her rosary beads in her hands and yet her head is turned towards the open window where a carnival is in full swing. This carnival represents all the carnal pleasures of the world outside the monastery grills. Through the open door we spy an old, decrepit nun, with the crosses of the cemetery clearly seen. This part of the triptych represents death, death to the world and all its pleasures and temptations, death to sin, death to oneself. During the ceremony for the taking of final vows, the nun prostrates herself before the altar and a black cloth is laid over her, to represent her death.

This novice has not been in the monastery long, and her white veil indicates that she has not yet taken religious vows. The open window indicates that she can freely choose to leave the monastery. What should she choose? The carnival or the graveyard? This was the conundrum that I pondered as I sat and gazed at this bewitching painting.

I have never been into popular culture, and I know practically nothing about pop music, but I recall a particular song that went, 'I'd steal chips for you.' I was rather taken with this line as it seemed to me so utterly romantic. Fish and chip shops are a prominent feature of northern life and I would often use this line in my prayers, as a way of telling Jesus that I loved him utterly, more than anything or anyone, without reserve and forever. Yes I would gladly steal chips for him. Now, it is all a phantom, I have been offering to steal chips for a phantom, I might as well have promised to love the tooth fairy.

CHAPTER SIX

Soli House

To be or not to be...

After uni. I was completely unsure about what path to take. As a teenager I had been a massive fan of Sylvia Plath who in one text writes about herself as looking at a fruit laden tree and because she was unsure which delicious item to choose and in the end she died of hunger because of a lack of decision.

I still wanted to be a nun but I had not found a community. I did visit a number of communities and although they were all welcoming they were not for me. So I started to look for a job. I explored the idea of becoming a prison chaplain which I think I would have found difficult but satisfying. In the end I plumped for a job with teenagers in a residential setting set in the magical world of Stratford-upon-Avon. Shakespeare here I come.

I was so excited to live just thirty seconds from the bones of the Bard. On my days off I could just trip to the theater and a whole wonderful world was opened to me. I am an early bird and so I would get up early, make a strong cuppa in a jar (putting the lid on keeps the tea warm), and go and sit by the river Avon and it was just heavenly.

The house where I worked was a retreat center for teenagers aged fourteen to eighteen. They would come from the local Catholic schools on a Tuesday morning and leave on a Friday afternoon. My team consisted of young adults who were having an experience of volunteering for a year. Gosh my team worked jolly hard and I have never, ever come across such dedicated, joyful, tremendous, lovely, wonderful, fantastic, tiptop, A-one, marvelous, phenomenal group of young adults. I have never been 'cool' or 'down with the kids' but my job was to organize, tell the rules, get up at three am when a teenager thought if hilarious to set off the firm alarm with an aerosol can (this happened at least twice a week), make sure everyone was A-Okay, enforce child protection guidelines (I did not like that because it makes one look at everyone as a potential pedophile – yuck), take people to hospital or anything else that required doing.

On a Tuesday evening we held a session entitled 'Grill Bill'. Bill was the priest and it was an opportunity for the teenagers to ask him anything they so desired, no reservations. Every week there were the same questions, on homosexuality, women priests, married priest, contraception, sex before marriage. Occasionally there would be an original question that showed the kid was really pondering matters of faith.

One week a teenager asked what if one lived their whole life as a Christian and then at the end of life one discovered it had all been a lie, a big fat lie. What would one do? Another woman who worked at the center replied that it would not matter, if one had truly lived a life according to Christian values and then discovered that there is no Christ to underpin these values then ones life has not been in vain; it was still a life well lived. I was horrified (inwardly, not vocally). No, it was not the Gospel teaching that I loved, but Jesus, a person, man and God incarnate. When I prayed, I prayed to a living being, without Jesus what a waste of my time. I might as well have spent time practicing my juggling skills.

I really loved that job. The only problem was a lack of sleep which has always affected me very negatively. I was never a Maggie Thatcher who could survive on five hours a night. I ended up on sleeping tablets for the first time in my life and I knew that I was not able to remain on them permanently so with a sad heart I had to say good-bye. Soli House is now closed. Another example of the Church putting money above the needs of the soul. We had a massive house in a prime location, with a stunning garden, so the pound signs were too great for the bishop to resist. Never mind the loss to the kids who came to us with a wary air but who left four days later proclaiming undying love for Soli. Shame on you bishop.

I had not abandoned the idea of being a nun; I still presumed that this would be my final destination. During my time at university I was still on the convent hunt. I had popped over to Eire a few times to visit a monastery of Dominican nuns. Then when I finished at Soli I went to live with the nuns for a month. This was a vibrant community with young women and I really liked the whole experience. Dominicans are known for their academic slant and this appealed to me. However, you know when something is right, right? And this monastery, though lovely, lively and perfectly nice, was not for me.

I had also been visiting a community of Dominican sisters (not enclosed) in England. On paper they seemed just my cup of tea, but they were actually really, really unfriendly and so I walked away and bided my time to find the right community for me.

I wanted to live in a Christian community and I knew of a lay-community in Scotland so I went to visit. I wanted a life where I could pray and serve and although my ideal would be religious life I thought a lay-community would be a sort of half-way house. It turned out to be very providential. I went to stay in the lay-community for a week to see if I fitted in, if I wanted to join them, and if they wanted me to join them. When I was up in Scotland I spoke to the woman who had originally founded this community and I told her that I wanted to be a nun but I was having trouble finding where God wanted me to be. She told me about a community of sisters who were based in Wexford, Eire. These sisters had occasionally been to this retreat house when they were on a trip with teenagers. From what she told me, these sisters sounded that they fitted the bill and coincidentally I was visiting Ireland the following week to see my brother. So whilst I was in Ireland I went to stay with these sisters for a few days and I knew instantly, from the moment I stepped into the convent that this was my home. I was finally home.

I loved everything. Young sisters, beautiful habit, work in the community, prayer, rosary, everything. So there and then I signed up. I went back to England and informed my folks that instead of cold Scotland, I needed to re-pack my suitcase, remove the thermals and prepare for life in sunny Italy. On the thirteenth of May 2010 I returned to the convent in Ireland where I remained till the thirty-first and then I got on the plane and that is how I ended up in a convent in Italy. The superior of the community in Ireland, Mother Light has since left the Order and the last I heard she was living in Scotland.

CHAPTER SEVEN

Bella italia

Paridiso, paridiso, preferisco paridiso....

Let me explain a tad about this Order I was just about to become a member of. Okay, in Carmel, we were just nuns, enclosed, contemplative, but The Servants of the Lord and the Virgin of Matara (the name of my new family) has quite a few branches. Okay, first came priests, founded in Argentina in 1984, then there were monks, who are the male equivalent of nuns, (enclosed and contemplative). Then in 1988 the sisters were founded and then monasteries of nuns. So that is four branches of one religious family. Then there were aspirants (girls as young as eleven who want to be sisters but are too young to enter the convent, so they live in the convent but are also home-schooled, or go to a school run by our priests). There are also minor seminarians, who are the same as aspirants, but boys instead of girls. Now we are six. Then there is the third order, who are men and women who live a regular life, without a habit, without a convent, seminary or monastery and without the religious vows of poverty, chastity and obedience. These were usually married people, who often had family members who were priests or sisters. Then there are the consecrated virgins who are women who want to live a semi-religious life but without actually entering the convent. They do not get married but as it says on the box, remain as consecrated virgins. So, let's see if my math's is up to scratch, which makes eight different ways of belonging to one religious order. This makes sense (I hope) of what I am going to scribble on the next few pages.

Hi ho, hi ho, it's off to work we go...so here I am bella italia on the thirty first of May. I had absolutely no idea what to expect when I arrived in Italy, but I was not afraid, rather it was an adventure as this was the life God had ordained for me. I was met at the airport by the superior, who was incredibly pretty, so young with an exquisite smile...and thank God she was fluent in English. Also in the car was a postulant from Albania; she spoke no English and although we had some heated moments over the coming months because I am your usual stiff, no hugging English lass, she was incredibly tactile and I had no way of telling her to basta! However, she became one of the sisters to whom I drew close to and we became good friends. I learnt Italian (painfully) and as we grew to know each other, we grew to love each other. She was the complete opposite of me but eventually we just clicked. She is one of those people in life who take suffering (and boy did she have a lot of woe in her life) and turns it into compassion for others. For various reasons her education was cut short and the exams were a source of distress for her. She had the most incredible gift for languages and could hear phrase once and repeat it.

Shpressa also loved playing practical jokes. I had only been in the convent a few days when I was on duty for lunch. I needed one of those lighters to light the stove, one of those make a clicking noise to light the stove. Shpressa was showing me how to use this lighter and she pretended to be electrocuted, all the body spasms and everything. I started to scream as I thought she really was about to die. Boy did that girl laugh at my reaction. This was a joke she liked to play on all newbies and she never seemed to tire. She had a simple soul, a pure, innocent, generous soul.

So then we were three. The superior and I chatted amicably on the way back to the novitiate. I did not know what to expect and when we arrived I was both thrilled and horrified at the same time. It was a big house rather than a purpose built convent. It oozed poverty. Downstairs there was the chapel, a kitchen, the superiors bedroom, a small library, a spare bedroom for guests, two toilet cubicles that also contained two showers and a large dining room where we would eat, have classes, study, do plays, dance, play games,. Upstairs there were two bedrooms, seven of us slept in one room, in bunk-beds that where three high. In the other room there were four, two aspirants, a postulant and a sister. There was also a W.C.

Everything was cheap, the windows did not fit properly, there was no heating, and if you used the basin upstairs the water came up through the bidet. Oh, here is an amusing story about bidet. Bidets are found in every toilet in Italy. When I moved to another convent I overheard a conversation between two non-European sisters who were discussing the purpose of a bidet. One said it was for men; the women would pee in the big toilet and the men would pee in the small toilet. This particular convent was purpose built and so no men would ever be using these bathrooms. The other sister disagreed and said that it was for washing your veil in! I never disillusioned them. I am glad it was poor, after all we were preparing to take a vow of poverty and so we should live it in practice.

I was on the bottom bunk of three and it was somewhat rickety; every-time one of the sisters above me turned over or got up to go to the toilet in the middle of the night it was if I were on a boat in some very choppy seas. We had some funny times in that room even though for the most part we kept silence when we were in the bedrooms. In the morning one sister would ring the bell and the rest of us would spring (crawl) from our beds and kneel down and say three Hail Mary's. We were so conditioned in this particular act that once in the middle of the night one of the sisters started to pray the Hail Mary out loud in her sleep and the rest of us sprang out of bed and dutifully dropped to our knees. Then we realized it was three in the morning...oh my goodness, it was so nice to slide back into bed with the knowledge that I could have another three hours of slumber.

There was another time when the sister who was meant to ring the bell in the morning overslept and when the priest arrived to celebrate Mass we were all still in bed; that was awkward. I eventually grew accustomed to sleeping in a dormitory and even now I find it slightly unnerving to sleep with me, myself and I.

We were rather a mixed community. Top down it went, the superior (from the U.S.A.), two helpers (sisters who helped the superior run the house, one Dutch, one from Argentina), five postulants (two Dutch, one from Albania, one from Italy and me) and two aspirants (both Italian). It is a pertinent question to ask whether it is healthy for such young children to be living in a convent, far from their family and in such an overwhelming and intense religious environment. In some countries such as Argentina, Egypt and Brazil there are numerous aspirants, but in Europe there are only a few. Also, why is the aspirancy not on the web-site for the communities in Italy? They are mentioned on the web-sites for other countries, but for example, on the website of the USA the aspirancy is merely called a house of formation, but it does not point out that these are young girls. When I was in Scotland one summer, myself and some other sisters were staying with the Sisters of Nazareth and when I went to mention the aspirancy to these sisters, my superior quickly told me to be quiet and not mention that we have young girls staying with us. We did not have a lot of space for all of us, but we muddled along peacefully, if not always happily.

As a postulant I wore a long gray skirt and any top, but if I was going to a celebration or to Rome, I would don a white top. We washed our clothes by hand so I preferred darker tops, and the bane of my existence in Italy was bloody olive oil; it is so flippin' hard to get it out of clothes, especially when hand-washed.

The day we received the habit was simply horrid. So much went wrong. We all had holy cards made for us that we could give to our family and friends. I chose the biblical quote, 'I have ransomed you, I have called you by your name, you are mine' (Isaiah 43:1). But all the letters 'e' were omitted. I sent a card to a friend in England and she replied, what has the computer got against the letter e?

Then we did not have enough money to buy material for the habit. Eventually, we got some material but it was late in the day and so when I my habit arrived I had not actually been measured for it and it was about a foot too long, so it was sent back for modifications (a sister at the Juniorate made my holy habit). When I went to bed about eleven the night before the day of investiture I still did not have a habit. Then the following morning, a habit had arrived but there was no belt, so a mother of one of my fellow novices who had come from Albania for the ceremony passed her morning making me a belt.

In Italy I was not permitted to write any letters, but my parent's could phone me once a week. My folks only travel between England and Ireland for holidays, there was no way they were going to make it to Italy, but I did make it back to Manchester a few times (my folk's had to buy the plane ticket) as we were generally permitted two weeks holiday a year.

I recall the first time I returned to Manchester for a holiday I was told by my superior not to watch any Harry Potter films and do not be seen out in public alone with a man, even if that man happens to be a brother as it may cause scandal. I am sure I was told a lot of other rules that I had to follow, but I can only remember these two because I found them so ridiculous.

Then the veils. We had to sew our own veil which actually sounds like a good idea, and it would be if we all knew how to sew by hand and we were given sufficient amount of time to produce our masterpiece. The veil was white and we had to sew them when we were sat at the table after we had finished our grub. Both these reasons resulted in a white veil that was rather grubby. So when the big day arrived, I was still sewing the veil of another sister who had never sewn a stitch in her eighteen years of life and then we had to wash them by hand and try and dry them with an iron.

Oh my goodness, nerves were stretched to breaking point, with a superior who was shouting at us to hurry up, sisters who were rather emotional and poor parents who needed to be shown some form of hospitality.

Remember, my name had now transmorphed into Sister Mary, Our Lady of Ransom aka Rrrrrrrrrrrrraaaaaaaaansom

The journey to the Church was one of the most bonding times of my life. I sat next to an Italian sister whom I did not particularly get on with as her English was atrocious, but it was better than my Italian. However, although I did not know any details, in our small, poorly constructed convent there were no secrets and I had heard voices raised between her and our superior. I was to learn the details later, but that is our secret. Well, I sat in the mini-bus and quietly wept, not because I was upset, but because of the high emotions. Well, this dear sister whom I love so much took my hand and we held hands all the way to the Church. Nothing could have comforted me more than this kind act of compassion, to suffer with, and I miss her. I will never hold her hand again and I miss her. This act shows how close my little novitiate community was and I miss them all.

That evening, we all had our hair shaved, not a skin-head but very short. One sister was upset to say goodbye to her golden locks, but I was happy as it made taking a shower a darn sight quicker.

Every August we went on a little trip which we called convivencia, this word does not exactly translate into English as it was not a holiday, but the best translation would be 'time together'. This seems like an odd concept, after all where␣we not together all the time? But it was a special, intense way of being together, a time of increasing in virtue as there were physical deprivations that were unique to this time.

Let me expand. What we did was all of us, Novitiate and Juniorate sisters together, packed our ruck-sack and headed off to the mountains. We stayed in schools or other large buildings and every other day we took off our habit, put on shorts, tee-shirts and bandanas and headed for the hills. We left early in the morning and walked up the mountains, singing and chatting, in the manner of the Von Trapp family. It was physically very tough, and some sisters, such as the ones from Egypt (as girls in that part of the world were not raised playing sport), whereas the athletes from U.S.A trotted up the hills like gazelles.

On convivencia a priest from our Order came with us to say Mass and hear confessions. On this day long hiking excursions we often had Mass on the summit of the mountain which was a beautiful experience. I am not physically robust, so the first year I went on this special holiday I detested it, the pain of spending the day walking up a mountain left me depleted. It did not help that I contracted bronchitis after one week, so I spent the rest of the experience, trying to breathe and put up with the pain in my lungs. I never had bronchitis before and so I did not know what the matter was, and there was no doctor to visit so I had to wait till we returned back to the Novitiate before I received a diagnosis. I was to get bronchitis a number of times during my years in Italy, by the end of my four years I was completely used to the sickness, it had become normal to be poorly.

We were generally a thin group of women, in long shorts, tee-shirts and bandanas and a number of us were very white. One sister used to joke that I was so white I could be Caspar the Friendly Ghost. So often, other people would see us and come to the conclusion that we were cancer victims, or we were a bit soft in the head.

Once when we were climbing a mountain, one of the sisters felt ill so she sat in a park at the bottom of the mountain and waited for our return. A park ranger came and asked this sister to move because he thought she was a tramp! Another time some sisters were making a lot of noise singing and laughing. Another park ranger and asked them to be quiet as they were disturbing the other people in the park. One sister said to this man that she was a nun and he replied, 'yes, and I am Donald Duck!' Funny times.

One day we climbed a mountain, and then one day we passed by a river (wow, Italy has amazing lakes everywhere), where we would swim, play games, sing and generally be together. I recall one particular mountain we ascended. At base camp the weather was glorious and the green on the hills was something from a postcard, however, half way up we encountered snow and ice. We passed a number of tourists who we all clad in the correct clothes for walking on snow and ice and there we were in our faded clothes and cheap pumps, and yet here we were singing and laughing, we must have looked crazy. What made me laugh most was that a number of sisters had these little bags with them, like handbags, which contained an embroidery project. All sisters were meant to impart the skill of embroidery, so that we could make works for the Church and our priests. Some sisters took to this fine work like a duck to water and so they never wasted a moment. If we stopped for a break on our odyssey, then out would come the needle and thread. I enjoyed the peaceful past time of needle work, but I not so enamored with it that I would carry it up a bloody mountain.

Other sisters would climb with guitars, so that they could play tunes for us to sing along to. I really appreciated the opportunity to mix with this wide circle of sisters, especially with those who spoke English. If there was a day when it rained, then we still passed the day together, playing party games. Everything was more basic than we had at home, fewer showers, longer days, not enough beds for everyone and so on. I detested my first convivencia, but by the time I came to leave Italy I really enjoyed these mountain hikes.

When I moved to Ireland, we still went to Italy for this vacation as we sought the sun. No longer in the large group of the studying sisters, we came together from what is known as the Northern European province, which consists of sisters from the Netherlands, Luxembourg, Lithuania, Iceland and Ireland. We numbered about twenty-five. No longer did we rough it, but I actually found it luxurious, with my own lovely bedroom, plenty of bathrooms (some rooms were even en-suite), and jolly nice grub. It was like staying in a hotel. As we were older sisters we did not climb mountains but just hills, and just the odd one. We passed time by lakes or playing outside games such as volley ball. We visited cities, went to concerts and generally had jollies. It was really, really lush and was more than I ever thought possible in the convent. One part of me felt uncomfortable that it was rather plush, but I cannot express how wonderful it was to pass a few weeks with my sisters. I laughed so much on those few weeks, and after the tension with Knock and Grace it was peaceful, happy, jolly, relaxing, blessed and blissful. I felt like a real grown-up, having time to spend with my equals, whereas in Bunclody I was a pathetic nobody.

Rewind to September 2011, in fact on my birthday, we went to join the sisters who lived in what is called the Juniorate. This is the next stage on the path to becoming a fully-fledged nun. Strictly speaking, only sisters who live in a monastery or abbey who are fully contemplative and keep enclosure are nuns; women who live in a convent and who gad about are sisters, but thanks to *The Nun's Story, The Sound of Music and Sister Act* people are o fey with the term nun, so in this text I use it interchangeably. Capisci?

I am crap, crap, crap at languages and italiano was no different. I really struggled. I was asked if I would rather go to the USA to study over there, but leaning and struggling with Italian was nothing when compared to listening to people who destroy the beautiful English language; where slang is used by grown adults and every sentence seems to be a question. No the land of McDonald's could carry on without me and I would stick to the realm of the culture, il papa and pizza.

I am really shit at anything practical. Let me tell you about a few of my cooking incidents in the convent. So, there were fourteen meals to be cooked a week and we took it in turns. One day, it was Shpress' birthday and I was informed by the sister in charge of the kitchen (known in Italian as the dispensare, but dispensary sounds medicinal in English) to cook rice and courgette. I know, hardly the most exciting grub for a celebration, but there was a birthday cake. Do you remember Margot from *The Good Life*; well that is me, slow on the uptake and not suited to practical matters. Well, I did what I thought I was meant to do, but when it came to serving the food I realized I had not cooked any rice...so my lovely sister had courgette and bread for her birthday.

Then there was the time I had to cook spaghetti and red sauce (a staple in the beautiful land of artists and saints). Well, when it came time to serve I realized with horror that I had omitted the red sauce, so there I was, stood in the kitchen waiting to serve the evening meal and I only had spaghetti. Thankfully the Italian novice came to my rescue. She had been raised cooking so she knew what to do. She quickly added some eggs and oil and the heat of the spaghetti caused the eggs to cook and it was actually really yummy.

Then there was the time I had to prepare a white sauce to go with the pasta. I had never cooked a white sauce in my life. I do not think I had ever even consumed a white sauce. I followed the instructions (in Italian) and made a humungous pan of white sauce. It was disgusting. When my superior came to try the food she said that it just tasted of flour and water. But we were beggars and food could not be wasted, so every day we all had to have a few spoonful's of this wallpaper paste on one's food so as to finish it. There was a loud cheer after two long weeks when we finally reached the bottom of the pan.

Then there was the time I decided to bake a cake. How hard could it be? I had seen my Mum cook hundreds of cakes. It was for Sister Fons Vitae who was enchanted by castles (she is Argentinean and they do not have castles I understand). So I baked, and then constructed a castle, with four turrets. I covered it all in pink Angel Delight (sent by my Mum) and on the Sunday afternoon I presented this work of art for tea time. It was a rock, too hard to even cut and we had to eventually admit defeat and dispose of it in the bin because trying to consume it might have resulted in a fortune in dentist fees.

It was not just cooking that caused me humiliation...oh no, there were humiliations awaiting me at every turn. I was the sacristan in the novitiate and above the altar hung a very large, stunning crucifix. Every Friday we prayed the Stations of the Cross and this crucifix would be taken down so that all the sisters could kiss it in devotion of the sufferings of Jesus. One week, I lent the crucifix against a wall whilst I fetched a chair that would enable me to reach and place it back above the altar. The crucifix slipped because I had not secured it properly and it fell and broke into many, many pieces. You might think, well yes, it is not good to break a crucifix, but it is only a material object and you nuns with your vow of poverty should be detached from such things. But we were Pious (requiring the capital) and to break anything that belonged to the chapel was a major no-no.

My superior was in the shower at the time and as I awaited her I wanted to run away and come back in a few days/weeks/months/years time. When she saw me, my face told her that I had committed a grave fault, but I could not get the words out. Eventually she went into the chapel and saw the damage for herself. I know I got a stiff penance for that fault, but for the life of me I cannot recall what it was.

The crucifix was replaced by another of vastly inferior ascetic quality and I blushed with guilt every time I entered the chapel and saw it. When we moved to another house (we moved three times in my novitiate year) I was getting the chapel prepared. Anima had come to make an inspection and she was in the chapel with me and my superior and this is how it went:

Anima: 'Where is the beautiful crucifix that used to hang in the novitiate chapel?'
Superior: 'It got broken.'
Me: Silence.
Anima: 'How did it get broken?'
Superior: Silence (I loved her for that silence that showed she was on my side).
Me: 'I dropped it.'

Silence from all three.

To compound matters, in a Catholic Church hangs a red candle to indicate that God is present. Actually, the candle is white, but the holder is red and in Italy they often have small red bowls filled with oil instead of a wax candle. I was holding this red bowl in my hand as the above conversation took place, and in front of Anima I dropped this bowl, full of oil on the chapel floor and it smashed and the oil went everywhere.

No-one said anything.

Are you grasping by now that I was not your picture perfect nun?

Another time, I came home with the police. I had been to Rome to visit my brother and his family who were en-route to a family wedding. On the way home I had to catch a bus from the train station back to the convent. Of course, being me I got on the wrong bus promptly fell asleep and when I awoke, I had no idea where I was, but it was dark and I was lost in Italy, with no money, no phone and very little Italian (and even less common sense, negative numbers do exist).

I got off the bus which was now in the middle of no-where. A dark road. This was a Thursday and on a Thursday we had confessions in the convent. So mother superior told me not to phone the convent before nine in the evening so as not to disturb the confessions. Not that I had a phone, but I could ask someone if I could use their phone, and people usually said yes to us nuns. It was nowhere near nine o'clock so I just sat on the pavement and waited. I thought that as the time drew near to nine I would go hunting for a person and a phone. And that is what I did. About ten to nine I started to walk down the road and I discovered a pizza parlor (thank goodness the Italians are crazy about their pizza). I went in and asked a nice looking man if I could use his phone. I spoke to mother Nadiya but I had no idea where I was and therefore it was rather complicated working out how to come and fetch me. At this point the police arrive. Someone had seen me at the side of the road and phoned them. They were so lovely. I told them where I lived and they offered to take me home.

It was my first (and only) time in a police car. The seats were hard plastic and when I went to put my seat-belt on I discovered only handcuffs. Also, the car doors opened from the outside, so it was a very strange sensation to arrive somewhere and wait for a police man to open the door and free me.

When I arrived back at the convent (it later transpired that mother thought one of the people in the pizza parlor had kindly given me a lift home) a sister saw me get out of the police car. Well, I had endured enough for one day and when I got in I said my night prayers and went to bed as it was getting rather late. The following morning we had Mass first thing, then breakfast. I thought it prudent to wait till after breakfast to inform mother of the previous night's excitements. However, someone got there first. Imagine us all, seated at a long table, and with a priest in the middle and suddenly this sister announces in a booming voice, 'Ransom came home with the police last night.'

What a tumble-weed moment. All heads swiveled in my direction, mother said, 'Ransom, is this true?' The priest gazed at me with open mouth surprise (this priest happened to be my spiritual director which made the whole situation so much more humiliating). It was true, the police were my knights in shining armor, but my halo lost some of its sheen that day.

There was another day when my brain cells took a while to catch-up with reality. Our superior had gone away to a meeting for a few days and we were left in charge of her little helpers. One afternoon the convent phone rang and I had the job that week of answering the phone and door I picked up with the friendly 'pronto' which is how everyone in Italy answers the phone, it means 'I am ready' which always felt a bit rude, but protocol dictated such things. This is the dialogue:

Ring, ring.
Me: 'Pronto!'
Other person: 'Posso parlare con Foederis?' (May I speak with Foederis?)
Me: 'Me dispaiaci. Lei non sta. Chi parla?' (I am sorry, she is not here. Who is calling?)
Other person: 'It is mother.' (This was said in English).

I thought this was Foederis' mother, who is from the Netherlands and could therefore speak English, but not necessarily perfectly.

Me: 'Oh, hello, I will tell her that her mother has phoned her.'
Other person: 'Not her mother, your mother.'

Well, this left me flummoxed, as this woman did not have an Irish accent and I knew that my mamma could not speak Italian.

Silence...for quite a duration.

Me: 'I am sorry, but what is your name?'
Mother: 'Mother Nadiya.'

There the phone call endeth.

Oh dear, I messed up again. The other sisters had been listening to this strange communication and the roared with laughter at my stupidity. I bet you are wondering how I ever got a degree.

So, I am sure that these stories have indicated without doubt that I can be a very dull creature. However, I hope they also show, in a small way, that I tried to be a good sister, and I know I messed up but I tried and tried with the sweat of my brow and soul.

I am as stubborn as a donkey. Here is a tale to illustrate what a horror I was to my Mother Superior. Now in the universe of the convent, you get told to do things, not asked, not consulted, but told and with the vow of obedience one is always expected to acquiesce, no matter what the command. I can read music (flute player) and can play very simple tunes on the old Joanna. One day I was informed that the following week I was to play the organ at Mass. I did not know chords or how to play the organ and I said that I did not want to do this as I had hardly any time in which to learn some chords and practice. My refusal was ignored and I was duly informed that I would be playing one verse of a hymn at Mass the following week. I was as mad as a box of frogs, but I had to bow my head and try to humbly obey.

So, another novice taught me the few chords necessary for a hymn to the Blessed Virgin Mary, and every pause in studies and work I dashed to the chapel to practice. Well, the day of reckoning arrived and I did play the hymn, but without good grace. I had been told that I had to play one verse and I took the letter rather than the spirit of the law. It was a simple hymn, with simple chords, and after I had completed one verse I stopped, even though some of the sisters were still queuing for Holy Communion, and normally a sister would play the organ till all the sisters were back in their pew, but I stopped. I saw my superior turn and glare at me, but she had only commanded one verse and that is what I played so technically I was obedient.

Well, happily, I learnt my lesson and in the future I played with a better spirit. When I got to Ireland I had improved so much that I often played for the entire Mass and actually enjoyed it.

I am a very open person; you will not find me saying nasty things behind another's back. What you see is what you get. I learnt a painful lesson a few months after the organ debacle. A woman came to visit us from Scotland as she was discerning her vocation. She was about the same age as me and I was asked to look after her, so I sat next to her at meal times to converse with her in English and talk about things British. As this woman was thinking about entering a convent we passed the majority of our conversation discussing bits and bobs about the religious life.

Thinking that I was helping I told her about my struggle with obedience and the whole organ situation. I wanted her to understand that slightly older women have struggles that maybe younger sisters do not have, after all we had passed a number of years making our own decisions. I painted the whole situation in a positive light and I was the one at fault, my refusal to rely on the power of grace. I was a naive idiot. This woman who had seemed so friendly to my face returned to Scotland and told a woman who is the mother of one of the Order's priests and said that I had been bad-mouthing the convent and things turned messy. This mother contacted her son who told his superior, this superior contacted my superior and I got a right rollicking for saying negative things about the convent. This simply was not true; I said negative things about myself, but never about the convent. In conclusion, I imparted my lesson and this woman did not enter religious life.

1.　　Woman → seminarians Mamma.
2.　　Seminarians Mamma → to her son.
3.　　Son → to his superior.
4.　　Male superior → to my superior.
5.　　My superior → to me.

What a fiasco!

A major problem I encountered in Italy was my weight, or rather, my lack of weight. When people are stressed they get headaches, or indigestion, or heartburn or whatever...I struggle to eat when I am under pressure. This has always been the case. Food is my control stick in the game of life. I did not eat enough and a full day of work and movement (and sweating as though I was in a Finnish sauna) left only half of me. I went down to thirty-five kilos. When I came home for a holiday, my family was horrified and they did not want me to return to the convent. The convent did everything they could to help me gain weight and I cannot fault them. Mea culpa, mea culpa, mea maxima culpa.

In my final year of study some of the sisters came from the USA to complete their studies. They were lovely and holy but even though English was our common language, we were speaking double Dutch to each other. They were always getting together to talk about their 'feelings', just the thought of this made me want to vomit. One day I was drying some plates after lunch with some of the sisters from the US. One of the sisters said 'shall we talk about our feelings'? I thought she was joking; after all we were just drying the dishes so I started to laugh at this preposterous suggestion. The sister who had broached the idea got really upset and left the kitchen. Another sister informed me that I should be more aware of other people's feelings and that the sister was making a serious suggestion and was not speaking in jest. Next time I kept my lips sealed and laughed inwardly.

So rewind, rewind, back to the novitiate. Back to my failure to learn Italian. After one Italian exam, my superior took me for a walk in the garden because she wanted to inform me of my score...wait for it, I got zero! She thought I would be really upset but I just laughed. I mean zero. Even if I had just done ip, dip, do the Law of Probability would state that I would get at least one answer correct. I was not upset about such things.

At the table we had a rule that we had to speak Italian. The aspirants and one of the postulants had Italian as their mother tongue and they also used dialect. The other sisters had a good grasp of the language and there was just me sitting there like Billy no mates. I had no idea what they were waffling on about, it was all too quick and my mind worked so slow that by the time I thought of a response it was too late. I kid you not, from the thirty first of May two thousand and ten to the twenty fifth of September two thousand and eleven I spoke not one word at meal times. Can you imagine, four times a day (breakfast, lunch, afternoon tea and supper) I sat there deaf and dumb? After I left the novitiate one of the aspirants told me that she never thought I would survive the duration of the novitiate because I must have been really lonely. I replied that I was never lonely because whilst they chit-chatted amongst themselves, I spoke with God who thankfully understands English.

One of the philosophical questions I have enjoyed pondering is 'what is more important, truth or love?' I rejected the theology of Abelard because I find it too kissy, kissy, mushy, mush and theology should be logical at all times, directed by the head not the heart. One should do things because it is the right thing, not infected by feelings. So I concluded that truth must always be what we aim for, because it is sure path that will lead to true love, but if we only have love as the apex of our philosophizing then we can be led very far from truth. Just recall that teenage crush you had on the boy in the year above, where joy and agony held sway in your soul and you never thought you would love like that again. Yes it was a form of love, but truth was somewhat on the sidelines.

So, I believe that we must all think about the question of truth and although we may disagree, it is in the struggle that we arrive at some form of harmony. However, there is one aspect of my life that I would rather not see in such a truthful light. That is the truth about me. Let us get it out of the way, the truth about me is that I am a horrid person. Remember the childhood rhyme, *'there was a little girl who had a little curl, right in the middle of her forehead; when she was good, she was very, very good, but when she was bad she was horrid.'* Well, I lean towards the latter part of the rhyme.

I do not accept glibly this aspect of my character, we have free will and intellect and therefore I can choose how to behave. I have always tried to follow the Christian message 'do unto others as you would have them do unto you' (Matthew 7:12). I have tried to be kind to all those people I have come into contact, and many times, oh so many, many times I flopped and messed up, but I could say sorry and move on. Fall, rise, fall, rise, fall, rise; this is the pattern. Back to my frightfulness. During my novitiate year I fell far more than I rose. My novice mistress was a good and holy woman and I made her job oh so difficult.

It is much harder to enter a convent after one has experienced independence and freedom. To go from living independently, earning money, paying taxes and deciding how one spends one's free time, to living where every second of every day is ordained for you, to being told you could not have a shower today because you had to do some extra work; it is really hard. If one enters the convent aged just eighteen (or even eleven) then it is easier to take unremitting orders. I know because I have done it both ways.

I clashed terribly with my novice mistress. She was very patient and understanding with me and I did not give her an inch. I resented her rule over me and I resisted to the point of arguments. I acted childishly for the entire duration of my novitiate and I am ashamed of by words and actions.

A few years later I had the opportunity to spend some time with this particular sister and we were reconciled. It was a beautiful experience and although I know I will never see this sister again, I had a few weeks to try and rectify my past comportment and that brings me some semblance of peace.

Let me tell you a noviciate account that shows what a jolly lot we were. Once a month we had a day of retreat where we kept silence all day, prayed more and thought about our religious life. That was the idea anyway, but we failed every time.

In the afternoon we had merender (afternoon tea). We usually fasted that day apart from this small meal so we did gobble like a gaggle of geese. One of the superiors arrived with a spiritual book and told us that one of us had to read from this book whilst we ate but this is how it went,

Foederis: 'One of you has to read from this book. Shpress, you can start.'

Then Foederis left and we were left to our own devises.

Shpressa has an amazing talent for speaking languages but her education in Albania was cut short so she is very nervous to read from a text.

Shpress: 'I do not want to, Incoronata, please can you read?'
Incoronata: 'No, I am hungry.'
Me: 'I will read.'
The others: 'No, if you read we will just laugh.'

At which point we all started to giggle and the more we tried to desist, the more we laughed till we cried. Then we decided to be good and obedient and we all turned our chairs around so our backs were facing the table. The idea was that if we could not see each other then we would not cause each other to titter. Failure! We laughed and snorted and giggled and could not contain our mirth. We were like that all the time...any excuse to laugh.

After fifteen months or so I moved from the novitiate to what is called the Juniorate, and on the fifteenth of October (feast of Saint Teresa of Avila, the patron of the Juniroate), we novices took religious vows for one year, poverty, chastity and obedience and we ceased to be novices and became Juniorate sisters. This was a house of studies and we would be here for three years.

We numbered about eighty-five sisters from twenty-six countries. The building is a monastery, which belongs to the Poor Clare Order. It is such a beautiful building and to be in a purpose built convent was heavenly. The Poor Clare vocations had dried up and there was just one old nun left in this monastery, Sr. Maria Rosa, who was in her late eighties. She wanted to live out her days in the place she had called home for over sixty years. So, the head of the Poor Clare Order in Italy looked around for a religious community that could take up residence with Suor Rosa and keep the life of the monastery vibrant...and so we arrived.

Monastero
S. PAOLO
delle Clarisse
TUSCANIA (Viterbo)

You have to hand it to the Italians – they know how to build...

I loved Sr. Rosa and I spent a lot of time with her, sitting with her, chatting and generally looking out for her. Of, course all of the sisters had a soft spot for Sr. Rosa, but you could ask any of the sisters and they would admit that me and her had a special friendship. She had a television in her room and she loved some company, so I would sit with her when I could (I think religious television is soooooooooooooooo boring). I would often go to my bedroom and find a banana or some sweets left by her fair hands on my pillow, how adorable is that? I got bronchitis on a regular basis whilst I was in Italy and I spent quite a lot of time in bed. She would come and visit me a number of times throughout the day, and even if I was snoozing she would wake me up for a little chat. I miss her –

like a granny I will never see again.

Sometimes Sr. Rosa got confused, mixed up between reality and the story that played out in her head, but she was very elderly and after sixty years inside four walls it must have been somewhat disorienting for all these semi-wild sisters to suddenly turn up and invade the place. When we were on a religious retreat we would always get up in the middle of the night to do extra praying (never enough hours in a day). Often the sisters would go to the kitchen for a strong coffee before heading to the chapel, otherwise it was to hard to resist the pull of sleep.

I was working on one of these retreats, that is, I was one of the gaggle of sisters who cooked and cleaned for those who were on retreat, therefore it was permissible for me to chat. Anyway, one evening, Sr. Rosa came to me in a rather agitated mood and she told me that the behavior of the sisters was not proper. I was completely perplexed and asked for an explanation and she informed me that the sisters were getting up in the middle of the night (true), eating pizza (not true) and gadding about the town (most definitely not true). I tried to calm her fears but once she had an idea in her head that was that, I only hope that she soon forgot this outrageous notion and started to think about something else more in keeping with reality.

The building was just magnificent; it must be the artistic temperament of the Italians that inspired the architect. Look it up on Google maps. Tuscania, Viterbo. It was a poor place to live as we lacked heating, sometimes hot water and at one stage we even lacked electricity and we had to pray early in the evening so as to make use of the natural God-given light. I loved the poverty of our life, because I had taken a vow of poverty and that should be lived not just spiritually, but also materially. We washed our clothes by hand (cold H20) and we ate a lot of pasta and red sauce or pasta with white sauce, the way nuns should live.

There were two long corridors with numerous bedrooms. In these rooms were bunk-beds and we usually slept six to a room. I am a very light sleeper and I struggled with snoring, people going to the toilet, creaky beds, the cold in winter, the heat in summer, the bloody pigeons that insisted on perching on the window sills. Holy poverty and holy joy.

These bloody pigeons drove me crazy. I had a bottle which I filled with water and when these horrid creatures starting hooting (or whatever they do) I would get out of bed and throw water at them. They flew away but within minuets they had returned. A few months later the sister who slept in the bunk above me said that she had been wondering for months why I kept throwing water out of the window, and the penny had just dropped. Imagine, she had been watching me throw water out of the window with no idea what I was up to; she must have thought I was completely gaga.

The order that I had joined was founded in Argentina and the majority of the priests and sisters were Argentinean. When the Falklands occurred I was only four and so I have no recollections of the war. I came across the issue whilst I was studying A' level politics, but I would argue that for the people in Britain is no longer an important issue, not when we are at war with bigger fish. So, it never entered my little brain that it would be a elephantine subject when I joined the Servants of the Lord and the Virgin of Matara...naive.

All the sisters who were non-Argentinean wanted to visit the father-land. I was told in a very good natured way that I should never go to Argentina as I would probably get shot, nice. From the moment I signed-up, I had snide comments thrown at me; a sister would show me a photograph with a sign-post reading Maldives (I did not even know they were called anything but the Falklands). A sister would play a recording of the *March of the Maldives*, which I did not recognize.

I was never made very welcome which at the beginning I could not understand. The head of the female branch of the order is called Anima. Before I met her I kept being told what a special person she was, so friendly and warm, so motherly. I was really looking forward to meeting her, but what an anti-climax. I was in Rome for Mass with the pope (I forget what the occasion was) and it was raining heavily. I was taken by a sister over to Anima and I had such high expectation. This sister introduced me as the first sister from England and Anima looked at me and said, 'well, the English like the rain so you should feel right at home.' There was no welcome hug, no smile sister to sister, just coldness and then she turned away from me. Good job I was very confident with a tough skin that could deal with these unpleasantness's. Remember I was the only sister from the U.K and I was soon made aware that the English are most definitely persona non gratia in this particular order.

Things different in England and Italy -important thingies

1.   Salt and Vinegar are my favorite flavored crisps but they are hard to find outside the British Isles. One Easter my folks sent me a box of confectionery which I of course handed over to the common larder. One night a packet of salt and vinegar crisps arrived on the scene and everyone who tried this particular delicacy did not like them. Boy was I happy because I got to eat them by myself. Salt and Vinegar crisps rock.

2.   Chatting about the weather. Plonk yourself down at the table and say, 'che bell' tempo ogi' (lovely weather today) and you will be rewarded with a confused stare.

3.   Chatting about grub. Plonk yourself down at the table and say, 'che bella pasta ogi (lovely pasta today) and you will be rewarded with a gaggle of nuns all with an opinion on the pasta and tomato sauce.

4.   Personal space. When I get on a bus and I have a choice between a seat by myself, or a seat next to another passenger then 100% of the time I choose solitude. However, in Italy if I got in the mini bus and there were two available seats, one directly next to me or one at the other side of the bus, then the sisters would always sit right next to me. The English are not a tactile race and it used to freak me out when physical contact was the norm.

5.   This last one is what makes the fact that England is an island set apart so obvious. Now, nuns are friendly, all the time and to everyone. Even when you do not want to be cheery-cheery, it was not an option, smile at all times. We often went on trips to Rome where sisters would always meet people from their homeland and they were always jolly happy to see each other. Oh my goodness, if a sister from the States encountered a group of travelers from that land then it was if they were long lost cousins, with hugs and laughter and photographs and the exchange of addresses and more hugs and photographs. Now the people from the States were always the extreme but I observed that most nations were thrilled to encounter sisters from their land. Not so the English. I k now what the English are like, give them a polite hello and then walk away. My superiors did not grasp this aspect of my fellow country men and women. Here is one example. We were on our way to convencia and we stopped off at a service station to use the toilets. As we stood in the queue there was an English couple stood behind us. My superior told me to say hello to them and I said that I did not think they would appreciate me disturbing them. However the order remained and so this is how it went:

Me: 'Hello, are you from England?'
Them: 'Yes.'
Me: 'What part of England are you from?'
Them: 'Devon.'
Me: 'Are you here on holiday?'

Them: 'Yes.'
Me: 'Bye, enjoy your holiday.'
Them: 'Bye.'

I turned to my superior and said 'told you so.' My superior looked at me aghast that our interaction was so formal and cold. This is Blighty and we do things differently here.

I say potato,
you say pasta.
I say tea,
you say espresso.
I say space,
you say cozy.
I say rain,
you say pizza.
Let's not call the whole thing off.

One evening, when I was in the Juniorate, a group of about six of us were chatting over supper; the topic of conversation was typical summer holidays in our respective country. It was a rather light-hearted conversation and I failed to pick-up on the seething animosity. The sister from Italy said that most Italians stay in Italy for holidays because they have such stupendous weather and breath-taking coast-lines. So it went. I said that due to the weather climate in England, we often go to countries where the sun shines for more than one hour every other day. This sister (Argentine) who was sat opposite me said in an extremely hostile tone, 'well, it is a good job that you have stolen so many islands around the world. You can always go to one of them for your holiday.' I was so shocked, especially as this was a sister who had a position of authority in the convent. I have to admit that I did not react well to this comment as it made me see red, so I replied, 'look, you started the war, you lost, we won, get over it.' Granted, my comment was rather childish and the whole conversation was soured for everyone involved. It was a relief when the bell went for night prayer.

I will give a quick overview of the honorarium in the convent. Monday to Friday the morning bell went at half-past-six and we were expected to jump out of bed, kneel down and pray three Hail Mary's and think of our morning proposal. Every sister had her own personal proposal that she was working on, which she would discuss with her spiritual director (a priest). The proposal was a mode of correcting a fault; for example, if a sister had a dislike of a particular sister then she could make a proposal to be extra nice to this sister. Or, if a sister struggled with pride, she might make a proposal to never mention how well she has done in an exam. So a sister works on this proposal every day because perfection was the aim.

As we slept in dormitories it was never a case of nothing stirring, not even a mouse, there were plenty of bumps in the form of people snoring, going to the bog, getting up early to study, late to bed because of kitchen service, as the King uttered, etcetera, etcetera, etcetera. One of the frequent disturbances was sisters talking in their sleep. I think this was due to three factors, firstly, some people naturally chatter in the time of slumber; secondly, we all had a lot of pent up emotions that were kept under-raps during the day and found an outlet in the dark hours; and thirdly, when a sister was thinking about a certain subject during the day, for example her sins, then they would sometimes burst forth in speech when she was unconscious.

When you heard a sister starting to confess her sins, one of us would jump from our bed and shake her back to consciousness so as to save the poor soul any embarrassment. Well, the other night I was woken by a woman speaking and from what I could gather it was of a rather personal nature, so I jumped up and went towards the sound only to discover it was just the radio. I hate being alone, I hate silence and I hate the dark so I keep the radio on all night. It is the World Service and therefore speaking, but when I wake up during the night, as I frequently do, I panic in the dark and silence. I also have a night-light which makes me feel about five years old. I wonder, when will I ever be rid of the convent? When will I awake in the morning and not experience that panic of being trapped in a place of torture? When will I be normal?

We had corporal punishment. Scourging. Flagellation. Whipping. Many sisters slept on boards instead of a mattresses, and no pillow. Cold showers, lack of food, not sitting back on a chair, offering to do extra days of service in the kitchen, there were a hundred ways to subdued the flesh. We also whipped ourselves. On a Wednesday evening, we would get ready for bed and then sit in the corridors with our own personal whips in hand; then at a given time the lights would be extinguished and we would lift up our tops and the whipping would begin. The duration of the whipping lasted whilst we prayed a decade of the rosary and a few other prayers. Then we would go to bed in the dark. Sometimes we acted out this punishment on other days such as days of retreat or Good Friday. It was not just us, on a trip to Spain we went to visit another religious community and we saw the 'discipline' (what we call the instruments used for whipping) they used and they were made of metal and had sharp pieces of metal attached to it, it must have drawn blood when they used it!!

There was also a metal belt; it was made up of lots of pieces of metal that finished in metal spikes that we wore facing inwards and thereby inflicting pain. This spikes would pierce the flesh, not so deeply as to draw blood, but just so as cause constant discomfort. It was an effective method of keeping the flesh subdued. At all times, the evil, fallen flesh must be kept under control. Whilst I was in Italy I tended to get bronchitis on a regular basis so I generally wore this belt on my thigh rather than my waist because I did not want the doctor to see the puncture marks when she listened to my lungs.

I did embrace this corporal punishment idea. I got rid of my mattress, and got a wooden plank to sleep on. I got rid of my pillow. I wore my metal belt every day. I embraced it all. Cold showers, bare minimum of food, work during siesta time, no middle ground for me. I saw sisters around me doing this level of penance and I wanted to be just the same. However, I got really ill. I recall it was the feast of St. Joseph and I had not slept for a number of nights, because I was so thin that every time I moved at night, the pain of sleeping on a wooden board woke me up, bone on wood does not make for a peaceful slumber.

The sisters encouraged each other in this corporal punishment. When I got rid of my mattress for a wooden board, the sisters I shared a room with actually congratulated me. When I was getting ready to move to Ireland another sister asked me at supper time what extra penance I had adopted in preparation for the 'fight against evil.'

Well, on the feast day I could hardly function. I was told that my eyes where black (we did not have any mirrors so I never saw myself) and I felt as if I was walking through candy floss. About five in the afternoon I went to a superior and told her that I was not feeling well. I went and got a mattress from the attic, some pillows from the store cupboard and went to bed. The following morning my eyes were so puffy that I could barely see, but I rose with everyone else and did all my jobs. Eventually in the evening I again I asked to go to bed early and my superior said a very welcomed yes. After that I cut back on the corporal penance and got on with my life. Some sisters are physically robust but I was not one of their number.

Back to six thirty in the morn. We dressed as quickly as possible, I always wanted a shower but obviously that was not executable   There were often jobs to be done before Mass, for example, if it was your turn at kitchen service, you had to rush to the kitchen and start putting things on the table in time for breakfast that was consumed straight after Mass . The chapel was incredibly beautiful, so simple and classic; I loved praying in that splendiferous space where generations of nuns had prayed before me. (English is an ever evolving language, so it is perfectly permissible to create ones own word).

Here is a tale for not doing important work when one is still in sleep mode. It was my job in the morning before Mass to place the hosts for Communion in the correct place (ciborium) and put everything ready on the altar. One Sunday morning I messed up big time; imagine saying big time in a very slow Texan drawl because what I did deserves emphasis. On a Sunday we not only had ninety nuns, but also a number of people from the local town, so the chapel was bursting at the seams. All went swimmingly, the priest said his prayers, invoked the Holy Spirit and we lined up for Holy Communion. Then, oh my goodness, my heart, brain, lungs, bladder all sank. As the priest lifted the lid on the ciborium, he discovered it was empty, he had been praying over an empty container. I had forgotten to put the hosts out for Mass, and there was a room full of people waiting for this angelic bread. Praise the Lord, there were enough hosts in the tabernacle that had been left over from a previous Mass. The Mass was saved but I was in deep do-do.

Bella capella

We went for breakfast and afterward I stood in line to see my superior and receive my punishment. I play the flute and this was removed from me for three months. I think this was a just punishment...it could have been a lot, lot, lot worse.

After Mass we had breakfast which usually consisted of coffee, tea and biscuits. It sounds a bit fancy to eat biscuits for breakfast, but it is something that we were donated biscuits rather than bread, so that is what we munched on. You never left the table needing to loosen one's cincture.

The whole day was spent running from one thing to another. So then we ran (literally) to class. Some of our lessons were held at the seminary where our priests dwelt. We had a few mini-buses and cars and so the sisters would travel the twenty minutes journey to Montefiascone. After my first year at the Juniorate I was exhausted. I have always a rather delicate creature physically and the strain of keeping up with the younger sisters was just too much. In my second year I was given permission from my superior to not attend the classes at the seminary and I stayed at the convent; although I still sat the exams for all the classes that everyone else was doing. I would look the notes

54

that the sisters took in class and we had a class program (usually in Spanish!!! This is because most of the professors were from Spanish speaking countries so they wrote the notes to complement the lectures in espanole, ola! I do not speak Spanish, but it is very similar to italiano so I was able to muddle through). But muddle I did and happily. HAPPILY – what a beautiful word.

I still took all the classes, but now I could sit down a bit more. I adore studying so I enjoyed the way that philosophy stretches the mind to ponder new worlds and a radical way of seeing the universe. Opening one's mind is a truly beautiful thing. Dostoyevsky claimed that the world will be saved through beauty and I agree because if we do philosophy, that is think about everything, then we will make the world a better place. It is similar to going to Tate Modern and you leave a different person than when you first walked through those sugar doors; you might not care for everything you see, but it causes one to think with an enhanced appreciation of the capacity to think.

So the morning was taken up with lectures or personal study. Everything was ruled by the sound of the bell. I love playing practical joke and once I took the dong out of the bell so when the appointed sister went to ring it then silence would reign. I chose the day when the strict, scary superior was out of the convent and I would also be out of the house visiting the elderly. Everyone knew it was me because I had a reputation for playing jokes. I get that aspect of my character from my darling Daddy. I recall once when I was working in Stratford-upon-Avon, I went home to visit my folk's for a few days. I just had one of those small suitcases, but on the way back to Stratford the case was so heavy. I did not think much about it, but when I got back and unzipped the case I discovered my Father had added a few heavy stones to my luggage; so generous papa.

It was important that every moment of everyday was ordained for one. No free time to just relax and think...that thinking could be dangerous. Keeping people busy is a form of brain-washing. Too busy to think...

I also taught English to one of the aspirants. She was such an incredibly beautiful creature; she laughed and cried easily, was super generous and a real pleasure to spend time with, but she was not a pleasure to teach as she detested English and therefore never did her homework and clearly would have preferred root canal surgery rather than practice her verbs and adjectives. I was a strict teacher.

At twelve-thirty we prayed the rosary. If it was sunny, as it usually is in bella italia, we prayed as we meandered around our garden, if sister rain was making her presence felt then we prayed in the chapel. After we concluded the rosary we would make an 'examination of conscious' this is when we would recollect in silence and recall our proposal that we made in the morning and see how we were getting along (remember when I told you about the personal proposal?) We then asked God for the grace required to keep our proposal for the remainder of the day.

Then it was lunch. As my magical Mother has often said, 'hunger is indeed good sauce', so if you are hungry, we would happily consume the fare and lunch never lasted very long. If we were in service, then we would dish up the grub, make sure there was water on the table, if we had bread, keep the bread baskets full and generally smile and create a felicitous world. Service is a beautiful act.

Then from two to three there was that wonderful Mediterranean tradition of siesta...happy times. Even if I did not fall to sleep, it was wonderful to take off my habit as by this time my veil was usually wet with sweat (gross). A good trick was to soak the bit we wore under the veil in cold water before putting it back on my head and it kept me cool for about ten minutes.

After we had arisen from out rest, we all toddled off to work like the holy fraggles we were. Jobs were too numerous to list here, and over three years I did various things from cleaning, sacristy and for two years I was the librarian. I adored being the librarian; the books were kept immaculate and in correct order. There was no messing in my library and I guarded the books as if they were the crown jewels. I knew every book in that royal palace. That is why I get so distressed when I go into a public library and I discover disorder.

Every summer when the exams were concluded we went all over the world doing various works, such as youth camps. In the September of my third year I went with three other sisters to do a mission in Scotland, along with some of our priests, seminarians and minor seminarians. What a blast I had. The idea of a mission is that we work in a parish for a week or two and everyday a priest would give a talk in the Church (priests talked, sisters worked), we would go out in twos to the houses of the parish, run an after school group for children, have a pizza night for teenagers and generally spend our days reaching out to the people of the parish. The male members of our group stayed in the parochial house and we stayed with the Sisters of Nazareth who had a convent in the parish. Oh my gosh, these lovely sisters bent over backwards to be hospitable to us. We would return to the convent about midnight and they would always have lots of scrummy food waiting for us. We stayed in comfortable rooms and generally I had a ball. I adored being in a parish, mixing with the local people and going to my slumber at night with the feeling of a day well spent.

When we finished the mission I was kernackered. When I returned to Italy I slept for three days, arising just for Mass. This experience left me secure that I wanted to be a nun working in a parish, getting to know the locals and doing anything I was able to help everyone I came into contact with, it was heavenly.

In my third year two teenagers arrived from Scotland to live with the aspirants. I was asked to look after these two sweeties and I loved them with a passion that took me by surprise. There is nothing I would not have done to make their life easier. Their superior was not able to speak English so for the first few months, before they learnt Italian I was able to liaise with their families in English and then tell their superior in Italian. They were home-schooled so I did a lot of translation. I saw these two Scottish darlings as my primary concern and my own studies took a back seat.

I have to say I am rather clever (my head is now so big; I doubt my neck will be able to support it). I reach this conclusion because I missed so many classes and I still got excellent marks. I was crap at languages and italina and Latin fell flat, really flat, but all my other subjects were top notch. I was ecstatic when in the second term of my second year I was told that I would no longer be required to do Latin as I was going to help another sister who was struggling with her studies. This sister was not at all academic, but she was really lovely and I enjoyed spending time with her...although I confess, we did not fill our ten hours together with study but often ended up discussing other things of mutual interest.

After work we had some free time; not really free time but a space in the day when we could attend to our own personal jobs. It was here that we had time to wash our clothes (by hand and in cold water), have a shower, have a coffee, practice the organ or anything else that was required. Then back to classes and study till seven-forty but the last hour or so could be used for other things such as preparing apostolate work or catching up on other bits and bobs. There was always plenty of bits and bobs.

I am one of those people who attract trouble. Believe me, I know I can be a brat but I truly start with the intention to do everything perfectly. At the mo, I am staying at my folk's house for a fortnight as they are on holiday in Ireland and I am playing Saint Francis, looking after the animals. I broke the toilet seat as I was trying to clean it. Then I smashed one of the glass shelves in the fridge and I still have seven days to go.

Well, this trouble was my constant shadow in the convent. Granted, most of the time I was in trouble I was as guilty as a drunk in prohibition Boston. I took biscuits without permission, I was late, I just oozed bother from every pour. The most hurtful thing a superior has ever said to me is 'you need to try harder, make more effort', because I can say with my whole being that I always gave the best of me to every second of every day. I spent most of the time tripping up and falling flat on my face, but if there is a God, the deity will defend me because I always, always, always, gave my best...no reserves. I took comfort that God could read my soul and deep in there I was good...not a failure, but good and worthy and a success.

One thing that I found repulsive is the way that sisters would run to a superior and 'grass' over another sister. I know the sisters from the States said that they would go and tell their superior everything, if you had a cross word with a sister, go tell Mother, if you saw a sister doing something wrong, go tell Mother; go tell Mother was the key. E-V-E-R-Y S-I-N-G-L-E M-I-N-U-T-E T-R-A-N-S-G-R-E-S-S-I-O-N This was also true with sisters from other countries but maybe with my English schooling where telling tales was an anathema, I just could not do it. Only once in five years did I go to a superior about another sister and this is because I was worried about her health and she did not want to cause a fuss, but I think she needed to see someone.

Just take the punishment and suck it up (a phrase I learnt from the sisters from the USA).

I know that sisters often went and grassed on me because I was forever being corrected. On a Wednesday we played some sport in the afternoon after siesta. We had a large garden and at the other end the garden was a Church that had been converted into a music school. We could hear the music very clearly and one week a woman was singing *Gloria Gainer's 'I Will Survive'*. I had a bit of a sing along as we endeavored to play volley-ball. Well, someone (I never knew who) ran to Mother and I was corrected for singing along to modern music with immoral words; I happen to think it is a wonderful feminist tune...justifying oneself was not encouraged my dear.

There was a superior in the convent, not the Mother Superior, but another superior who we also called Mother and she had the enviable title Prefect of Discipline. It was her job to snoop. She had a little black book where she would jot down every misdemeanor that a sister performed and would dole out punishments; more about them later. She would go around all the bedrooms and make sure beds were made in proper nun fashion (we had lessons in the novitiate), make sure no towels, sock or any other brick-a-brac was out of place (a place for everything and everything in its place). Then during the day she would glide around owl like and note down any faults committed by us nuns in training.

Each Mother had what was called a secretary, but was really a dogs body, someone to wash her clothes, clean her room, make her bed and other errands. One day I was chatting at lunch with some of the sisters about this and that, when one sister said something about me being Mother Aracoeli's (who held the title, Prefect of Discipline) secretary; I replied that I was not, but she said that she often sees me with her, and I confessed that I was with her so much because I was usually getting told of about something.

Mother Aracoeli was seriously scary; the comment about being an iron fist in a velvet glove was created for her. She is petite, Argentinean, clever, and an amazing organizer, but scary. Imagine you see a glass of Bailey's Irish cream and it looks so smooth and creamy, so you take a sip and you get a hit of poitín at the back of your throat that causes a coughing fit; that is MA. You never knew when she was going to metaphorically hit you and whenever I left a room I would say, 'please God, don't let her be in the corridor.'

I am also on the petite side and once I picked up an incredibly large pan full of water and something in my back went snap. The doctor put me on steroid injections and these knocked me out so I for a week I slept a lot. One day MA came to see me and she was actually friendly; I was rather surprised but hey, don't look a gift horse in the mouth. Later that day she went somewhere for a few days and I remained in bed for the rest of the week. On the Sunday, as is fitting for the day of resurrection I did a Lazarus and came back to the land of the living. She also returned that day and when I saw her on the corridor I stupidly expected her friendly streak to still be flowing in her veins; no. She looked at me like I was something dirty and smelly; the smile I tried to give her died on my lips and the mistrust returned to my eyes and the disapproval to hers.

She was the mother superior you had to ask permissions from, to use the phone, go to bed early, have extra biscuits etcetera. I often did things without permission because I was just too scared to go to her; I did not know what mood she would be in and by this time I had lost my tough exterior. I never disliked her though because I always longed for her affirmation. I was not the only sister who was afraid of her. Even when my friend came to stay with me for a few days, she said that she was rather intimidated by Aracoeli.

For example, I wanted to use the washing machine because my back was still painful and washing my clothes by hand was a bit too much. After our brief encounter on the corridor I could not pluck up the courage to go and ask her (this was the same day), so chicken that I am I wrote her a note and placed it on her desk. That evening, I was on my way to the chapel for evening prayer when she collared me just outside the entrance and rebuked me for writing her a note instead of coming to her in person. Many a time she corrected me just before prayer time which is an awful thing to do because I would spend the next hour and a half thinking about the scolding rather than praying. This tipped me over the edge and I cried so much, but I did not want to cry in public so I went to another chapel that we had in the convent.

One afternoon when we were playing sports, I fell on some concrete and cut my knee. The following morning it was a lovely mix of blood, blue and purple. As a rule, we were not permitted to wear sandals until the first of April (no joke!), until then we had to wear winter shoes. This fall was before April, but my boots were rather cumbersome and so I put on my sandals as it was easier for my knee. That morning I got up, went to Mass, went to breakfast and then sat in the dining room to study (the dining room was the warmest room in the house as it was next to the kitchen, so many of us sought refuge there to study). After about ten minutes I saw the door open and in sauntered MA, but I actually sat there calmly because I knew, without a shadow of a doubt that I had done nothing wrong. I was where I was meant to be, I had not argued with anyone, I had not been late, and obviously she was here for some other sinner. I think you can guess where I am going with this. She came up to me, but still the penny did not drop, and told me off because I was wearing sandals before April the first. I wanted to scream. How could she in such a short time, with ninety sisters all wearing floor length habits, notice that I was wearing sandals? How? Should I be honored that I was so special to be singled out in this way?

Then there were her classes. She taught history of philosophy which was one of the most fascinating courses I took. Now she is a bright cookie, but...humility alert...she was not as bright as me. There were some sisters who were intellectually superior to me, but MA was not one of them. We had very different views to learning. For her it was all about rote learning. Only once in three years of lectures with her did I ask one question; I cannot even remember the question but it was during the medieval, scholastic period; the reply she gave was that Aquinas would not have posed such a question and that was the start, middle and end of that. However, in posing the question and I quickly understood that I was to absorb what she said and not query anything. *'It is the mark of an educated mind to be able to entertain a thought without accepting it.' (Aristotle).* No free thinking allowed here.

At Cambridge we were expected to do mainly personal study. Lectures were given, followed by a long book list and off we went to read, read, read, think, think, think, write, write, write, defend, defend, and defend. Mere regurgitation of lectures was not looked on favorably. At university I found seminars so exciting, where I would write an essay and the tutor and a few other students would rip it apart. So I am used to doing a lot of reading about a given subject and coming to my own conclusion; it did not matter if I thought completely differently from the fellow next to me, what mattered that was that I could defend my position. Not so with MA, her particular mode of teaching really flummoxed me, because study should be learning, thinking and not mere recall.

Due to the somewhat icy manner of MA I always made sure I knew everything that was possible to know about the subject, nothing in the exam was going to catch me off guard...naive. Oh, in Italy, the majority of exams are oral not written. In the first term of my second year I learnt everything from the lectures, but I also did a lot of independent reading. I was blessed that in our library we had the nine volumes *History of Philosophy by Frederick Coppleston*, who is the man to read on this subject. I went swaggering into the exam, overflowing with confidence. All went well, I answered perfectly, but then the question that was my undoing came; she asked me where I had got all this extra information from. I happily told her that I had been reading Coppleston, after all, which historian could not be in awe of Coppleston? I was quickly rebuffed and informed that in the exam she expected me to simply give the information she had taught in lessons, anything else was not welcome. I withered like a rose in the Sahara. I think she insisted on this mode of examination because I do not think she knew the subject matter deeply enough to cope with a student who knew more than she did.

In the second term of the second year the exam was like a high jump into a shallow pool. As the majority of our exams were oral we usually went in alphabetical order. The first few sisters would go to the examination room and the rest of us would sit near-by waiting our turn. As my surname begins with M I was usually somewhere in the middle, that usually meant a five to eight hour wait. So the exam began and about ten of us were sat in a corridor nearby, reading over our notes (and sometimes chatting, which we were not meant to be doing). After about half an hour a sister came (a snotty-nosed class prefect kind of lass) and called us all into the examination room where MA informed us, with a sickening amount of glee, that she was failing most of us because she wanted us to all be in the examination room at the beginning and then we could go outside to wait. As the majority of us were in the corridor, perhaps it was a break-down in her communication, but we were the ones who were punished.

In the end, she was not permitted to give us a big fat zero as some of the sisters had a low score average and it would drag them down to an overall fail. In the end most of us got an A for absent and had to bloody re-sit the exam about two months later. This was horrid as we had begun new courses and having to revise for an exam from a term earlier was fucking annoying.

I actually saw her just before I left for Ireland and she was friendly, but I had been bitten too many times by her and I was too nervous to respond. I never want to see MA again; I would actually go out of my way to avoid her as she is just too scary. Be afraid, be very afraid.

Generally I enjoyed the exam period. During this time the sisters were permitted to get up at five-fifteen to get in some extra study. I never got up early as I was tired enough with the regular honorarium so the idea of getting up early was a big no-no. Also, I loved the chats I had with sisters whilst we waited. There was one sister who was always directly in front of me. We had been novices together and we were both the sort of sister who did not run to Mother superior with every little of a perceived misdemeanor by a fellow sister in Christ. So we had a good old chin wag and we told each other secrets that we would never have trusted to another sister. It was a beautiful, precious time.

A little story I hope to show that although I was a failure as a nun in numerous ways, my intention was holy. As we were waiting for a particular exam, we were sat outside as it was a glorious Italian summer's day and we had a beautiful courtyard with a pond in the middle. Well, the sister in the queue in front of me was not very academic and she was very, very stressed during the exam period. This day, this dear soul was sat on a bench weeping as she awaited her execution. I saw her and my heart lurched as I saw my sister in distress, so I abandoned my revision and went over and I danced a silly little tap dance and I sang a silly little ditty to make her laugh, and laugh she did. I was not meant to be talking, let alone singing and dancing, but I could not abandon my sister in her pain. I could not believe it when I did not get in trouble for this misdemeanor, I got in trouble for everything and I braced myself for this rebuke, but it never came, and even to this day I am amazed.

We also had some very funny times whilst we waited for the exam. There were some sisters, who revised in the library to the last possible moment, but I was not one of them, and thankfully there were some other sweet-hearted sisters-in-arms who were always up for a giggle. For example, in the corridor outside one of the exam rooms there were three toilet cubicles, so whenever anyone went to the toilet we would bang on the door and make silly noises and when they left we gave them a guard of honor. This all sounds so infantile, but remember, these were very young women and stress is relieved in laughter. I had done the whole degree thingy and so I did not feel the pressure, I just wanted to be a good, holy, kind sister, exam marks were not all that.

Gosh, have I still not finished our daily time-table? So I left us in the chapel praying. We prayed till nine thirty and then we went for our evening meal, quick, quick, quick, munch, munch, and scrunch. At ten we returned to the chapel for our last prayer of the day. Then back to the library for more study. At this time at night I was zombie like so I often stared at my notes that had magically turned into double-Dutch. Then like the song of an angel the bell rang at eleven and we all rushed up to bed to be ready before the lights were extinguished at eleven twenty. As we were going to sleep we were instructed to think about Mass the following morning, so that we had God on our minds as we snoozed. I tried to get sleep super quick before the snorers started who created a cacophony to rival the last night of the proms.

On a Saturday we went out into the community to do some apostolic work. For my entire time at the Juniorate I visited the elderly and house-bound. I have always related well to the elderly and so this work was a delight. At university I looked after two elderly people and this sort of work is peaceful because I actually felt like I was doing some good in the world. These old fellows really appreciated a visit, someone to chat to and look at some old photographs. And boy, did they make great Italian coffee...I have not discovered anything but dirty water in inghilterra.

On a Friday and Saturday evening, instead of study we had a time of relaxation together, on a Friday we ate pizza and played games, danced, chatted or whatever caused us to be joyful. The majority of the sisters were just adolescents and were brimming with energy. There were just a few of us in our thirties and we often said how nice it would be to sit quietly with a cup of camomile tea and a pleasant Dave Attenborough nature program. Some of these youngsters would use the formal 'Lei' with me, which is used with the more mature of the population, they would say it in jest, and it made me laugh. Some of those sisters were complete darlings and it was a privilege to live with them, they were far more virtuous at eighteen than I will ever be and just thinking about them restores my faith in humanity. I laughed a lot, a great deal, a good deal, everyday in that convent. If I was ever feeling crap, there was always someone who would make me smile.

At Christmas and Easter we celebrated big style. Gosh, it was all so creative and I marveled at the inventiveness of it all. This is what we did. At Easter we had a week of Pasquetta and at Christmas we had Navidad. All of the sisters were divided into groups and each group would come up with a particular theme, for example, the 1950s, Kings and Queens, The Colors of the Rainbow, (where each person of each group had to come as a different color), Fat (I found this theme gross as everyone had to dress up as fat people, and all the food was fried and greasy). We had an abundance of fancy dress clothes in the convent, most of the clothes came from sisters when they initially came to the convent, I have no idea where some of the stranger items came from, such as wigs and hats.

These festivities would be held in the evening. Base-camp was usually the dining room, which would be decorated to within an inch of its life, but there were usually some form of party games that took part in other areas of the monastery, particularly our extensive garden (heaven knows what the neighbors thought). I recall one Easter a friend of mine from England came to visit. She had gone to bed, but we sisters were still partying. It was a nursery-rythme theme evening and we played a game based on the Pied Piper of Hamelin. Each of us was a mouse and we had a balloon attached to our ankles by a piece of string. A sister played the flute and we had to try and burst the balloons belonging to the other teams by stamping on them, whilst defending our own team. Can you imagine the noise? The flute, sisters screaming, the bang of balloons...and this particular game was played on the corridor in the guest wing. So my dear friend was lain in bed listening to all this noise. She told me the following morning that she had no idea what was going on and was too scared to peak outside her door. How we laughed the following morning when I told her what we had been up to.

We were not limited with our theme, and as a group we created decorations, posters, games and so forth from what we could find around the monastery. As we were beggars, we had no money, so we either had to use the food that was in the monastery larder, or we asked the good folks of the town for food. Of course, the food had to fit in with the theme, on a budget of zero; it was a wonderful opportunity to have fun for nothing. The night usually finished rather late, and everything had to be tided up before going to bed, so that when the priest came for breakfast the following morning, the dining room was restored to its monastic order. I recall a few evening dancing till four in the morning, and then getting up a few hours later for morning Mass. It was tiring, but exhilarating.

In Italy, they have these massive Easter eggs. No small one Euro eggs for them. A few kind people bought us these eggs at Easter and there was enough chocolate for every sister to have some yummy confectionery. One evening, a few of us took the wrapping from one of these eggs and wrapped me up as an egg, and then they carried me into the dining room and placed me on the main table, after three I jumped out and surprised all the sisters. Now, this may sound rather childish, but we laughed and laughed. Laughter came very easily to us.

Another celebration was when a sister was preparing to take her final vows. It was a mock wedding reception, where the sister in question wears a bridal gown (either borrowed, or donated to the convent). It was not a hectic evening like Pasquetta or Navidad, but a more civilized affair, with a nice meal, all the sisters dressed as wedding guests, maybe some singing and dancing. It was a beautiful to celebrate with a sister who usually returned to her own country for the actual taking of vows, so this was our celebration. The whole bridal thing made me feel slightly uncomfortable. All these brides, and one bridegroom (Jesus) which made me feel part of some harem. However, it was always a special evening as we loved our sister and wished her every good thing possible. We did have fun.

One example of how I tried ever so hard to be a diligent nun is once when I went to bed and tried to be quiet, only to wake most of the corridor. When one was on kitchen duty (about twice a week) one was often still in the kitchen, washing, drying, cleaning floors and all those normal domestic duties when the lights had been extinguished and the first nuns were beginning to snore. So one evening we were given a lecture on the charitable act of being as quiet as possible when going to the land of nod. Take shoes off before entering the dormitory, do not bang bathroom doors, and remove one's habit before entering the bedroom and so on. I know I have claimed this before, but I really, truly, verily tried by best, I wanted to be a saint.

So the following day I was on kitchen duty and this appeal to quietness was at the front of my mind. I was going to be the quietest nun ever. Not only did I remove my shoes before I embarked upon the long corridor, off they came before I even walked upstairs. I also removed my habit on an upper landing and used a bathroom well away from the sleeping beauties. So far, so good. I was pleased with my practice of charity and started towards my dormitory where my aching body and contented soul could slumber till the morn.

Then it all went wrong. Sisters often left their habits outside the dormitories because in the mornings there was too much flesh for us all to change in the bedrooms. Also, some sisters got up early because they had to go and collect the priest for mass or various other reasons that made changing in the dorm somewhat impracticable. So as I reached towards my door, in the pitch black, I fell over a wooden chair that was the hanger for someone's habit. As it was as black as the eyes of a spaniel I went right over the chair, causing it to crash to the ground and sending the habit to a jumble on the floor. The crash was also accompanied by all the noises associated with the occurrence of someone falling over a chair in the dark.

One time I recall that after night prayers it was my job to make all the coffee for the following morning. We did not have time to make all the coffee in the morn so we made it the night before and reheated it in time for brekkie. Now, I was tired and I am ultra crap at anything practical and so my coffee making did not bubble successfully. So, there I was, gone midnight, burning coffee. I wanted to go to bed and tell everyone to have tea for a change. I was in a bad, black mood with little patience and in walked a superior (in her pj's) and informed me that it had gone midnight and I should have finished the coffee by now. I did not reply but in my heart I was screaming at her, 'do you think I want to be in the bloody kitchen at this time of night, making bloody coffee when I could be in bed ?????' I have absolutely no idea what time I made it to the land of nod that night but there was coffee at breakfast the following morn, and no one was poisoned.

I tried so hard to be good, to be charitable, obedient and quiet and I literally fell on my face, thank goodness there were no eggs.

Life in the convent was not an indulgence of femininity, cleanliness was expected but nothing more. In Carmel we did not have shampoo or deodorant and the soap came in the huge green blocks that required one to cut it up into more manageable portions. We only had a bath or shower once a week and the sanitary towels did not have wings (this seems like a minor thing, but wings to sanitary towels is what butter is to hot toast, not exactly necessary but oh it makes life far more pleasing).

In Italy, when I was a novice I often had to skip a daily shower due to lack of time, and when it is the height of summer that is just gross. When I went to the 'big school' we were instructed to have a daily shower but there are only so many hours in the day and the time allocated to showering was severely curtailed. If I had another job to do in my free time then adios showering, but at least when we has a shower there was soap and shampoo. Again the sanitary towels usually lacked wings and washing bloody knickers in cold water was not exactly pleasant or particularly hygienic. Rather than posses our 'own' things such as cream, toothpaste, shampoo, these items were held in common which meant that they remained in the bathroom for general use.

One day I had a shower and as usual I was rushing, always rushing, I did not even turn the light on. After the shower I grabbed what I thought was the face cream and shoved some on my cheeks. Annoyingly this tin of cream was actually in English, but I just plastered it on without reading the label, mistake. The cream felt awful and would not rub into my skin. Only then did I turn on the lux and read the label only to discover I had caked my face in shoe polish.

I am European and body hair does not faze me; leg hair helps keep the pins warm during the winter months. Cultural differences are absolutely fascinating. We Europeans were not that bothered about unwanted underarm hair but the sisters from the USA were obsessed about being hair free. To them, removing leg hair was as basic as cleaning one's teeth. I think I am too lazy for all that jazz.

They were disgusted that there were women who kept their hair just as nature intended. There was even one sister from the States who entered the convent with a mono-brow and before she received the religious habit she was whipped off to a beauty salon to get her eyebrows seen to; a sign that the convent has too much money?

I can understand the sisters from Asia or Egypt removing facial hair because they had very dark hair and it can be upsetting if you are talking with someone and they keep staring at your chinny, chin, chin. These sisters helped each other and removed hair expertly with some cotton thread. We also shaved our hair on our head (not bald but extremely short), but that was a practical matter as long hair cost shampoo and would stick out of the veil. We usually shaved each others hair as it was easier, but the shavers were so incredibly loud and sometimes when we had visitors they would ask what that loud noise was. I never gave the secret away, but they must have been ever so perplexed.

Another way that the convent's desire for mammon that was utterly distasteful to me was the reading out of donations on a Thursday evening. Every Thursday we had what is referred to as Chapter where various announcements would be made and the accounts of the convent would be read aloud. We were constantly seeking monetary donations for the Order and if a sister had managed to obtain a large enough donation (about two hundred Euros plus) then her name would be read out at Chapter and she would be praised. This always left a sour taste in my mouth. How could a sister from Egypt, ever hope to ask her family for so much money? Whereas, a sister from an affluent European family could raise so much dosh. Why should one sister be humiliated that her family was poor and another praised because her kin were rich?

It reminds me of a story that my Father told me. My paternal family were poor, very poor and yet they would scrip and save so as to be able to make their small offering at Mass every Sunday. There were of course rich families in the parish and they too would make their ostentatious offering. Somehow, the amount that each family had contributed was reckoned and the parish priest would read this notice of pride and shame from the pulpit. A family who had only contributed a pittance, even though this pittance was formed from sacrifice, was embarrassed by the parish priest and the richer families showed their plume like strutting peacocks. My God, had this priest never read the Gospel story of the widow's mite?

Another thing was the disproportion of material items that each sister owned. Some sisters had sandals held together with elastic bands, and some sisters had kindles and tablets and even their own lap-top. This cannot be right. In the religious life the attitude that 'I am okay and have everything in abundance' in detriment to my sister who does not own a single pair of socks without holes is abhorrent, yet this is what happens.

The sisters from Egypt were amazing and they taught me so much. Most of them had come from the rural parts of Egypt, generally were unschooled and as simple as they come. Imagine, most of these women could barely read and write in Arabic, and here they were, speaking and studying in Italian. In the past the Egyptian sisters did not come to Italy to study as it was generally too hard for them, but in 2011 it was decided that it was too dangerous for them to remain in Egypt so they came to Italy as a refuge...and I am jolly glad they did because otherwise I would not have met them and my life would have been impoverished by their absence.

Most of the Egyptian sisters had no documents such as a birth certificate and so when they had to get passports it was rather complicated as most of them did not even know how old they were. One evening I was chatting with a Egyptian sis and her cousin had entered the convent at the same time so here they were together in Tuscania. Sister F told me the tale of when they had to get their passports. Due to a lack of documentation they all trapsed off to the doctor who gazed into his crystal ball and was able to discern how old these women were, however, this was not a fail-safe method and Sister F told me that her passport it has her date of birth and on her cousin's passport her date of birth is given as a few years older. The thing is, these cousins had grown-up next door to each other and she knew that she was born before her cousin, a few years before. How weird is that? So here were these women, with false information on their passports...not that it matters, but it is highly interesting.

One day I received a parcel from home. Post went straight to the superior, and once she had looked at them they would be left on our beds. I was in a dorm with an Egyptian lass and she asked me what the parcel was on by bed, not what was in the parcel, but what was a parcel itself. I explained that it was a gift from my folks in England. She could not grasp how it had got from England to Italy. I explained about the postal service, but she was completely perplexed. I inquired if her family never received letters, bills, documents in the post. She said that if her folks required something, they had to go to Alexander for it, which was one heck of a journey for poor people.

Another story that this sister told me that had a massive impact was about the toilet in her home. She belonged to a poor family and they did not have doors in their home, but rather they had curtains. One day, a group of sisters went to visit her family and one of these sisters was from a more affluent family and she was verbally horrified that she was expected to use a WC that did not have a door. The mother of this family turned round and stated, 'Jesus was born in a stable. What is good enough for Jesus, is good enough for us.' What a woman. True sisters must imitate Jesus.

Sunday was the day I disliked the most. It was not a day off, but a day of sport, cleaning the convent, yuck. I was always glad when the light on a Sunday dimmed and Monday was fast approaching.

I tell you about two of the most beautiful people I have ever met, very different, but I was honored to call them both Mother. The first one is Mother Salut, she is a proud Castilian and oozes holiness from every pour; I love her. She became my Mother when I moved to the Juniorate and as you have already gathered, I was not the most perfect of nuns, and although I had to be taken to task a number of times by her, she would correct me, give me a punishment and then we moved on. She never belittled me or made me feel broken; rather she would speak to me as a true Mother to daughter and I would realize my error and she would make me want to be a better person.

She is actually younger than I am but she has the wisdom of a gray-haired granny. She had so many talents it is hard not to be jealous that she got such a large dose in the talent queue, when I got a dose the size of a grain of sand. Yet, one was never jealous of her because she used her gifts for the good of others and so it was such a privilege to have such a woman looking after you.

She was far more intellectually gifted than any other sister I encountered; she was really, really funny and could entertain a room full of people as if she were just having a chat with her neighbor. She could sing and like a true Spaniard was like a super-star when she picked up her guitar. She was also really 'cool', she came across as a mere teenager, she would slouch in her seat and her shoe laces were always undone. In the winter she would don a gray hoodie over her habit and invariably the sleeves were too long; and yet, she was always the Mother Superior, there was never any doubt that she was in charge, not in the sense that she was walking round with a 'look at me' attitude, but rather, in the sense that allows you to sleep in peace because you know you are safe when she at the helm.

I sometimes had to go to her office to deliver a book that she had requested from the library and I was always so excited, like a puppy that wags a tail when the owner comes home. Once, when I had been rebuked just before evening prayer I just happened to be sat in the same pew next to her in the chapel; and just to be near her made me feel so calm – only a Mother can do that. There is a Russian saint called Seraphim of Sarov. He lived alone in the forest and his notoriety for holiness drew many people to come and speak with him. One day, a man came to speak with Seraphim but when he arrived, Seraphim was asleep and so this man sat and waited for him to awake. After the night passed and the morning dawned, Seraphim was still asleep, but the man realized that simply being in the holy man's presence had answered his questions and brought his soul to a place of peace. That is how I felt about MS.

I was not the only person who felt like that, everyone felt like that; all the sisters, all the people in the town, all the visitors to the monastery. When she left the Juniroate at the end of my second year, for a new position in Madrid there were many wet faces. Actually I was not sad, because I believed that it was God's will and that was the only thing that mattered. Also, I looked at this amazing, beautiful, talented, generous, holy, kind, gentle, wise Mother and it was only right that other people should also have the special experience of knowing her.

The second person I want to write about is the Mother who came to replace MS, also an MS so do not get confused, this time Mother Siluva and although she was very different from the original MS she was also worthy of the title Mother. She is the nearest I am ever going to get to living with royalty, not in a haughty manner, but in the sense of Princess Di or Kate, friendly but with an obvious inner gravitas that cannot be denied; Princess Grace of Monaco had nothing on this Argentinean lass.

She is very tall and slender and everything about her was perfect; her habit was immaculate, her veil hung like French lace, nothing was ever done in undue haste and I swear she did not walk like mere mortals do, but sort of glided around the room like Fred Astair and Ginger Rodgers. Once I even saw her eat an orange with a knife and fork...amazing.

When she spoke to me she really listened; she looked at me as if there was nothing else in the world for her to be doing except converse with me, she made me feel important and I loved her. I love her. She was ever so different from MS but she was a worthy successor. Nothing was going to go wrong with this special bundle of motherliness.

I struggled at being a good sister and yet she made me feel that I could do it and she never spoke harshly to me. I remember one difficult evening and I had gone to bed early, it was a Friday evening and I knew that it was pizza night and everyone down stairs would be waiting for her and yet she came and spoke with me for a long time, only a heart full of compassion would do such a thing. She had ninety daughters to care for and yet she supported for each one of us as if we were an only child. I know she will never read this and therefore will never know how much I think of her, but her goodness will be her own reward.

I love philosophy, in fact that is what the word means; philo means love and sophy means wisdom, like the name Sophie. I loved having my mind stretched and thinking about things I have never thought about. Have you ever had that experience when you go to a modern art gallery like Tate Modern and as you stroll around the various installations you feel as if you have walked into another world? One is taken outside of one's self and one's own narrow world; that is what philosophy for me. I am aware that we had to learn exactly what we were taught and regurgitate it in the exam. However, I had to think about these things, not just learn them as one does the eight-times table, and this got me into trouble.

I listened, read and learnt, but I also disagreed...horror. It was during one exam period and I had taken a particularly difficult exam and I got full marks, but a number of sisters had failed, including sisters who were considered top notch students. MS asked me how I had got full marks and I jokingly said that my parents are really rich (not true) and I bribed the examiner. I do not come across as an intelligent person because I like to laugh and laugh at myself. As Mr. Shakespeare stated, *'The fool doth think he is wise, but the wise man knows himself to be a fool.'* All my life people have always been surprised that I do so well at exams. I have never had a chip on my shoulder about my image as a fool; why should I care what other people think of me?

The next day I took another exam that was considered one of the most difficult and again I got full marks. Again MS asked me how I did so well and I again laughed it off. By now I was starting to worry because I learnt the material perfectly, but I also realized that I did not believe all that was coming out of my mouth...scary. I wanted to say what I actually believed, but I knew that I would probably fail, and what was the point of that?

I will give you an example. In the Catholic Church, when a person is baptized they receive an indelible mark on their soul. This is a mark that can never be erased even if the person (like me) does not actually practice their faith. Even if I commit every mortal sin, the mark remains. This indelible mark is only gifted with sacramental baptism, which is with water and the words, 'in the name of the Father, and of the Son, and of the Holy Spirit.'

Now there are other forms of baptism, such as baptism by blood (martyrdom) or baptism by desire. So if there is a person in a Muslim country and they want to be a Christian but there is no one to baptize them, they can be baptized by their desire. However, this is not sacramental baptism and they do not receive an indelible mark on their soul. In the Catechism of the Catholic Church, which is a sort of A to Z of Church teaching, it states that a person who dies without sacramental baptism is not guaranteed to pass through the pearly gates but are entrusted to the mercy of God.

What a terrible teaching. If God created every soul, then God must be held responsible that the good people of Tibet have never heard of Jesus and baptism. They practice Buddhism because that is what their ancestors lived and that is all they know. In this world the majority of people are not Christians through no fault of their own; for this crime should they cast into the fiery furnace for all eternity? Think about this for just a moment, what kind of God is portrayed by this teaching? *'Men create gods after their own image, not only with regard to their form but with regard to their mode of life.' (Aristotle).* If God is love, then every soul must be loved equally, not just the favorite ten percent of the world. If I believe in a deity, what kind of God do I want to worship? If God is love, then he cannot love one person more that another.

The Church argues that this is why we need missionaries, to go to these places and convert the infidels. Harry S. Truman when he was President, had a note on his desk in the Oval Office that read, 'The buck stops here.' I think God should have this note on his heavenly desk, the buck stops with the one who created us, and not leave all the results to mere mortals who are limited creatures. I am not omnipotent, omniscient, omnipresent...on God's school report it would read, **'could do better.'**

In the exam I waffled on about metaphysics and indelible marks and Aristotle's ten categories, but what I really wanted to say was, 'this version of God is not appealing and I have so many doubts, what shall I do, where shall I go to find the truth?' So I got a hundred percent, but my soul and mind were unsettled. Intellectual freedom?

One day Anima came to the Juniorate and as it was the time of the year when sisters started to discover where they were destined to after we finished our studies. Anima saw me on the corridor and called me into the superior's office and there she informed me that I was headed to Bunclody. I was thrilled. My heart leapt with joy. This was it, I was finally growing up and was going to be a real nun. All the sisters were attending a conference in the dining room so I sneaked into the darkness and there at the back of the room I spotted one of the little Scottish stars and I whispered in her ear that I had a destino. It was top secret where I was going, but the butterflies in my belly needed some form of outlet. This wonderful girl came out into the garden with me and there we jumped, leaped and laughed on the trampoline. I was so happy.

1.   I get to work in a parish just as I hoped.
2.   I get to move to Ireland, a country I love.
3.   I get out of the library and get to actually help people, concretely.
4.   I get to live near my extended family.
5.   I get to speak in English!
6.   I get to have visits from my folks and big bro.

Life continued as normal but the excitement grew as we became aware of more and more sisters receiving their future path. We did not know who was going where, but this was what we had been training for during the ups and downs of the last four years. One evening the superior arose and told the community where each sister was going, an evening full of hugs, laughter and tears. We loved each other deeply, and we knew that this was a final goodbye, we would probably never see each other again in this life, but our eyes were on heaven and we knew we would be reunited on the other side of the pearly gates.

The night before I left Italy I discovered my bed covered in gifts and balloons. I arose in the middle of night, said goodbye to Tuscania and headed to England for a holiday with my family before I went to Ireland...with high hopes. Ignorance is bliss, and if I had known what was waiting for me in Bunclody I would never have got on the plane.

CHAPTER EIGHT

Ireland 2015

Abandon hope all ye that enter here...

I am going to digress for a few moments to make some comments about swearing. I grew up in an Irish household in a working class town and I went to Ireland every year for my holiday so I was raised surrounded by foul language. It does not bother me in the slightest; I was more offended when people blasphemed. I did not swear as I never felt the call for it; live and let live is a wonderful motto to adopt but when it came to the odd curse my lips were sealed. This sprung principally from my faith.

Now I am going rather pious – sorry if it is so sickly sweet that it causes you to feel nauseous. I tried to think about God every moment I was awake and I liked to think about Mary, Joseph and Jesus in their daily existence in Nazareth. I pondered on how they would interact, especially in their mode of speech. How lovingly Joseph would address Mary and Jesus, how happy they would be in each others company because they all cared for each other. (Do you feel nauseous yet?) I did not think that swearing would be heard under that hallowed roof and therefore neither would I have recourse to these words. This can be demonstrated by a syllogism;

Major: All Christians imitate Christ.
Minor: Christ did not swear.
Conclusion: Christians do not swear.

Thank heavens we have confession to repair our soul when we fall short of such lofty ideals.

So, I did not care for swearing, but nor was I shocked when others partook of such vocabulary. However, I was shocked if I heard a priest or a nun swear (which I did hear, unfortunately). When I was a novice we were running a summer camp for children. Italian kids are spoilt brats and therefore horrid. Many families only have one child and consequently they are treated as royalty. They do not say please or thank-you but they are well adapt at cussing. When I moved to Ireland the children were like angels. I was stunned the first time I asked a group of children to form a straight line and they actually did it without a murmur. Every time I worked with children in Ireland I was overwhelmed at their manners and respect. Imagine when all those Italian brats grow up, Italy will become a very selfish society. Anyway, back to my first summer camp in Italy. One of my fellow novices had clearly reached the end of her tether and she said the 'F' word. I was stunned. Now when I reflect on this moment I feel sorry for the sister but at the time I was disgusted.

The worm has now turned. I never uttered a swear word whilst I was a sister, but when I returned to England I was so depressed and my brain had gone on holiday and my vocabulary dwindled to the level of Bill and Ben. There were times when I was so frustrated that I found great relieve in swearing. I talk to myself all the time (I still do) because I find that this lowers my anxiety. I waffle on about nothing but a constant stream of consciousness helps me function like a relatively normal homo-sapien. Sometimes when I am out in a public space and there are lots of people I walk down the street with my eyes down, clenching and unclenching my fists saying 'fuck, fuck, fuck fuck, fuck, fuck,fuck, fuck, fuck, fuck fuck, fuck, fuck,fuck, fuck, fuck, fuck fuck, fuck, fuck,fuck, fuck, fuck, fuck fuck, fuck, fuck,fuck, fuck, fuck, fuck fuck, fuck, fuck,fuck, fuck, fuck, fuck fuck, fuck, fuck,fuck, fuck, fuck, fuck fuck, fuck, fuck,fuck, fuck, fuck, fuck fuck, fuck, fuck,fuck, fuck, fuck, fuck fuck, fuck, fuck,fuck, fuck, fuck, fuck fuck, fuck, fuck,fuck, fuck, fuck, fuck fuck, fuck,

fuck,fuck, fuck, fuck, fuck fuck, fuck, fuck,fuck, fuck, fuck, fuck fuck, fuck, fuck,fuck.' You get the idea. Yes I must look and sound like a nutter, but I think of myself as a nutter. God might be in his heaven but all is not right with the world.

The first time my parent's heard me swear was rather amusing. My parents have a bloody over-sensitive fire alarm that fills their bungalow with the cries of hell. One Saturday I was visiting them and the fire alarm came to life and screamed at me. We did the whole thing of waving tea-towels in front of it, opening doors and windows, but it refused to be silenced. My head was exploding and I said, 'please turn off that fuckin' alarm, I cannot stand it.' My Father looked at me and just chuckled. My Mother looked aghast; poor critter, I know she does not like me swearing but she has heard it so much since then that she keeps her disapproval internal.

So, now I am a woman who swears and I do not feel guilty about it. I would try not try not to swear in front of a child or elderly person, but beyond that I think anyone is fair-game. My vocab, or rather lack of a decent vocab. is still a source of frustration so there are times when only the 'F' word will suffice to assuage my anger and pain. So there will be swear words in this memoir, because that is my reality. I have no desire to offend.

In July 2015 I moved to Ireland. I was happy to finally be a 'real' nun – no more playing, here I would be putting into practice what I had be training for over the last four years...and I would be able to be a hundred percent sure what people were actually saying to me (well, maybe eight-five percent of the time!).

That day there was a problem with the plane engine so we were delayed in Manchester for a few hours. After a very bumpy flight on a replacement plane I arrived in Waterford. Ireland is so familiar to me that when I arrived on the Isle of Forty Shades of Green that it was felt that I was only natural that I was sent there. Of, course I had been in Bunclody a few years previously and I knew the Church that would be my base for the next few years – or so I thought at the time.

Mother Knock who was the superior in the convent collected me from the airport. She is a very pretty woman with a delightful smile, quite tall and incredibly thin (as she ate practically nothing). We chatted amicably on the way to the convent and nothing was a surprise or particularly uncomfortable. When I arrived at the convent I was actually pleased to discover that it was placed directly behind the Church next door to the parochial house. It always seems wrong to me that women and men who have taken a public vow of poverty live in what is a relatively palatial dwelling. A convent should be poor and any physical deprivations should be embraced as our solidarity with the poor. I think that those people who waffle on about poverty of spirit as opposed to material poverty are rich Christians who do not want to be challenged by the Gospel message. Of course there is a place for poverty of spirit, a humble, peaceful people are lights in the world, but this does not exclude the call to be materially poor so as to help our poorer brothers and sisters.

So I was pleased with the house. There was absolutely nothing wrong with it, lots of bathrooms (three) and four toilets, double glazing, heating, a nice kitchen, plenty of rooms; it was a nicer house than many people have, but it was poorer than many convents I have visited. I shared a room with Sr. Grace, it was a large room with two sets of bunk beds and an en suite. I was glad I had to share a room because of the vow of poverty; a room of my own would be incredibly comfortable and luxurious. Naturally I would prefer my own space, but as I have mentioned previously everything a nun does should be aimed at becoming as poor, chaste and obedient as possible and material deprivations aid this journey.

I started my life in Ireland running and that summer we had a camp for children, plenty of visitors and I loved it. I particularly enjoyed chatting to the people who came to Mass. After Mass had finished I would go to the back of the Church and have a little chinwag with the delightful people in the parish. I felt at home with these wonderful, friendly and generous people and I felt that I was doing what I was born to do; and I envisaged that I would be doing this work for a number of years to come. I was so alive, full of peace and purpose.

A thin me with some fat Irish pigs

Only one thing struck me as odd, Knock (I am just going to refer to her as Knock from now on because I do not think that she is worthy of the appellation Mother) and Grace were very, very, very close and I did not feel welcomed into their community. In one way it was only natural as they had been together for a few years, but this was my home now but it was definitely them and me and I was shocked that Knock, as the superior of the convent did not make more of an effort to help me become part of the community.

One example of this was a summer fair that took place in the parish a week after I arrived. We had been asked if we could help on the burger stand. There were two other sisters staying in the convent for a few weeks trying to learn English. So Knock told me and the other two sisters to go and work on the burger stand which was okay with me, but I was shocked that all day we worked on the stand (and it was hot and messy) and I saw Knock and Grace walking around together just looking at things and drinking tea. They had arrived late and left early and did absolutely no work. I had no problem with working on the stand but I had always lived in a convent where everyone helped each other and we all shared the work. However, this was a pattern that would repeat itself many times over the next year.

One thing that is vital to religious life is the intrinsic relationship between the inward community life and the outward apostolic life. No matter how diligent a sister was in her work outside the convent walls, if her relationships with the sisters who make up her home life are not strong, loving and happy then her work is useless in the sight of God. It would be like the Trevi Fountain without water or a football team without a goal-keeper or a library without books; possible but in reality useless.

That is why in Italy we all worked so hard at forgiving each other, trying to support each other when the other is sad, or accepting the hand of sisterhood when one needed support oneself. Why we pushed back the table and chairs on a Saturday evening and danced, swirled, laughed, played music and healed the wounds of stress and exhaustion. I miss my sisters so much, but I know they are lost to me now.

When I moved to Ireland there was no community life for me. Grace and Knock were so devoted to each other that there was no place for me, the unwanted third child, the black sheep. Grace would have done anything for Knock. In the beginning when Knock was around Grace was careful what she said to me, but when we were alone then she did not hold back. As time went on and Grace realized that I was persona non gratis with Knock she would also berate me in front of Knock.

Just a little act that struck me as odd was one Friday night a box of chocolates was taken from the larder and placed on the table. So far, so normal as we often had sweets after supper on a Friday, Saturday and Sunday evenings. Knock never ate sweets, but Grace and I did. So the box was opened and there was a love-heart shaped chocolate right there in the middle; Knock leant over, took this choco and gave it to Grace. They shared an 'ahh' moment and I felt like a third wheel. Weird, really weird.

This caused me confusion and worry. Where was the necessary cohesion between the community life and my work outside the convent? After all, I enjoyed immensely my work, visiting the elderly, drinking lots of tea and consuming vast amounts of apple pie. Trying to interact with the travelers, especially as Knock and Grace acted as though this part of the town did not exist. To kneel in homage during Mass, thanking God for bringing me to this splendid small town in Wexford where I loved the people, and felt loved by them, where I could imagine myself living for many years quietly spreading the gospel message of love, kindness and hope.

However, as my community life unraveled I had to question if anything I was doing outside the convent was actually of any value. I was like a woman who got wed. to the man of her dreams, bought a large family home that she planned to fill with seven children only to find that she is sterile and as the years pass her marriage turns into a one act drama full of recriminations, bitterness and pain. To the outside world, they have the most wonderful marriage, fancy holidays, big house, two cars and a yacht. At cocktail parties they seem so happy and close, her with a Chanel dresses and him with his distinguished gray hair. Oh how true is the saying, 'no one knows what goes on behind closed doors. No one could imagine what was going on behind the convent door in Bunclody.

Another example that caused me a lot of distress was that sometimes, after we had finished our night prayers (Compline) we would go to bed and Grace was in charge of turning the lights off at a specified time. I am a light sleeper and Grace is very noisy so I always knew if she was in her bunk or out of the room. So after lights had been turned out I would hear her leave the room and go to Knock's room which was just across the corridor and I could hear them laughing together. I heard Grace returning to the bedroom a long time later. The next day there would always be lots of sweet wrappers in the bin so I knew that they had also been having a party of two. I was never invited to these community socials and it made me feel so unwelcome in the house, as if I was just there to work but not invited into the inner circle of the community.

As a nun, we view suffering as a positive thing so I could 'offer it up' but we were also taught that if the life in the convent is not healthy then the work outside the convent in the community will not be effective – and life in our convent was far from healthy. When you have a problem in the community it is not as though I merely have a problem with my boss who I can moan about when I return home; or go out for a cuppa with a friend and tell her all my woes, those things do not happen in a convent. I could not tell my family as I did not want them to think I was unhappy. So I kept silent and hoped that as time passed I too would become an appreciated member of the sisterhood. Alas, this hope was ill founded...

Every day flowed, we arose, prayed, ate breakfast (always the most difficult meal for me because it was then that I would ascertain if Knock was in a good mood or not). Then Mass, study, housework, lunch, siesta (a strange concept for Ireland, but because the order was founded in Argentina we kept a lot of their customs). In the afternoon I would usually go house visiting. I became a Catholic Jehovah Witness. Grace would give me a list of street names that I should go and visit and I would start at the very beginning (a very good place to start) and knock on doors explaining that I was a religious sister (which was stating the obvious as my habit was a bit of a give away in a Catholic country) and if there was anything they needed then they could contact us. Most people were friendly but did not invite me in for a cuppa, only the travelers invited me in, but that is something I will write about more extensively later on as it was a real bone of contention in the convent.

For those of you who know Ireland, you will know that the weather is not always clement and there was me walking around in the rain and cold for a number of hours every afternoon. I am not a shy and timid creature, but I cannot force people to invite me in, however, when I returned to the convent and informed Grace of where I had been she was always really annoyed with me because I had not actually made it into the dwelling. Mamma mia! Also, the town was new to me, and as anyone who knows me, I am rather ditzy when it comes to practical things and I could get lost in my own back garden. So, I often got lost. This was a source of amusement to the good people of Bunclody as it is a very small town and the idea of losing one's bearings was ridiculous – but the fact is I often got lost. When I told Grace that I had got confused about the street I was meant to visit she would get really miffed with me.

Later in the year I started to make house visits with Grace which in one way was more comfortable because she drove the car and so I did not get wet all the time, but I also felt very on edge because Grace would always criticize me after a visit for the things I spoke about during the visit. I am a great chatter box and I love nothing more than sitting down with an old lady, a cuppa and a bunch of old photographs. I can talk forever (as my Father would say, I can talk the hind legs of a donkey), I talk to anyone, at the bus stop, in the supermarket, in a cafe – and I talk about anything. So visiting an elderly person and chatting away for an hour or so was no problemo. I also tend to make a lot of jokes as I think laughter is a beautiful thing. Grace was not keen on my jokes and comments and after the visit I knew that there would be negative comments and there was no way that I could make Grace see my point of view so I just accepted the criticism in silence. I have proof that my so-called failings were reported back to Knock.

When I started to get sick I found that I was unable to chat away for an hour. My mind went into a fog and I found that I was unable to think quick enough to hold a conversation. I wanted to curl up in bed with my duvet over my head and never interact with another person. At this point I found that I cried easily and often and all this made house visiting incredibly difficult, and some days it was impossible. As the year drew to a close and the days became dark early I was usually sent to house visit by myself and Grace got to stay in the warm, light convent with Knock who hardly ever did any apostolic work.

When I was cast out of the convent in the afternoons I would usually go for a walk down by the river and ponder if I would ever have the courage to actually cast myself into the water and fight against the natural instinct to rise to the surface and inhale air. After this I would head across the road to the Protestant Church.

So I was in a conundrum. It was cold, dark and usually wet and I had been sent out to knock on doors, but inwardly I was in a miserable coma. Bunclody is home to two Churches, one Catholic and one Church of Ireland. The Church of Ireland is up on a hill and has a graveyard attached, with no through traffic and this is where I usually took myself on these miserable afternoons. I would escape to the hard, cold steps behind the Church that looked onto the graves and there I would sit in the rain for hours till I had to return to the convent. I became numb physically but that merely mirrored my inner state of being. I saw the houses with their lights on and they looked so cozy and inviting and I thought that I would like to live in a home where I felt welcome and safe – but I did not.

This Church was placed on the top of a small hill and the graves where at the back. If it was light enough I would wander through the graves, reading over and over again the names, dates and biblical inscriptions on the cold, wet stone. How I envied those corpses; whatever misery had been their earthly lot was now ended. They had fought the good fight and now had their crowns in heaven with Jesus, Mary and all the saints.

At the back of the Church there were some stone steps and these became my tuffet as the darkness became ever so dark and usually the drizzle would seep into my habit and cause my bones to turn to stone. Sometimes I wished that some nice, grannyish woman would find me, take me to her house, place me next to the warm range and place a large cup of soup into my hands that would restore life to both my body and soul. This never happened and I would have to sit there for hours before the time allotted permitted me to return to the convent where no one cared how wet or cold I was.

The darkness in the graveyard was rich and heavy. I would sit on the top step with my knees tucked in trying to keep warm (pointless). I did pray in my misery. I prayed that things would miraculously be healed in my fractured community, or that I would be sent to another community, or that Grace and Knock would be sent to another country and be replaced with a superior who would be a true mother. Mostly I just prayed to die, a car accident, a problem with my heart that had gone undetected, an electric shock, struck by lightning, pneumonia, anything that would make this horror story stop. I did not want to upset my parent's, but I could see no way out.

This evening (December 2016) R4 did an excellent piece on bullying and its effects. There were two people giving their personal accounts of bullying. One was a young man who was badly bullied at school and who twice attempted to commit suicide. The other was a mother who had the heart-breaking account of her son who was also bullied on social media and successful committed suicide.

The man's story resonated with mine and I stood transfixed as I listened to his account of hell because if you just changed the pronouns and tweaked it a bit, he was telling my story. He said that he imploded and became numb. That sums it up really. I too imploded because I had no one to tell what hells that bitch put me through. I too became numb because the pain was too much to feel and I died inside. That bitch bullied me into a breakdown and I am not sure I will survive.

GRAVEYARD BUNCLODY

My settle is ordained for me.
A cold stone step
is more comfortable than the chapel pew.
Everyone here is dead,
including me.
The cold seeps into my bones
and joins with the coldness of my soul.
As the rain falls
I wish it were acid
that would strip

73

the flesh from my bones
and leave a mere skeleton.
I long to lay down
and become the bed-fellow
of the corpse of Agnes Fitzgerald.
As time drifts to seven thirty
I walk away from the graveyard
and my body returns to the convent,
my true mausoleum.

At this stage I realized that there was something seriously the matter, both with me and with the community. One thing that I have practiced for a long time is trying to be aware of the world around me; I could sit and look at a single flower for half an hour, or make a conscious effort to escape my own internal video and listen to the birds chirping as they went along their merry way. The walk around the golf course was incredibly beautiful with a canopy of mature trees and the dappled sunlight as it shone down among the leaves. As you turned the first corner of the walk there erupted a feast for the eyes because the trees in autumn were a magnificent display of red, orange, yellow, green and brown. On the other side of the river were fields where sheep grazed and beyond them were hills as grand as any Hollywood could produce. I would often brace myself as I prepared to turn this corner as I wanted to be startled by the beauty as I had been every time I had sauntered down this path previously and yet, nada, nada, nada. I looked at the trees, sheep and hills with, well with nothing. My senses had ceased to function. You do not have to stop breathing to die.

On my ramblings around the golf course I would think about what I could do to rectify the car crash of my vocation. I could ask to move from Ireland to another convent, for me it was irrelevant where I was in the world, as long as I was doing God's will. However, I knew that my family was very happy that I was in their home county and would be devastated if I moved to another country where they would be unable to visit me. Also, I believed that God was calling to serve in Ireland and therefore I had to find a way to cope. My hope lay in the fact that both Knock and Grace had been in Ireland for a few years and they might move to another convent and two new sisters would be sent to Ireland. Grace had family in the U.S.A and she went to spend some time over that side of the pond during the Christmas period...so I hoped that she would soon be moving. Also Knock complained about Ireland and Irish people all the time so I thought that she would not stay in Bunclody for an extended period. She had been in New York before she came to Europe and she was always spouting how great it was compared to Wexford.

The parish of Bunclody actually consists of two Churches, the one in Bunclody and another in a near-by hamlet named Kilmyshall. When I had first visited Ireland it was our priests who had run this smaller parish. Then, about six months before I went to Ireland in 2014 there had been a scandal. There were two I.V.E. priests (who were actually cousins) from Argentina. The parish priest got a parishioner pregnant and he left the priesthood and moved to Spain with her. The other priest also left the parish with no prior notification and because of all the child abuse that has plagued Ireland there was a diocesan investigation. No impropriety was discovered but the I.V.E priests will never be permitted to run another parish in Ireland. Knock said on a number of occasions that the sisters should have left Ireland at the same time as the priests. Throughout all this it never occurred to me, not even for a nanosecond that I should leave the convent, this was my vocation, this was my faith, and this was my life...forever.

I have to press the rewind button now and take us from December back to September. Knock went to visit her family in Argentina during September which was initially going to be for one month, but there were some issues about her family so she stayed a few weeks longer, but that is her story so I will not elaborate. I was left in charge. I am sure this must have been a humiliating thing for Grace as she had been there for a few years and I had only been there a matter of weeks, but hey ho that is how it went. Grace is an incredibly strong character and she would come down on me like a ton of bricks all the time. She is also physically incredibly large, tall, big and overweight, so in all ways she was an intimidating creature.

She criticized everything I did, and I mean everything. It became absolutely ridiculous and I had no idea how to deal with her. A silly but telling example is the water tap in the kitchen. It needed a new washer and it tended to drip. Physically I am rather weak, I did not eat all my spinach as a child, and I could not turn the tap enough to stop it dripping. One lunch I turned the tap off (Grace had a problem with the skin on her hands so she was unable to do any washing up; I do not know why she could not just use washing up gloves, but Grace was Knock's pet so that was that). Grace told me that I had not turned the tap off properly and I replied that I was unable to turn it anymore. Oh my goodness, she was like a Jack Russell with a rat. She kept telling me that I could turn the tap off if I just made more of an effort, I said I could not and she said I could and on and on it went till I just asked her to please stop criticizing me all the time. I am sure if she ever saw me on the toilet, she would criticize the way I wiped my derriere!

I felt that as the sister-in-charge my main role was to keep a happy, peaceful community. But Grace had different ideas. Her adopted role was to make my life as miserable as possible. If we were talking at the table (and as there were only two of us it was imperative that I initiate a dialogue) and I said something like 'I was chatting to so and so after Mass and she said blah, blah and I replied blah, blah' no matter what I had said Grace told me that I should not have said it. One Friday evening I did not have the resolve to keep talking as I knew how it would go. Grace told me it was really boring and I said 'Grace, I do not know what to say anymore because whatever I say you just criticize me.'

If she went out and I asked her where she was going (remember I am in charge of the convent) she would just say 'out' and refuse to tell me. I am not telling you all this as a form of character assassination, but as a way to build up the picture that would eventually lead to my break down. As I write this it sounds so petty as if we were children in the playground, but it was not petty, it was horrid and I felt drained and depressed and wanted to cry all the time and I had no support. I knew Grace was in contact almost daily with Knock as she would use Skype in the office (but the door was shut so I did not hear the conversation). In the six weeks Knock was in Argentina she phoned me twice – the second time was the day before she was coming back to Bunclody. I was unsupported and on the slow train to a terrible place. *'Fear is pain arising from the anticipation of evil.' (Aristotle)* I was full of fear and pain.

I knew I was being spied on. I do not use the word spy lightly, but it is the most apt word for the situation. I know that Knock needed to know what I was doing but it was more than that. There was a good friend of the community who would do odd jobs for us around the house. He was incredibly generous with us regarding money. One day, when I first arrived in Bunclody he came to me and told me not to trust the sisters, especially Grace. He said that the sister who had been there before me was a really lovely sister (I actually knew her from Italy as she was one year ahead of me) but Grace and Knock had been horrible to her and in the end she left the order and returned to her parent's. He knew all about it as this sister had confided in his blood sister. He said that she had gone to his sister crying that she could not take it anymore.

There is a beautiful saying about home by I. Crawford that reads: 'Home as a safe place, a loving place an a creative place.' I could have cope without the loving and creative bit but I needed the safety aspect. I was not safe with Knock and in fact I was in danger.

From our time together in Italy I was actually very friendly with this sister and I considered her one of the nicest, most generous people I have had the pleasure to be acquainted with. Knock painted a rather different picture and she told me on a number of occasions that this sister was lazy and the people of the parish did not like her. I did not confess that I knew this sister and I just kept silent and nodded my head. I have never spoken to this woman since she left and so I do not have her side of the story, but I can well imagine Knock saying the same lies about me now.

This same man came to be a few months later and said that Knock had asked him to stand near me outside the Church after Mass and tell her who I spoke to, the duration of the conversation and the subject matter. Oh please! At daily Mass were just a few old dears and we spoke about the weather or what they were having for lunch. No cold war secrets were traded. He said that he wanted to tell me what was going on as he liked me and did not think that it was a just way to act.

It was also at this time that I did something wrong that led me to discover that there was a spy within my own camp. The computer that we used in the convent was a common use item, that is Grace and I used the same computer and Knock had her own laptop. So we had a general email account, which meant that I was unable to send private emails to anyone. On the computer there was a file named confidencial (confidential in Spanish, as if I was not able to work out some simple espanol). I should have left it well alone but I did not and what I read lead to me losing part of my mind. This confidential file was actually daily emails between Knock and Grace and they were all about me. So Grace was sending constant emails to Knock informing her of my every move, when I used the telephone, how much I conversed at meal times, what I ate, who I spoke to, everything. Then there were the daily replies from Knock that were just so friendly and encouraged Grace to continue to spy on me. During the same period, the emails between Knock and I were scarce. Grace also informed Knock that she was doing most of the work around the house and I was doing sweet f.a. Lies, lies, lies.

When I read this file I felt that I had fireworks going off in my brain. I did not know what to do. I could not tell a friend as all my emails were public (all the emails I wrote were also sent without my knowledge to Knock in Argentina) and I knew Grace listened to my phone calls. I could not tell my family as that was just not the thing we did in the convent. I remember sitting on the stairs in the convent with all this confusion in my head and I did not know what to or who to turn to. The obvious answer was to turn to God in supplication, but I felt a little bit crazy at this point and I really had no concept of how I was going to get through this. Later, I would tell a superior in Italy some of the cruel things Knock had said to me, but she replied that she did not believe me. So to top it all I was considered a nun who lies – what is a girl to do?

So what I did was to get a razor and cut my thighs. This was the start of my self-harming that would rapidly descend to a dangerous level. I sat on the stairs and slashed at my legs and out poured into action all the pain and confusion that I felt inside. However, as I was the sister in charge I felt that the most important thing I could do was to keep a happy and peaceful home (even if this was not the case for me); so I turned my frown upside down, went to dinner and I could have won an Oscar for my wonderful portrayal of a nun who is the embodiment of all that is joyous and calm.

Life started to become something of a blur after this time. I know that Knock returned from Argentina and I was desperate to lay aside the mantle of responsibility, let her deal with Grace, even though Grace would never have spoken to Knock the way she spoke to me, she only attacked those she thought she could overpower. I needed Knock desperately at this point, I needed to talk to a mother. The day after she returned her and Grace went out for the day (I do not know where but this was a common occurrence, but I hoped that she would split the time between us and help me make sense of what was going on). I was left alone, again, had lunch by myself and was coming to realize that hope does not always spring eternal in the Christian breast. Over the next few days I was alone most of the time as I was sent to do door to door canvassing and Knock and Grace remained together in the convent. Lady Di said that there were three people in her marriage, well there were only two people in this community and I was simply the court jester.

I am going to write about the traveling community as this was a major bone of contention in Bunclody. When I had visited the community just before I entered the sisters worked a lot with travelers. A third of the children in the local primary school were from the traveling community and therefore they were a sizable minority. However, it was like there were two communities in the town and there was limited interaction between them.

It was extremely rare to find a traveler marrying a non-traveler (a settle person). One couple in Bunclody consisted of a traveler man and a settled woman. I was told that when they first started a relationship there was a lot of trouble with their extended families. I presumed that it was the woman's family that were upset, but no it was the mans! The traveling community did not want one of their men marrying a settled woman because if there was any trouble in the marriage a settled woman would leave her husband whereas it was almost unheard of a traveling woman leaving her husband and community.

Once they marriage, that is it for life, and even after life. There was a young traveler woman (twenty-one) in Bunclody who had married aged eighteen, got pregnant, gave birth to a lovely little boy and then her husband died in a car crash. I was told that this woman is never allowed to re-marry and if she did then the whole community would shun her. I felt so sorry for this young woman, mother to a boy who would grow up and leave home, a woman with not enough education to get a job and no prospect of re-marrying because for the travelers a woman must be a virgin on her wedding night.

When I returned to Bunclody in the summer of 2015 there was a marked change in the attitude of the sisters to the travelers. I am the sort of person who would strike up a conversation with a chicken on the street and so when I went to work in Ireland I was full of optimism and zeal and wanted to talk with everyone and help anyone I could.

The travelers are generally Mass goers so I would often have the opportunity to speak with them at that point. My main interaction with them was when I went door knocking. The people in the town were extremely nice to me, but generally when I went door to door people did not invite me into their homes; but the travelers always did, without a single exception, invited me in for a cuppa, cake and often dinner. When it is cold and dark I was grateful for this warm hospitality.

I am not so naive that I am not aware of the issues that concern the traveling community. When I was at university I would sometimes go to a traveler site to give catechism classes to children who were preparing for First Holy Communion. I know there are issues of alcohol abuse, violence and so on. For me, the guiding light of my actions has always been to follow in the path of Jesus. Not a comfortable middle class interpretation of the Christian manifesto, where dropping a few coppers into the collection plate of a Sunday, whilst wearing my Marks and Spencer's outfit, suffices. I have always been a person of extremes, both in good things and bad. I understood that my religious vows were a way to radically live the Christian message.

In practice this means that I sit down and chat to the homeless. I stand up for those who are weak and vulnerable and I fight against injustice. I go to those of the margins of society and tell them that they are welcome in society. Now, I know what you are thinking, 'yeah right, who actually lives out that?' You would be correct. I do not live out these ideals, I am not even close, but they remain my ideals that I want to live by. That is why the Catholic Church has confession, because we fall so, so short of what we should be. Catherine of Sienna said that if we were what we are actually meant to be we would set the world on fire. I really like tattoos (please excuse my tangents) and I want to get one that simply reads, be kind; because if we were all just kind to each other than what a beautiful revolution we would cause.

So, when I met the travelers, I had a good background knowledge of the them, both from my Irish family and my work in Cambridge. If there is someone who is alienated from society, for whatever reason, you have to reach out to them to make them part of society. Otherwise the status-quo continues to the detriment to all citizens. If children get an education, the world opens up to them, but if they live in on the outskirts of the town then their world is oh so small.

I got to know a number of traveler women and they have very tough lives. They have not received an adequate education, they married very young and have a number of children. There is a big drinking culture among traveler men and this leads to crime and domestic violence. I heard stories from some of the women that would make the hardest of hearts weep with pity. There was little I could do except listen. I did advocate to some of the women that they should take their children and go to a woman's refuge, but this was unthinkable for them as shame was a major issue, so they kept their problems secret. If they left their husband then their children would not be able to remain part of the traveling community and therefore not able to wed within their culture. These women spoke to me in confidence; how could I turn my back on them? Yet that is what I was required to do.

I was told by Knock and Grace to stop going to traveler homes and if they came to the convent I was not to let them in and I was to discourage them from knocking on our door. Apparently, because we were financed through the parish, and we received a lot of financial donations from the 'settled' people we had to work with the parishioners who were not travelers, as the travelers were not financially beneficial to us.

We had a kid's club on a Saturday and a lot of traveler children came. I thought this was perfect opportunity for us to teach them some skills that would help them integrate better with the settled kids. Yes, their behavior left a lot to be desired, but if nuns were not willing to do this work, who would? Yet we not only discouraged some of traveler children from coming to the club, we actually bared some of them. I was mortified and there were unpleasant scenes with the traveler mothers being (understandably) confused, upset and angry.

One incident demonstrates this attitude to the travelers perfectly. It occurred during one of Knock's absences and I was in charge. It was a Sunday evening, I remember because on a Sunday we prayed in the Church rather than in the convent so that anyone from the parish could join us. I was sitting near the rear of the Church when I was approached by two traveler women. One was heavily pregnant and both seemed very young. They told me that due to domestic abuse they had decided to leave their husbands and they were heading to some family who lived in another part of Ireland. They had a car full of children and they asked me if I had any food I could give them. The cupboards in the convent were constantly overflowing with food and we never knew want. I went to the convent and filled two carrier bags with biscuits, sweets and drinks. We would never miss this food and if I asked myself 'what would Jesus do?' then I had to help them, for me, these women came to me whilst I was praying and therefore they were Jesus for me in that moment. 'Whatever you do to the least of these my little ones, you do unto me.'

I gave the food to the women, apologized that I could not do more for them, promised to pray for them and I returned to prayer. When we got back to the convent I told Grace about this incident whilst we were having our dinner. She hit the roof. She told me that I should never give the travelers anything as they would just keep coming back for more. I was shocked at her attitude and hurt that a woman of God could adopt such an position.

A windy day in Wexford, wearing my Dad's hat

Another incident that disturbed me was when a woman in the parish committed suicide. It was an horrific incident that affected me deeply. Even now, I think about this woman every day. It was just before Christmas and she drowned herself in the river that was not far from the convent. As I stared at the river, the frigorific, unfriendly water, I thought about this poor woman's state of mind that would permit her to walk into this bleak blackness that would consume her breath, I felt such pity, and if I felt such pathos for her, God who is love must have looked on her with infinite compassion. Yet that evening in the convent we were discussing the tragedy, Grace said that this woman would now be in hell. How could she think that? I know what the Church teaches, that to commit suicide is a mortal sin against the virtue of hope. What a load of shit. These theological concepts were created by men who dwelt in an ivory tower removed from women and society.

79

However, no matter how much I disagree with what the Church teaches and I believe that God either took this woman to heaven with infinite tenderness, or if God does not exist, this woman merely died, for myself I worry that I will be condemned to hell, and eternity is a very, very long time.

'By my sins I have deserved
death and endless misery,
hell with all its pains and torments,
and for all eternity.'
(Hymn)

Then a very black day occurred. One of those days when you suddenly realize that the situation you are in is not going to improve, no matter how hard you try because the others are out to get you. Now I know from my time in a psychiatric unit that people with mental ill health often indulge in conspiracy theories, along the lines that the government has put something in their brain in order to monitor their whereabouts and this results in craziness, and all the docs and nurses are in on it. Now, my conspiracy story was not of this genre, I was living with two women who were actually, objectively and tangibly out to get me. How could I combat against a superior and her beloved side-kick? It would take a stronger woman than I.

Well, this black day. Knock and Grace had gone out together (surprise, surprise) and I did not know when they would return. I was left in charge of lunch. Grace decided what was on the menu and Knock would sign it off, so they were both aware of my work load. The kitchen was just your regular, run of the mill kitchen found in thousands of regular houses on regular streets up and down the country. The oven (electric) only had three of the four hobs in working order, and one of this was so weak as to render it practically useless. Lunch was usually, some meat, potatoes and veg (and salad for Knock). I was informed by Grace that I had to cook three types of veg (yes, for three people), all of them boiled, but boiled separately – do not mix the veg – then boiled potatoes and boiled ham. Seriously, all this for lunch! What they used to do was get me to cook more than necessary and then when it was their turn to cook all they had to do was heat up the left-overs. How could I on two working hobs cook what was the equivalent of five pans of food (remember I had to prepare this entire food first, peal bloody everything except the ham). I only had an hour and yet I would have to cook some food, wash the pans and then cook some more...impossible.

Then I got a phone call from Grace informing me that her and Knock would not be back in time for lunch (gosh, I never saw that coming!) and I was to eat on my own (I should have been used to this by now) and then go house visiting, again, on my own. I had enough, but I had no one to tell or help me. I left the veg half-boiled on the hob and went to bed. I did not sleep, I was too anxious to rest, but I pulled the duvet up above my head and for an hour I hid from this horrible world I found myself inhabiting.

The stress stared to take its tole on my body and I started to feel weak and tired. One evening after I had returned to the convent I asked Knock if I could go to bed early. I could not face another evening meal where I tried to enter the conversation but where I really felt that I had swallowed some magic dust that made me invisible. Knock was not happy that I requested this early night but she said that I could go. Did I go to bed and fall into a peaceful slumber? Did I flip. Knock insisted that I leave the door open to my bedroom and the light on. Also Grace came into the room and my goodness can that woman make noise. Even when they both went to munch in the kitchen they left the kitchen door open so I had the pleasure of listening to their chatter and laughter, but not the pleasure of sleep. I think sleep is so important in times of difficulty as it allows us to escape for a few hours where the nightmares occur when one is awake. Grace even came to use the en suite in our room at one point, even though there were two toilets downstairs and Knock had an en suite in her bedroom. So I was well and truly put in my place.

What if this feeling, or rather numbness is the human condition and I have been kidding myself that life is like a weird Disney movie? I read a quote donkey's years ago that we can never be sure that we are not really living in a mad house and our 'lives' are just our fantasies. I thought 'no problem' I am content, find meaning in my day, if this is just a figment of my imagination then I have done a rather satisfying job.

When I sat down at a meal table at the convent in Italy the conversation was natural and full of companionship. Sitting in silence never occurred; in fact sometimes a superior would stand up and ask us all to speak a tad more pianissimo. The conversation was friendly and full of sisterhood and I failed to appreciate it at the time. I stupidly thought that this was 'normal' in all convents.

Whenever I imagined my perfect life as a nun it is what I had in Bunclody. What I really wanted is to live in a small community, in an ordinary house among the people we served, in a town small enough that I would get to know everyone, in a town that was on the poor side with a melody of social issues. So Bunclody should have been perfect. A community of three, a house attached to the Church so everyone knew where we were and we were easy to find, Bunclody was a mini town so as I walked down the road it was a constant stream of hellos, there were the travelers who made up a third of the town and all the social issues that went with such social diversity. I had the idea that I would spend my days working in the community, drinking vast amounts of tea and listening to joys and woes. Then in the evening I would return to the convent which would be a sanctuary, where I could relax and sit in peace. The evening would conclude with the last meal of the day as the three of us laughed and chatted as three people content to be in each other's presence and bonded together by sisterhood. Oh no...

What is loneliness? It is isolation and exclusion. I dreaded returning to the convent as I was isolated from Knock and Grace; they formed a community of two and I was never invited to join them. They were constantly together, whispering in corners and talking behind closed doors. I lived in a community. I spoke to numerous folk every day. I had a direct line to God. I was isolated and excluded and I was oh so lonely.

Knock did not talk to me about what had occurred during her absence in Argentina and then a week after she returned she went to the Netherlands where the provincial house of the northern European province is located. I cannot recall now how long she was absent but I was again put in charge. Again I had little contact with her and again I knew she was in constant contact with Grace. I do recall one email where I was rebuked. Grace had informed Knock that I was not pulling my weight and that she was doing the majority of the work...it was like living in a parallel universe, *'earth calling Orson, come in Orson'*. I received a harsh email telling me to make more of an effort and not to leave everything to poor Grace. I did reply defending myself but I knew that I was wasting my typing skills and I may as well take the blows.

I am aware of the phrase 'first world problems'. I do not know what it was like to be persecuted for my faith, or to have my home torn apart by civil war, or to be considered a second class citizen simply because I lacked the male member. This is merely my account of my helter-scelter descent into madness.

By now I was crying a lot and had started to self harm as a way to cope. What I would do is pour boiling water over my legs. Large blisters would appear and a few times they became badly infected. I restricted this self mutilation to my legs and stomach as they were areas of my body that were constantly hidden from others. Once I burnt my arm because I was in hospital at the time and I had to be quick so that the nurses did not see, but the rest of the time I hurt myself in secret. If I had no access to boiling water then I would use an iron to burn my stomach. This did not hurt nearly as much as the water so if I could I would scald myself. A few times I had to receive medical treatment for the infections.

When Knock returned I knew that things were not going to change and so I asked if I could go to my G.P. He was excellent and listened to me. I was embarrassed confessing to him my depression because I was a nun and in my world nuns should be happy, happy, happy. But I was also desperate so I opened up to him. He gave me some tablets, but I had to tell Knock about this as I had no access to money and so I needed her to give me some Euros. She insisted that she buy the medication so that she could find out what was the matter with me. I wanted to say, 'you, you are the problem you heartless, thoughtless, cruel excuse for a mother', but of course I kept my lips sealed and bowed to her command.

People say that there is a gradual decline into a mental breakdown but there was one particular day for me. Looking back I see now the warning signs but at the time I could not see the wood for the trees. One of the side effects of the medication was sleepiness. This particular morning when the bell rang I felt terrible, I was tired yes, but it was more that I just could not face another day in the convent, or rather this particular convent, or rather with this particular community. So when Grace put on the light I lay there and hoped that no one would notice my absence. However Grace came over to me and told me to get up. I went to Knock's room and asked permission to get up later in the morning as I was not feeling well; by this point in the narrative you can probably predict her response; no. My D-Day had come. I had been unhappy for months, under incredible stress, verging on madness, lonely, confused and unable to cope, then BANG! I could take no more.

It happened at breakfast. We usually ate in the kitchen as there were just three of us and on this particular morning all was as per usual except I felt as I was walking through treacle and I know I was crying and I did not care. I have no idea if I ate or drank anything, but I do know that neither Knock or Grace spoke to me. After breakfast we had an hour of prayer in the chapel, I said to Knock that I could not move and she told me to get to the chapel. I remained at the kitchen table in the dark. Grace came to the kitchen at one point and told me to go to the chapel but she might as well have told me to jump over the moon singing Abba. I just sat. It is a strange experience to sit perfectly still and let the world revolve around one, to be in the world but no longer of the world. This stillness and incapacity to move has happened to me a number of times since I have got ill and I imagine it is what the experience of illegal drugs are like (not that I have ever done drugs I hasten to add. I have smoked some weed in my time but it never had much of an effect on me).

So I sat, and sat and sat till Knock stormed into the kitchen, put on the light and precede to berate me along the lines that I was acting like a child and I need to make more of an effort. Still I sat. The rest of the day, and the following days I am unable to write about because they are hidden in the black hole of my mind and I do not know if they will ever appear again.

I think things must have continued as normal except I no longer spoke. In January Knock took me to see a psychiatrist in Dublin. This doctor helped me immensely, giving me a diagnosis of depression and hope that one day I would be better. I could speak to her about life in the convent, my self harming and the chaos of my mind. Unfortunately I was unable to be treated as an inpatient because it was a private hospital and although we had private health insurance, Knock had not paid all the installments so it was not valid.

I continued to be ill and eventually Knock took me to the A&E department in Waterford hospital and I was admitted to the psychiatric unit. I had no idea of what to expect. I was relieved to be in hospital because I knew I was ill and I would have walked the Great Wall of China bare footed if I was told that it would make me better.

I state here that the treatment a patient with mental ill health receives in Ireland is first class. Compared to the N.H.S the doctors, nurses, occupational therapists, even the cleaners were outstanding. I am now going to praise the Irish medical system and then I will give my personal experience.

The actual facilities such as the bathrooms and dining room were not as modern as I have experienced here in England but boy was the treatment vastly superior. The nurses were gentle and friendly, the doctors went the extra mile and all the other members of the mental health team would win a gold medal if they were in the Olympics.

Rather than individual rooms we slept in wards of about six. This is a wise decision because mental ill health can be very alienating and by having other people around it forces one to interact with the world outside one's miserable cave. Also, the nurses insisted that the patient's get up for breakfast. Even as I lay there with my eyes squeezed shut and with no desire to venture from beneath my duvet, the nurse nagged and nagged till I wished a sink-hole would appear in the middle of the room which would swallow up the source of torment, I knew that it was for the sake of my recovery. So not only did I move from my slumber I also ate breakfast.

There was a large room on the ward where there was a full timetable of activities. In this room there was a pool table that the male patient's made full use of. There was a large table where one could do art or other activities. There were some couches and a C.D. player and a small library where we could just hang out. A little kitchenette allowed us to make tea and coffee and there were cookery activities throughout the week. There was a washing machine and dryer which we were allowed to use, and this also forced us to take some responsibility by doing our own laundry and participating in occupational activities. There was yoga, meditation, art, cookery, jewelery making, music, healthy living. It was truly beneficial to the patient's, a holistic approach that complemented medication.

I saw a psychiatrist a few times a week and other health professionals such as a social worker and the occupational therapist would also come and see me. I did not have to fight to access these members of the mental health team, they came to me and they did a life-saving job. England could learn so much from the Irish health care system. The English system is in melt down and if they would only look over the water to the land of saints and scholars they might actually learn something about how to treat ill people. When I was in hospital for a month in England not one therapy was offered to me or any patient.

My faith was still really strong and all consuming at this stage of my journey. As I lay in bed I would hold a wooden crucifix and my rosary in my hands. I would ask if I could go to the hospital chapel and I would sit there and pray. There were questions asked of me from the psychiatrists inquiring if life in the convent was a contributing factor in my illness. I firmly rejected the suggestion that I leave the convent. Never, for a mere nanosecond did the thought of leaving the convent occur to me. Yes I was sick, but I thought of it like other illnesses, that I take the medication, make use of the therapies and I would emerge from the other side of the tunnel and resume my life as a nun. My faith was strong and the day I took my religious vows I intended to keep them for life. God and I were gonna remain faithful to each other.

I should have seen a warning sign in that I preferred being in the hospital than in the convent because I felt safe in the hospital and I did not feel safe in the convent. You know when there is someone who scares you at work and the mere thought of encountering them on the corridor makes you break out in a cold sweat? Well, that is how I felt about Grace and Knock.

Yet, I still desperately wanted things to change. I needed a superior who cared about me. I was not a hermit living in a cave where I would be Little Miss Independent; I was a sister in community who needed the support of the others members of that little cohort. Knock did come to visit me occasionally, as did other sisters who were visiting Ireland. I actually felt relaxed when they came to visit me because I knew that no-one would say anything cruel in front of the nurses and the other patients, and they would leave and I would be safe, safe, safe, what a beautiful word that is when you have known it's opposite.

The Servidoras is a very traditional Order, believing that practicing homosexuality is a sin. I am in fact very liberal in my thinking, but I had to keep this under wraps whilst I was a member of the Institute. I have no problem with homosexuals, and I believe that they should have equal access to marriage and civil rights. Why should we get so freaked out because two people love each other, surely there are more pressing issues in the world to get stressed about. Two women a week die in this country from domestic violence, now that is something to make the blood boil.

Anyway, one day Knock came to visit me in Waterford hospital and when she arrived on the ward the first thing she said was that she felt nauseous because she had seen two men outside the hospital kissing. I thought this was so OTT. Even if a person does not agree that people should practice homosexuality, to go as far as to claim that two people kissing makes one feel like vomiting is ridiculous. A person mistreating animals makes me angry. A parent who abuses children makes me was to decapitate them slowly and with maximum agony. A dictator who treats the citizens of his country as pawns in a game of chess makes me cry for the injustice that I can do nothing about. The idea that women are second class citizens created for the pleasure of man makes me rage at God. The election of Donald Trump makes me confused. Two people kissing makes me hope that they are happy.

I stayed in hospital for a few weeks and I know that I returned to the psychiatric unit twice more in the following few months, but I cannot recall dates, the fog blurs the calendar. I alternated between the hospital, the convent and a wonderful unit named The Sanctuary. Convent life was horrible and I became more and more alienated as I was made to feel like a freak and unloved. I stupidly kept seeking Knock's affirmation but I might as well have tried to swim the channel.

The Sanctuary was a sort of half way house. There were ten bedrooms, all individual with en suite. There were always nurses present but they did not wear a uniform. So, the nurses still dispensed the medication. We were not allowed to return to bed during the day, we were not permitted to remain in our pajamas during the day. We were permitted to leave the unit and we were expected to take responsibility for ourselves and our own recovery. This place was the most amazing institution and I think that it saved my life. The nurses helped us to see that we could one day recover, or at least learn to live with our condition. I spent a lot of time in this unit and the compassion I received was the complete antithesis of what I received in the convent. I wish I could repay them in some way. I believe in karma, what goes around comes around, so what those nurses did for me will be repaid in some manner at a later time. I found more love outside the convent.

During one of my stays in this unit Knock came to visit me. This unit was not far from Bunclody and Knock did come to visit me occasionally, but there were a number of days when I phoned Knock and asked her to visit and she never came. The power games continued. For example, I saw a psychologist every week and a psychiatrist every month and for all my appointment Knock wanted to be present throughout. The doctors and therapists always said no, I was the patient and it was not beneficial for my therapy that she be present. I was between a rock and a hard place (I adore cliches), Knock was hassling me and getting angry that she was not permitted to come to my appointments as she was convinced that it was my doing and if I really wanted her present then the therapist would concur. I did in fact ask the therapists but I was glad that they said no as I was now so fearful of Knock that with her in the room I know I would be too intimidated to say anything.

As she insisted eventually my psychologist said that he would arrange a special meeting with Knock, me, himself and the head of the department. Knock knew the date as she mentioned it on a few occasions and even mentioned it to an aunt of mine whom she had spoken to a few days previously. So on the appointed day I went to the meeting but Knock never turned up. I was mortified because these two professionals who had a heavy work load had arranged a special meeting at my request and all I could do was apologize. I tried to phone Knock but she did not answer the phone. Eventually later that day a nurse from the unit contacted her and Knock claimed that she did not know about the meeting which was a lie. She implied that it was me who was either lying or crazy, but she had spoken to my aunt just two days before and told her about the meeting, so ha, ha Knock, I am not a liar and you have egg on your face!

One evening Knock arrived at the unit and told me that when my religious vows expired on the twenty-seventh of October I was not going to be allowed to renew them. I felt as though someone had punched me really hard in the chest and I could not breathe. After she had told me this information she did not remain to chat, she just told me and left, as if she were a postman whose job was to merely deliver a letter and not a religious superior informing a member of her community that she was not wanted any more. Vi via! I was in pain, not just in my soul but there was a physical reaction that made it hard to breathe normally. I did not cry, I did not shout or get upset I just went to the television room, sat down, put my head on the arm of the chair and tried to breathe normally. It is funny how so much of this period is a blur, but I remember clearly that evening. *The Big Bang Theory* was on the television. A nurse came and asked me if I was okay and I said yes. Later, I went for a walk around the hospital ground and sat for a long time looking at the grotto of Our Lady and St. Bernadette that was in the garden next to the unit. That evening a nurse gave me a Valium to help me relax and get to sleep; it did not work and I was awake all night. I did not cry. I was in shock. Even, after all this razzmatazz I still wanted to remain in the convent, being a sister was my whole life.

I had been taken into the hospital a few days previously because of the burns on my legs. My Mum had asked me what would happen if I had to leave the convent. I told her not to overreact as that was not a possibility. I was still convinced that I had a religious vocation and it never occurred to me that my community would throw out like rubbish, a sister who was ill and needed care to get better.

So Mum was right and I was wrong. So the twenty-seventh of October was THE END, the day when they would cut me lose like needless baggage and the world would see my crazy failure.

When I left the unit and returned to the convent boy oh boy was I persona non gratis. I was told to sleep downstairs in the spare room and I was not meant to go upstairs because that was only for the nuns. One day I went upstairs to go to the cupboard where all our coats were and I wanted my rain coat and the bedroom doors were locked. Why? I was informed that I was not to take any food without asking permission. I had always been in charge of the laundry in the convent and in good nun style I always did it to the best of my ability, folding all the sisters clothes neatly and putting it on their respective beds. However, now I was told I was not permitted to use the washing machine and if I wanted clothes washed I had to leave them in the laundry room. Yet, when I did leave clothes to be washed they would 'miraculously' be returned to my room unwashed. When I asked Knock about this she denied it and told me that I had not put them in the laundry room and it was pointless to argue with her. When eventually my clothes were washed they were put in a large pile on my bed, nothing folded, it spoke volumes of how I was now not valued as a sister or even a human being.

I did a lot of cleaning in the convent and one evening I was in the process of cleaning bathrooms when Grace arrived with a slice of white bread with some margarine on it and told me that was my merendar. In the convent, we ate lunch at the normal lunch time, but we always ate our evening meal late and so about five in the afternoon we always had something to eat. Knock usually had a bowl of porridge and Knock always made sure Grace had something nice and tasty such as cheese on toast or cake. I do not like white bread, but as Grace does not like brown, we had to have white. So downstairs Knock and Grace were sharing a friendly tete-a-tete with tea and coffee and I got a slice of white bread with marg. and nothing to drink. Now as a nun I did not mind the white bread because it was unfitting for a nun to have a table ladened with goodies.

So, I was presented with this offering, with no drink and I was expected to eat it upstairs on my lonesome. I did a terrible thing. I was so tense inside that I could not have swallowed these crumbs so I threw it away in the bathroom bin and as I was in the process of cleaning the bathrooms I presumed (wrongly) that no one would discover my act against poverty. I did and do feel guilty that I threw away the bread, a nun should never be wasteful of anything.

I emptied the bin and threw the contents outside. Knock must have gone through the bin bag. She went ballistic. After her outburst (and she was right to correct me) I went to the bathroom, locked the door and lay on the floor, afraid and shaking. The hard, cold floor comforted me. I have no idea how long I lay there crying but I was left alone, thankfully. Eventually I pulled myself together, I exited the bathroom, was informed by Grace that I was to have my evening meal by myself and then go to bed. No-one spoke to me and I did not know how long I could survive. The writing, as they say, was on the wall, but I was too ill to read it.

Let me interject here with an account of what breakfast was like in convent sunny. Every morning Knock had porridge, made in the microwave by whoever was on kitchen duty that day. I would have appreciated a warm bowl of yummy porridge on many a frosty morning, but that was not on my menu. Grace and I had white bread, margarine, jam, cake (which was a favorite of Grace's). We had neither an electric kettle nor a toaster as Knock claimed that these two appliances used too much electric and were therefore too costly. However, when we had sisters visiting, the kettle and the toaster miraculously appeared and the price of electric was ignored. Knock loved her porridge and as she ate practically nothing at lunch or tea apart from salad or boiled vegetables, at least she ate something in the day apart from apples. In Italy the breakfast was crap, but at least we all ate crap, not just the Dobbies. I eat porridge every morning now.

Monday to Friday I would go to a day center which was great. Honestly, the N.H.S should really look to Eire. At this center we did various activities such as quizzes to keep the old gray cells working and art to keep our soul ticking over. I got a bus to the center as Knock informed that she was no longer willing to take me to places. Also, I rose later than the other sisters and I had no breakfast as Knock was over in the Church by the time I got up therefore I was able to ask permission to take food. Knock insisted that I leave the convent before nine in the morning even though the bus did not come till half past nine. There was no cover at the bus stop so if it was raining (as it often was) then I had the pleasure of waiting in the rain and cold. I have absolutely no idea why I had to leave the convent so early.

Here is a story of outstanding kindness. One day I got this bus to Enniscorthy, but I was actually going to see my psychiatrist which was a long way from the bus stop. It was pouring with rain, but as no bus went near the clinic (and I had no money for an extra bus ride) I had to face a long wet walk. I was the only passenger that day and the bus driver asked me where I was going. When I told him he said that he was going to drive me there, right to the door. I still think about this kindness, a kindness not offered me from the convent. So I did not have a long treck and this wonderful, amazing and generous man even gave me my money back so that I could go and buy a cup of tea to warm up. One day I had to pay for my bus fare in coppers, so I think the bus driver ascertained that I was a bit hard-up financially.

The center was free but we had to leave for an hour at lunch. Most of the service users went to a cafe but of course I was not given any money so I usually went and sat in the Cathedral. Every day the women would ask me to join them and I think they realized that I had no dosh. Oh my goodness, I have received such kindness from people who have come across my path, and these angels offered to buy lunch for me. How ironic that the 'holy' women were bitches and the people outside the convent walls were the ones really living the message of Christ. I did not accept money for lunch but I did agree to them buying me a coffee which allowed me to sit with them in the cafe.

The center closed about three but my bus back to Bunclody was not for a few hours so if it was raining I went back to the Cathedral, and if it was sunny I walked around or sat down by the river. When I returned back to Bunclody I hated to return to the convent as I knew what I was going to encounter. I had no key to let myself in so I would ring the door bell and Knock would let me in but she did not speak to me; she opened the door and walked away in silence. I went to my room and usually went straight to bed, fully clothed as I was too depressed to even try and function like a normal sister/person.

One Wednesday I returned to the convent and my aunt was there. I was told to go to the dining room. Imagine a rectangle table; at one end sat Knock and I sat at the other end; one side sat my aunt and on the other side sat Mercy (another ironically named nun) who was a superior from Italy and was visiting Ireland. So all three of them could see me and as they were facing in my direction but I was the only one who could see Knock and I was told that I was to return to Manchester on the Friday and I was not welcome to return to the convent. Another thump in the chest. I tried to argue and say that I wanted to remain in the convent till my vows expired. Mercy was the one doing most of the talking but Knock could not hide her pleasure. She who had accused me so often of acting childish was herself a parody of a seven year old brat. She had a look on her face that children get when two children have been squabbling and one of them gets in trouble and the other one gets away with it. All that was missing was that she put her thumb to her nose, wiggle her fingers and say 'na, na, nana,na.' So there was me getting treated like an old pair of shoes and she was like a bitter person who takes pleasure in other people's misery. It was so horrid that I asked her to stop and she replied oh so sweetly that she wasn't doing anything. As Mercy and my aunt were looking at me and not at her I had no way to defend myself.

It was Mercy to whom I had told earlier what Knock had been saying to be and she accused me of lying, Knock would never say such things. I learnt in that moment that I was fighting a losing battle so I stood up, smiled and even laughed, said goodbye to my aunt, went to my room and cried for hours. This was the end of the journey that I was not ready to conclude. Is this is how someone feels when they are married and one of the couple says they want a divorce but the other person is still in love with them? Unrequited love...well, words fail don't they?

There was another community of sisters (Faithful Companions of Jesus) who lived in Bunclody, they ran the secondary school. I wanted to go and stay with them for the last two nights, to get away. Knock hated the other sisters because she thought that they were not real sisters because they did not wear a habit and their convent was more luxurious than ours. Not a day went by when Knock or Grace did not say spiteful things about them. This was a real shock to me as in Italy I did not hear sisters criticizing other people, it was considered as an act against charity. In Bunclody I did not know what to do when the sisters were bitchy about people in the parish. I could not take the moral high ground and tell them that they should not say such things, that would have made me as popular as a Donald Trump at a Clinton birthday party wouldn't it? I did not want to join in as I knew it was a sin and sins lead only downwards to the netherworld. So, I did not have the opportunity to speak with the other sisters. I also had no time to say goodbye to my many friends in Bunclody. That was it, another life over...

I am not sure about God at the moment. My life has gone from the big philosophical questions to dealing with the minutia of daily life; but if there is a God then one day Knock will have to face her judge.

So Friday arrived. I did not know what to do with myself, who to say goodbye to, how to prepare to leave. I only had hand luggage so that did not take long to pack, so I decided to go for a walk around Bunclody as it was just too intense in the convent. I met a man from the parish (the one who told me about Knock wanting him to spy on me) and he took me for a coffee. I was very grateful to him for occupying me for an hour. As we said our final goodbye he gave me a hundred Euros which was wonderful as I did not have any money. In fact, Knock did give me fifty Euros as I left and the first thing I did when I reached the airport was to go and buy food. Tumultuous times...

Knock took me to the airport as she was also taking Mercy for her flight back to Italy. They sat in the front of the car chatting for the whole duration of the journey and I sat mute in the back. We said a brief and uncomfortable goodbye and that was that my friend...as we parted Knock tried to give me a hug, hypocrisy; it sums up what my time in Ireland had been, we had to be all jolly, fake and holy on the outside, the way we portrayed ourselves to the world, but behind closed doors it was all horribleness, unkindness and wicked.

CONVENT IRELAND

Why did they not want me?
What is it about me
that is not good enough to be a nun?
I tried so hard,
I promise,
cross my heart and hope to die,
stick a needle in my eye.
I wanted to belong to You alone
since I was seven.
Nothing else ever caught my eye,
I had set my heart, mind and soul,
on entering the convent
and a forever goodbye to the world.
I put You first.
I cast aside my family, friends and
everything.
Why did they not want me?
Why did You not want me?
What is it about me

that is not good enough to be a nun?
Am I not good enough to be anything?

When I became a postulant in Italy I was given a spiritual director. This was a priest who belonged to our Order and with whom I would meet once a month to discuss my spiritual life. Every sister had a spiritual director. I received the most wonderful priest to be my guide. He was in his fifties, incredibly intelligent, wise in spiritual matters, a wonderful preacher and I was so grateful to have this holy man help me on my way to perfection. Boy, did he have his work cut out, for I was far, far from being good, let alone perfect.

When I moved to Ireland I asked Father L. if he would continue to be my spiritual director and to my joy he agreed and so we would speak once a month via Skype. When I left the convent, I hoped that he would contact me via email as I saw him as an anam cara and I missed his advice. He has never contacted me and this makes me sad. My value was only as a nun and now I have no worth to them.

CHAPTER NINE

England - 2015

On the Friday evening I returned to Manchester and my wonderful parents came to collect me from the airport. I have no idea what I would do without my family. My parents are my rock and together with my eldest brother Andrew their support has been constant and life saving. In my darkest moments they have held me secure and they will never know how grateful I am. I was so broken, so out of my right-mind, so depleted that if it were not for my family I would have ended up on the streets. Maybe there might have been places I could have gone for help, but I did not have the strength, physically and particularly mentally to seek them out. I would have just lay down and ceased to be.

Of course, the convent would not have helped; they were just content to get rid of me. People argue that no-one needs to be homeless; there is help out there for them. Sure, there may be some people playing the game – whatever that game consists of, but the problem of homelessness is not simply about a shortage of housing, it is far more messier that can ever be conceived in the warm corridors of Whitehall. People on the street are a mixture of mental ill health, broken families, abuse, an inability to cope with the demands of the adult world, lost adults with lost children, sex crimes, drugs, alcohol, illness, tragedy, the weak, the sad, the desperate, as Stuart Little stated (himself a homeless man), 'Homelessness – it's not about not having a home. It's about something being seriously fucking wrong.' The fucking wrong might be a number of issues, and as a society it is so much easier to turn one's gaze to the shop window display and ignore the poor, cold critter huddled on the floor.

It is easy to pontificate when it is not one's problem; give the poor women in Africa sterilization then there will be no children to feed; send the migrants back to Syria, Afghanistan, and Yemen, then we can close our eyes to the problems we have created in the Middle East; take all the Palestinians from their homeland and make them move to Muslim countries near-by, then Israel will not have to deal with the two-state solution. How easy it is to answer questions on a quiz show when one is sat on one's backside at home. When I left the convent I was given fifty Euros, where else could I have gone except the streets?

I returned to Radcliffe, but what was meant to be a few weeks holiday turned into infinity. I took up my position on my parent's settee and there I became a couch potato for the next few months. When we had the inquisition before I left Eire I asked Mercy if the convent would support me financially till my vows expired – nearly three months. With great reluctance she said yes, (remember, by this stage I knew that the community in Bunclody were not short of a euro or two). It was something of a battle to get anything from them as Mercy said that she would not respond to my emails and that any dealings I had with the Order had to go through Knock. I said that this would be stressful for me as Knock and I had such a volatile relationship, but she just shrugged her shoulders. In the end they gave me eight hundred pounds but I had to battle for this sum.

I watched vast amounts of daily television. Even as I stared at the screen I knew that it was crap but I had no motivation to shift by bottom. Depression, was my constant companion. My Mum fed me, my dear Dad tried to make me laugh and the dog became my couch buddy. My family is very close to another family and they gave me another home. I slept in their spare room and boy did I sleep those first few months; even at eleven o'clock in the morning I had to drag myself from the bed to the couch. I had always been a morning person but I was just so, so tired. Sleep can be a great companion as it allows one to have some respite from the inferno, sweet oblivion.

I went to my G.P. and he made a referral to the psychiatric unit at the local hospital. I carried on with my medication, went to see a psychiatrist and had absolutely no hope that things would ever improve because I had no will to forge a new existence for myself, I just did not care about anything.

What about faith? Every time I thought about going to Mass I started to panic; the place that had been my true home for over twenty years had turned into a mausoleum. Every Sunday I went to a different Christian Church, Anglican, Methodist, Unitarians, United Reform, Baptist and Quakers and I did not feel comfortable anywhere. So I had to desist. My faith has dwindled to nothing. More about that later. Now back to Radcliffe.

I could not face my life, at this point and so I escaped into a fantasy world. Not for anything particularly exciting, but just anything that was not reality. I was a teacher in a girl's boarding school; I was PhD student, all consumed with my thesis; I worked in a dog's home where I would spend my day's taking attention of all those lovely creatures; I was a nurse who cared for my patient's with loving care; I was an artist lost in my world of colors and hues; I was anything except what I really was; a failed nun with mental ill health who watched crappy telly and adopted my parent's couch as my personal throne of misery.

I adore reading; I will read anything, fiction, non-fiction, shampoo bottles, cereal boxes, even if it is a book that is way over my head, I will give it a go as hey ho, I might learn something. Every day is a school day. I will even read the yellow pages if there is nothing else to hand. When I got ill my ability to read, or rather to concentrate was severely affected. Whilst I was at my parent's I tried to read the daily newspaper, but by the time I got to the middle of an article I had forgotten what had occurred at the beginning. It sounds odd, but I would go to our local library (one of my favorite places in the world, it reminds me of many happy hours as a child spent in that hallowed space) and just walk around. The librarians must have thought I was loca (and they would be right). A government that closes public libraries and cuts its funding rapes the intellect of society. A library should be the center of a community and a necessity to any civilized society. Not all of us can afford to buy all our books from Waterstones; bloody tories. As I write this my local loca councilors are planning on shutting eleven of the fourteen libraries in my borough.

My local library not only gives citizens access to the world of books, but also gives access to a number of educational courses. One such course was an art class on a Monday morning. I am not an artist but I went to these classes as they were free and they were a reason to get out of bed. I am a rather disciplined creature, and if I have said that I will be somewhere at a particular time then I will be there. My illness depleted this self discipline, but it was still there. On a Monday morning, as I lay in bed, desperate to hide under my duvet, I would haul myself to the shower and the library. Oh, oh, oh what a wonderful revelation. The woman who ran this course was one of those angels who one sometimes finds on one's path, with a heart of gold, a beautiful smile, and an artistic talent that should be exhibited in the finest galleries in this land of hope and glory.

Have you heard of religious scruples? If not then thank your little stars because there are the psoriasis of the soul which itches all the bloody time. I have had the company of this bugger since my teenage years when suddenly youthful eyes gazed on the world anew and instead of seeing beauty and pleasure, I saw pleasure and guilt; all consuming guilt took of my rose-tinted spectacles and donned me a pair that had YOU DESERVE HELL across the lenses.

Let me explain by a few examples. Imagine, me a jolly fourteen year old heading home innocently after a productive day at school and suddenly the guilt hits me like a stray cricket ball; guilt, because there I am sat staring out of the windows when I should be praying the rosary for all the sinners in the world. Now, I haven't prayed for them and so they will not convert and are on the fast track to the hot place; and because I am the reason they are going to hell, I too will join them in the burning inferno because the sin of the world is my fault.

M: If you do not pray, sinners will go to hell.
m: I do not pray.
C: Sinners will go to hell.

Result: GUILT!

So, I was a Catholic and we have a solution for sin, namely one of the seven sacraments, confession with a priest. I go to confession at every opportunity. Does this help? No. What does the priest invariably say when I stutter my deadly sins, 'you have scruples and it is a sin of pride to think so much of myself.' So I skip home with the sin of pride now added to by worries and I want to scrub my soul with a brillo pad.

These scruples never left me but I discovered the answer to them; enter a convent. This is my logic, I sin because I do not do God's will; nun's do God's will; therefore I must become a nun. Simple. So I did. Now I had the relief that every moment of every day (and night) I knew that without a shadow of a doubt I was doing God's will. God wanted me to scrub the floors? Viola, here I am O Lord, I come to do your will. God wanted me to eat carrots every day for a month? No problem, I gobble them up on my way to heaven. I could lie down in peace at half past ten because the honorarium states that lights are off at that particular time.

In the convent okay; out of the convent my psoriasis had a party. From the moment of rising there was nothing but unremitting guilt; I should have got up earlier, I am lazy, I ate too much at breakfast, I should eat food I do not care for because I am gluttonous. I should think more about God and less about the trivia of life, because I am worldly (anything worldly is a big no, no). It never ended; I was like an athlete that was obsessed with being better; instead of Olympic gold I chased heaven and yet it was like reaching for a star, forever out of reach.

I recall once at university a professor said to me in passing that he felt guilty because he did not respond to all his emails. I told him to become Catholic, because we feel guilty all the time so an extra bit of guilt about disregarded emails makes no difference.

Now I am a free woman. That all consuming guilt has dissipated because I am no longer a Christian and the Christian ideals are no longer my concern. Here is a banal example; the other day I was in cafe and as I was finishing my coffee a song came on the radio that I like (Oasis). As a devout Christian I would normally leave the cafe instantly because by denying myself the pleasure of hearing the dulcet tones of the Gallagher brothers I could make a prayer of my sacrifice and practice self-denial. However, on this occasion, as I automatically rose from my seat I realized that I could sit and listen and enjoy the tune and the walls of Jericho would not come crumbling down. So I sat and so I reminisced about when I was sixteen and so I enjoyed.

I am not sure what I believe about God – I will come back to that subject in a later chapter. I have always been a Catholic and so Catholic teaching is firmly established in my brain. Even if I doubt the existence of heaven, I am still consumed with the fear of hell. It seems impossible that I will avoid hell and that scares me. Pascal wrote about a wager; if you are not sure there is a God you might as well act as if there is and worship because if there is a God you have done the right thing and if there is no God then you haven't lost anything. What a load of crap. Truth is what matters; living according to your truth to the best of your ability seems to me the most honorable way to live. If you believe in God then bow down and adore; if you are an atheist then be true to your beliefs rather than going through a Sunday ritual of smart clothes and sore knees. After all, I believe that this search for truth must be the guiding light of humanity, the arts, science, religion, philosophy, ethics, everything. If there is a God then the one who made us must know what is going on in our minds and hearts and I just can no longer sit and kneel and sing and pray because it is not my truth anymore and I refuse to go to Church as a mere 'bet' that God exists.

One day I was having breakfast with my big brother and he started talking about some philosophical what not and I said that I did not want to think about the major philosophical questions as it hurt my brain which had gone on a world cruise and left just some gray porridge in its place. Later I said that I thought it was terrible that the government did not call the new boat (boat? Submarine thingie...? I am not sure) Boaty McBoat Face when that is the name the people had chosen, the bloody tories, against democracy blah, blah, blah. My bro laughed and commented on the fact that I have gone from spending my days pondering on the eternal questions to thinking about the name of a boat.

There are two emotions that I have never really experienced, boredom and loneliness. I was one of those kid's with a fab' imagination and an endless ability to occupy myself. I was just never bored. Even if I had to sit quietly I could occupy myself in either reading (I was always a voracious reader thanks to the example of my Mother) or thinking. I have always loved to think. I can remember the exact day when I sat down and thought of communism; I was only about seven and had never heard of communism but I thought 'why does not everyone work, each to their own physical or mental ability, and then pool all their resources and then each person would receive what they required?' This was the time of innocence, before I realized that some people are lazy, selfish and dishonest, it was a sad, sad day when I discovered that fact of life.

Now I know boredom because depression sucks out one's life force. Many a day (month) I just sat on the settee or lay in bed because 'I just could not be bothered.' I could not concentrate on reading, I did not have the energy to have a shower, I did not care enough about anyone to make the effort to speak to them, my musical instruments lay unused and day time television is like a drug that destroys the brain cells. When one believes in God then there is always something/someone to think about.

The phrase that best suits depression is 'never enough.' There simply is never enough of anything. A thousand people could tell me every day that they love me and it would not be enough; I would crave a thousand and one. No amount of material possessions would fill the landfill sites of my desire. Black holes do exist, you do not have to ask Stephen Hawking about this, just ask anyone who knows about depression and they will tell you that the black hole of 'never enough' is a reality and it could gobble up the whole universe and not leave a single star.

Loneliness. Again, not an emotion I was acquainted with as a child or adolescent. There were people who came and went in my life that I missed, but it was not loneliness. When I was about seven a good friend of my Mother's moved from Radcliffe to Inverness. I had seen this woman every day of my short life and I loved her with an unlimited love. The ache I felt as I watched her drive away that dreary morning was just miserable. It was an ache of missing someone, but my life was full and it was not loneliness. She would frequently return to England for holidays and she always stayed at our house. She has a lot of problems with her spine and cannot get upstairs so my bed was always moved to the living room and that is where she and I dwelt for a few brief but happy weeks. It was always painful saying goodbye, but I knew she would return and we also went to Scotland.

I recall one time when she was due for a visit and there was some issue in her family (I was too young to understand what it was) and the day before she was going to arrive she phoned up to say that she could not visit. I was so, so mad with God. How could God allow this to happen? Every evening as I prepared to go to sleep I dutifully said my prayers; 'Matthew, Mark, Luke and John, bless this bed that I lay on. Four angels round my bed, four angels round my head; one to watch and one to prayer and two to watch my soul till day.' That night I was still full of anger towards God and I said 'I am not speaking to you God, so I am not going to say my prayers.' Apart from a few drunken nights as a teenager, that was the only time I deliberately did not prayer. And yes, I did feel guilty the next day and said extra prayers to compensate! This still was not loneliness.

When I was in Italy another friend of my Mother and Father died. I still cannot accept that she is gone. I do not like going to visit her house because she is not there and it is all so wrong. She was another Mum to me and I think about her every day. I am friends with her daughter, who is more of a sister than a friend. I was not able to come home for her funeral and that is a major regret of mine. I feel guilty that I was not there for my family at this horrific time. I have a tattoo on my ankle as a mini tribute to her. Her name was Rosemary and so I have a ring of red roses around my right ankle. She was the kindest person you could every meet, one of those truly good people in life who just make the world a better place just by her presence. I liked to be near her and the thing I miss most is her laugh; she had one of those full throttled, unselfconscious laughs that made those near her also laugh. A number of people in my life have died, grand-parents, aunts and uncles, but Auntie Rose was the first person whose death affected me profoundly because we were so close and her death was sudden and unexpected. However, this still was not loneliness.

There were days in the convent when I longed for the nearness of my friends and family. There were many days when I was sad and home-sick. There were days when I would receive a photograph in the post of a family occasion or a friend's wedding and I wanted with all my being to be part of the crowd and not far away. This still was not loneliness because I had my faith. A saint once wrote that a Christian should never be lonely because they have the blessed Trinity dwelling in their soul. I imagined my soul as a place deep inside me and I spent all my time trying to dwell in that place so that I could be one with God and therefore I could spread the Gospel message with every fiber of my being. This place was one of tranquility and no matter what storms were raging externally I could retreat to my inner sanctum and all would be well. Even this is not loneliness.

I do not believe in God anymore. I have lost my hope (which is a sin against the Holy Spirit, and is therefore unforgivable). I offered God my whole life, a blank cheque that could be cashed at anytime. There is nothing I would not have done if I felt that it is what God was asking of me. Go to China where I would spend years trying to learn the language? No problem, I would have gone in a heartbeat. Go to Egypt where women are second class citizens and Christians are the persecuted minority? No problem, I would have gone in a heartbeat. Go to the U.S.A where I would struggle constantly with the decimation of the English language (I even turn the radio off if someone from the States or Canada is waffling on) and the McDonald's culture? No problem, I would have gone in a heartbeat. What my superiors told me to do was the will of God and I only desired to die to myself daily and belong only to my beloved. That is why I did not want to leave the convent, even in Ireland, because I had made my vows and given myself unreservedly to God and what was God's reply to my offer?

'I do not want you; you are not good enough.'

So that is how my vocation and faith ended. I had given my all and every single day I gave one hundred percent. I am not such a fool to think I was a good nun, I only had to look at the little saints around me (in Italy, not in Ireland) but I could stand up in court under oath and say that I always gave my best. Yes, my best is more Accrington Stanley than Manchester City, but I knew that God could read my heart and that there was nothing left for me to place on the altar. I am a crushed woman who was rejected by God and now I feel that if there was such a being as an omnipotent, omniscient and all perfect deity then I would have been treasured as a child, not put out on a Wednesday night for the bin men to take to the tip.

God permeated every moment of my day. It was more than a marriage because even when two people are wed they still have separate jobs, friends, and interests. God invaded my thoughts. If I was playing the organ I imagined that God was sat beside me. When I was on the bus I raised my mind and heart to God in prayer. When I lay down to sleep I thought of God and the instant I rose I knelt by my bed and offered my whole day to God's service. God, God, God, everything was about God and now there is just a void and I do not know how to fill it, the light in my inner sanctuary has been extinguished and nothing can light it. Do I have to live with this emptiness till the day I die and then just become worm fodder? I am exploring every means to heal my depression, but I do not believe that it is possible. This is loneliness. I am so lonely without God because nothing has any meaning anymore.

I just want to wax lyrical about Manchester for a mo. I adore Manchester, the people, the history, the culture, I am like the pope, when I step onto Mancunian soil I want to fall to my knees and kiss the hallowed pavement. I have lived in many cities and none of them come remotely close to my home. I accept that other people feel the same way about the place of their birth; my folks are Irish and still after fifty one years in England they still talk about going 'home' for a holiday. I think it is because in our home town we know exactly where we are.

When I lived in Cambridge, I was working one summer with a woman who I guess was in her mid-fifties. She was the epitome of middle class, with her Marks and Sparks clothes and Clarke's shoes, her holiday home in France and her preference for Chablis. Sorry, I accept I am an inverted snob; I am a working class socialist to my bones. Well, one day she said that she had just been to a wedding in Durham and she was really surprised by the north because she expected it to be congested with litter and decorated with graffiti. Alas, she found a pleasant, clean and civilized town where people actually use knives and forks (that last comment is mine). She claimed that she had never been to the north and had spent her life actively avoiding it because of the horror stories she had heard.

Then yesterday, I was watching a program on the television when a woman from Essex said to a man from Blackpool, 'but in the north you only eat fry-ups and food out of a packet don't you?' Stupid bitch! I mean Essex, where all the women wear short white skirts without tights (even in December), white stilettos, dyed blond hair and at least three fake things on the face! See, northerners are capable of stereotypes too.

My town is rough, but it is mine and I love it. Have you got the message yet that I love it? I often get the bus and never, ever, ever, never have I been sat at the bus stop with other people when a conversation has not been initiated. We are super, super friendly. We chat, we help, and we are friendly. I like being called 'love' and 'pet' and 'chicken' and 'sweet-heart' by shop keepers. I like having a joke with the bus driver. I like putting the world to rights with the check-out lady. I like smiling at strangers on the street. I like stopping to chat with people walking their dog. I like it here...

When I first moved to other towns in England, I quickly learnt that it was not socially acceptable to smile at strangers on the street. The key was to keep one's head down, one's face straight and never even consider the thought that you can pass a mere comment to a fellow passenger. Once, when I was still naive in the ways of aliens, I was in York and I smiled at a lady on the street, she stopped and said in a terribly haughty manner, 'do I know you?' I stuttered 'no' and in the moment I learnt a lot.

I am a passionate reader of books and I always have one (or four, just in case I finish one two or three) in my bag. Sometimes when I am sat by myself at the bus stop I read my book and many a time when another person joins me they just ask, 'what is the book about?' and so the conversation is initiated. I am glad I moved away from Radcliffe because I have learnt so much about different cultures; I am glad I have returned to Radcliffe, because the people here are the salt of the earth (I am not sure what that means literally, but as a saying it means that they are the best people you will ever have the privilege to encounter). We might be a bit rough, but boy we are friendly.

Oh God, I cannot stop crying. I have crashed in a spectacular way worthy of a boy racer doing a hundred and fifty in a Cortina around a built up housing estate in the rain. I have been keeping busy, not a moment spare, busy, busy, busy, thinking about anything but the shit in my brain. It was going well. I knew I was not happy but I was learning some coping strategies, well, the one about just keep as busy as possible and then go to bed as soon as I could. Every week I went to talk to a psychiatric nurse and I thought I was making progress; what a stupid fool I am. Talking to M. and the new medicine, Quetiapine (along with Alzain and Venlafaxine), I saw that even if I had abandoned all hope of becoming a smiling advert for a toothpaste advert, I could at least get through the day without wanting to physically hurt everyone who was unlucky enough to share the same geographical space as me. Talking to M. felt like a breakthrough, he is kind and intelligent and although I was aware I was only scraping at the top layer of my issues, at least it was a start.

Then I felt it coming, slowly but surely, everyday it was stronger and then I got up one morning and I wanted to annihilate every cell of my being because I was an idiot to think that I was making progress. I thought I was getting over being evicted from the convent, getting to a point where I could wake up in the morning and be satisfied that I was not filled with fear. In the convent in Bunclody I would wake up and dread the start of the day; I would long for the rising bell not to ring because I would have to go to breakfast and face ridicule or even worse, being ignored by my so-called community. I thought I was getting there, but I am not.

For the last couple of weeks I was hyper-aware that it was coming up to a year as a no-nun. I kept reminding myself what hell I was living in this time last year, and yet instead of relief I have dropped again to the bottom of my black hole and I am just so, so, so sad that I am not a nun. I want to be a nun, I want my faith back, I want to live in a convent, I want to live in a community where my presence is acknowledged, I want to listen to and be listened to, I want to laugh the way I did in Italy, I want prayer time where I can sit still and feel peace, I want my life to have meaning, I want to have an identity, I want to go to bed at night, exhausted from living at a hundred miles an hour, I want to go back to before it all went wrong with the knowledge I have now, I want to ask to go anywhere else apart from Ireland, I want so much and I cannot have any of it. Is this what unrequited love is like? This pain, this despair, this unremitting hopelessness...There seems like no way out apart from annihilation. What do I do?

Lies

Aged 38 I have discovered
that everything is a big, fat, fucking lie.
I have be conned.
Flimflammed.
Swindled.
Winston had his black dog – lie!
I like doggies,
and no dog could be this black.
Others have their monsters – lie!
Monsters do not exist
and nothing has ever been so existent.
Others have their clouds – lie!
Clouds are fluffy and fly away
and no cloud was ever this dense.
Hawking's black holes
are not as deep
consuming
dark
as this.
Try exercise,
the cheerleader chant,
healthy eating,
pills,
positive thinking,
talk, talk, talk.
All fucking lies.
Nothing helps
and the truth is
nothing ever will.
Will death really
be
a final
end?

When all I was interested in was God, I was not at all worried about the world, God would take care of things and in the end all will be consummated. Now, I am struggling to live in this world, I find the world scary and overwhelming. The last few days I have not been feeling well. I am having trouble with my legs; they are getting weaker even though I am exercising. Last Monday I was in the library in Manchester and my legs gave way. Thankfully I was able to sit down and read a book so as not to be conspicuous but inwardly I was going crazy; how was I going to get home? I could phone Dad but he would have no idea how to find a library in central Manchester. Was this just a momentary relapse or was this the final countdown? What the hell was I going to do without drawing attention to myself? Eventually the feeling returned to my legs and I was able to waddle like a duckling.

So, on Tuesday morning I phoned the docs. You have to phone at eight in the morning to get an appointment. I duly phoned from eight until ten past nine. I gave up the ghost then because I presumed that all the slots would have been filled. I went through the same rigmarole this morning with no joy so I went in person to the clinic. I do not like that particular clinic and on a number of occasions people have advised me to change, but life is stressful, with paperwork, questions, examinations; so I have always kept the status-quo.

This morning I encountered a little Hitler, otherwise known as a doctor's receptionist...power corrupts. She informed me that I would have to phone at eight in the morning to obtain a few precious minutes with the demigod doctor. I told her that I have gone through that pleasant system for two days and the phone was constantly engaged. No, twice it did actually ring, but no-one responded and it rang out. I said all this in a pleasant tone, I was not criticizing, I just need to see a doctor. She told me that I had told a lie because she knows that there were receptionists present at the allotted time and so there was no way I could have rung for an hour and ten minutes. No, I could not have an appointment; I would have to phone in the morning.

I crashed. I walked away and cried. The frustration. The anxiety. The stress. I walked downstairs to the clinic where my folk's see their doctor (with no problems) and asked to become one of their patients. I am sat with the paperwork beside me. When something like that happens it is though I am a balloon and someone decides that I am blocking their view and they take a pin and whoosh, my air escapes and I twirl and swirl and make a 'neighing' sound till I fall onto the earth and wait to be washed away by the rain into some unknown drain where the rats piss on me.

I hate feeling like this because it is as though I cannot cope with the basic functions of life and I wonder how I will ever be able to get a job and operate as a normal member of society. If I crash over something so banal what will happen if I ever become a teacher and have a class to interact with? If a student upsets me, I cannot leave them to their own devises, go home and hide under the duvet. I must look like a crazy woman as I drag myself down the street, muttering to myself as a way of keeping calm, just to get from A to B.

I wish now that I had shown the cow my phone so she could see that I was telling the truth, but hindsight is a great thing. My nerves are now stretched to a degree that is horrid; on the bus on the way home I wanted to scream, every time the driver beeped his horn the noise reverberated in my skull, every time a person spoke in a loud voice I wanted to holler at them to be quiet, every time an innocent child made a peep I felt hate towards them in my soul. This is the time when I am most grateful for sleep.

Two weeks ago I got knocked off my bike, I hold my hands up and it was my fault because I had a lapse in concentration (which is a common state of being for me). It was not a bad hit and although I got up worse for wear with bruises and my bike needs a bit of t.l.c. but, after a short duration of sitting on the pavement crying I got up and carried on. However, I have not been back on the bike since the accident which is not like me. I have always pushed myself to get up and carry on, if I make a blunder then I must not give up but I must gather up my bundle of courage and as they say, get back on my bike.

Once when I was playing the organ at Church I messed up because I had not secured the music properly and a gust of wind came through a window and whoosh, paper all over the floor. I was also singing into a microphone at this point and without the music or words it was a disaster with an audience of a few hundred people, how humiliating. So the next day I put my bum back on the organ stool and practiced and the following Sunday I had another go; it never occurred to me to lie down and admit defeat because where would that get me? So it has shocked me that I did not force myself to get back on the seat of my bike the following day, but I have pleaded bruises, pain and fear and that is a slippery slope to inertia. I must try and push myself and not constantly use my failing body and depression to do nothing.

I am a politics junkie. I desire to get involved in the local political world, but this is another thing I have failed at. I do not use social media such a Face book and nor do I want to; I use the internet as a necessary part of life, but I take no pleasure in the electronic world. I do not have the internet at home (too expensive and I do not want the temptation of constantly Googling random things) and so I go to the public library to use the computer, which has a time limit so I must cut my coat according to my cloth. However, I have been trying to encourage the people of Radcliffe to make contact with our councilors and MP to get things done, because left to their own devises these politicians must spend most of their time dunking biscuits and congratulating each other. So far I have only wrote a letter to our local paper and made some comments (about pot holes, the need for extra bins and so on) to the official complaints procedure on their web-site. I think this has been a failure.

My brother who is computer literate has shown me the errors of my ways and has advised me that social media is the way to go and I agree with him. In today's contemporary society the majority of folks have embraced the internet revolution, even if I insist on being a Luddite. So I bought a cheap camera and have been snapping mad. Not that I wanted to create a Face book page that is just moan, kvetch, complain, because there are many wonderful aspects to my home town, lovely parks, a stunning Victorian library and it oozes potential, but the councilors do neglect our town and we are the poor relation compared to other districts of our area such as Bury and Ramsbottom.

I cannot do it; I am a weak, pathetic, lazy loser, it is beyond my capacity. Not just because it is about using the internet, but I cannot command my thoughts in order to get this show on the road. It will take more energy than I have and I just want to lie on the floor and admit defeat. Every day I have battered myself to do this bloody thing, do it Deborah, do it today, do it now, stop procrastinating you lazy cow and so on. As I write this I feel exhausted, both mentally and physically. I might as well try and run the London marathon tomorrow than organize my thoughts, go to the library and sit down for an hour, download my pics and make a face book page. Then there is the constant updating the bloody page. I am just too tired. I hate that I am like this and I want a sell-by date on this depression and know that by the 8/10/2017 it will have expired and I will again be in control of my mind, body and soul; but that is not going to happen is it?

CHAPTER TEN

England – 2016

'And did those feet in ancient times,

NO!

Last week I went to a group for people with mental ill health. It is a drop-in group where we drink coffee and scoff biscuits. I was sat in between two blokes, one about my age and one well into his seventies. This poor old bloke waffled on about his school days and I was content to sit in silence and listen. Then I had a conversation with the whipper snapper on my left. He was a born-again-Christian and wanted to convert me, a hopeless sinner. I informed him that I was raised as a Christian but that I no longer believed in all that; I did not offer any more of my autobiography. He looked shocked and solemnly said, 'have you committed the ultimate sin?'

I know all about the ultimate sin. In the gospel it states that all sins can be forgiven except a sin against the Holy Spirit. This sin is usually interpreted as a sin against hope, that is, despair. This is why the Church teaches that people who commit suicide will go to hell because they have given in to despair. I worry that is I commit suicide I will go to hell. It is easier to believe that there is no God than there is no devil.

So I asked this messenger of joy what was the ultimate sin, just to hear his concept, and he replied that I once knew Jesus and now I have rejected him and the only place people like me will end up is in hell for all eternity. He told me that I needed to pray, but I asked to what or whom am I meant to be praying to? God? The trees? Faeries? I was given a card and invited to join his congregation on Sunday morning, but I declined the offer and the card went in the recycling.

This conversation did not disturb me as the thought of suicide fills my waking hours, as does the fear of hell for all eternity where I would be forever separated from my family. What a nice concept of God the Christian Church preaches (sarcasm).

Now, the studies I did in Italy were first rate, they challenged me intellectually and made me think more than ever before. Metaphysics, anthropology, history of philosophy it was all wonderful and I am very grateful for all I was given. However, I disagreed on some aspects of the studies and one of these was the theory of evolution. Yes it is a theory and we are still looking for the missing Lucy but I am open to the possibility that it is true or perhaps false, I cannot dismiss it and the story of Adam, Eve and the Garden of Eden just falls short of satisfying my inquiring mind.

We often had three day seminars in the convent, focusing on a particular aspect of either philosophy, theology or spiritually. In my finally year in Tuscania we had a seminar on creationism, that is the biblical story, (note STORY), of Adam, Eve, and all the creatures that dwelt in that Eden. There was a scientist from the States who tried to convince us that it was genetically feasible that all humanity sprung from the loins of one woman and one man. All the seminarians and sisters sat there and lapped it up as heavenly nectar and I was disgusted. We have a brain and it is wrong for us not to use it to its utmost capacity.

I was sat at the back of the room and happened to be next to another sister who I knew had a first rate intellect. At one stage our eyes met and we could see the doubt and I whispered that I did not believe what the scientist was claiming and she concurred. That was the end of our conversation, but afterward I was terribly worried that she would tell one of the superiors what I had said and I knew that I had to tow the line and keep stum on what differed in my mind from what was the official party line. It was never mentioned to me but I will never know if my file received a black mark. After all, as they say, it is all academic now.

English folk love to talk about the weather. In Manchester it is usually a moan about the rain. We listen with rapt attention as the weather woman tells us if tomorrow will bring rain. Even when it is sunny, we talk about how it will not last. English folk love to talk about the weather. What County-File says on a Sunday evening about the weather in the coming week is quickly whispered on mobile phones, 'it is going to be nice on Thursday, be able to get the washing dry'. English folk love to talk about the weather. We love to talk about the effect the weather has on the garden. The suburban gardens all need a good downpour. I sit at the bus stop and it is the favorite topic of conversation among strangers, really sisters-in-arms when faced with the weather. Yes indeedie, English folk sure do love to talk about the weather.

As the only English woman in the convent, there was no one to discuss the weather with me. If I sat down at breakfast and mentioned that it looked like rain, I got no reply and a few perplexed faces as if they presumed I had just mixed up my Italian. Every nation has their own particular topic of choice and in Italy it is food. I have sat through twelve course meals (yes twelve; it takes hours) and for the entire duration of the meal food was the sole topic of conversation. Every tomato was discussed; every ball of mozzarella was analyzed; every olive was raptured over; every drizzle of olive oil was beheld as if the finest bottle of French red wine.

At home my Mother would cook, and my Mother is a damn fine cook. She would work all day in a shop and then she would come home and cook a meal from scratch (meat, potatoes and veg. with fish on a Friday as we were dutiful Catholics). However, we would consume each fluffy King Edward's with pleasure but silently. Only at the end of the meal would we dutifully thank our wonderful Mum for her mothering in producing such fine fare. That was that.

Every evening our mother superior got up to address us upon some aspect of religious life, how to live more poorly, more chastely and more obediently. One evening we were delivered a sermon about the evils of moaning. Moaning about anything was a sin because we were meant to mortify our inner and outer selves on all occasions. Talking about the weather was held up as an example of complaining. After all, each day God gave us in the provision of divine providence, exactly the weather that was required and by making a comment about the weather we would not make the sun turn to rain or the snow to a heat-wave. So the only way to desist from sinning in this respect was to keep stum about the weather.

When these words fell upon my ears I wanted to stand up and say, 'but I am English, it is abnormal for me NOT to talk about the weather'. After all how many bloody things can you say about a tomato? It is red and juicy, move on. Of course I sat in my pew and never more mentioned the weather. See I tried so hard to be good and 'one of them' but I remained the freak of the group, the one that was a bumble bee among butterflies.

Everyone relies on something, it is human nature. I read a book by a Buddhist where he claimed that every human being requires a god figure, that is something to worship. Now, for some people this takes the form of main stream religion, for others it is a more pantheistic home brew spirituality, for others it is materialistic items such as shoes, phones, jewels, for others it is addictive substances such as alcohol or drugs and I could go on for another fifty pages but I am sure you get the gist. The key thing is, according to the wise man in the orange robes, is that we as individuals are aware of the god we have chosen to erect an altar to, where we come daily to lay flowers of homage.

Here I am in my little conundrum. I had chosen the Christian God because I believed it to be the most truthful of all the deities. Now I look at my altar and the flowers have died and the candles have blown out and the whole image is somewhat drab. I have to choose a new god. What shall it be?

When I am in the full grip of depression I can see no pleasure in anything. I j'adore paris. When I was at university and when I was working I went to Paris quite often for a long week-end. All by myself. I did not have any yearning to go to the most romantic city on earth with a male to hold my hand. I had Jesus; he consumed all my thoughts so I was never lonely. I would stay at some cheap hotel, rise early in the morning, eat warm pane-o-chocolate for breakfast and spend some wonderful days walking the streets of the French capital. Of course there was Mass at Notre Dame or Sacre Coeur or my favorite haunt, Rue de Bac where it is claimed that Our Lady appeared to a young nun, Catherine Laboure. There is nothing about Paris I do not find endlessly entertaining.

Then I would eat onion soup which is only tasty in France. I have tried it in restaurants in England and it is just dirty rainwater which a lump of cheddar on top. To finish off it has to be crème brulee. When you get this in England it comes in tiny ceramic pots that are meant to look rustic. The cream is too yellow and the brulee just like a teaspoon of demerara on top. Well, it is worth heading across the English channel just to partake of this heavenly manna. Contrary to the notion that French cuisine means petite amounts, a large dish is presented just for one, and as you crack the delightfully burnt sugar your spoon disappears into a whiteness that could rival a new born lamb. To say it is yummy is as weak as claiming that Donald Trump is a misogynist.

So, why am I rabbiting on about Paris? I want to show that I love to travel. I love everything about it; packing my suitcase and choosing my reading material for the journey; airports and the excitement of jetting off; arriving and that first rush of air that smells so differently in every country; the possibility of it all; staying in a hotel (though I draw the line at dirty sheets which I once had to endure in one cheap joint); meeting new people; learning from different cultures; returning home intellectually, spiritually a richer woman.

It is different with depression. I think about going to Paris (not that I would, just the thought of it) and I know that my intellect and spirit would increase by nothing because I am a dead person incapable of pleasure. I would look at the Seine and think about drowning. I would wander the streets late at night in the more lugubrious parts of the city and hope that I would be stabbed to death and become a mere crime statistic. I would sit on the plane and deliberately ignore the safety warnings because if that travel machine is going down, then I have no desire to bob about on the waves till my hero rescues me.

However, I have had a break-through. The other day I smelt some cut grass and I found that my senses were stimulated and it was a live person smelling and not a corpse. This is a major break-through, on par with a Brit winning Wimbledon; not a frequent occurrence and should therefore be cherished when the opportunity arises. Yes, I smelt the cut grass and it gave me pleasure.

When I read theology I always ask the same question, 'what kind of deity is portrayed here?' Often it is not the sort of deity that I would ever want to worship. The Christian tradition has always referred to God as Father because this is how Jesus addressed the almighty. So far so good. If one fasts forward one sees a distortion of this father figure. If God is father then in so much of Christian theology he becomes a mean, miserable, petty, unkind and a most definitely unloving father.

I fall physically quite often and today on my way home I had a bad fall on the road. As I stepped onto the pavement I caught my foot on the edge and could not stop my stumble. I have cut my knee and ankle and they are throbbing. Now, a true father would come and help me up and make sure I was okay; he would not leave me there to my pain and humiliation and let me feel only his absence.

101

Is a heavenly father so much less than an earthly father? Yet it is odd when we read about God and do not see our father.

Pleasure in pain

Ha, ha, ha.
You fell.
You cut your knee
and hurt your pride.
It will be good for you.
Don't sniffle,
offer it up for the salvation of souls.
I leave you there.
I will never help.
I will make you feel abandoned.
You will cry
and no-one will comfort you.
You will pray
and I will not answer.
You will want to die
but I will not reach out to sooth your weary soul and body.
Because I am your loving father.
The one you can always trust.
Ha, ha, ha.
This is the real joke.

Serendipitous: even as a child I loved this word. It is beautiful. It rolls around the mouth. Just the feel of the word is beautiful. Then I learnt the meaning and it was the same feeling you get when you walk from a dark corridor into a garden and it is so sunny that it blinds you and you can do nothing but stand still and wait for your eyes to adjust. I love the word serendipitous, the sound, the feel and the meaning.

I knew the word but I never had an occasion to use it, no event in my life has been worthy of this preeminent word, until now. Leaving the convent in Ireland was a serendipitous event. At first I was devastated, as though my life had stopped. All the other stages of my life were wonderful but they were tunnels to pass through and enjoy along the way. The convent was the final destination, nothing outside, nothing beyond, the eternal now of the religious state. So when I was unceremoniously chucked out (let's call a spade a spade) the eternal became finite and ceased to have meaning.

The major, oh boy, the majorist turning point in my recovery from crazy-hood is that I am glad I am no longer in the convent. When I was sat at the bus stop this morning I was thinking about philosophy and I felt my mind moving freely; jumping over hedges as a horse in flight. There is no restriction to what I can meditate on and whatever flows through my little brain is welcome. Therefore, I conclude, being thrown out on my ear was, no is, a serendipitous event.

Okay, so where am I? I am finally glad I have been emitted from the convent and I have started to get my life back on track. I am doing some courses and voluntary work and I have started to appreciate the variegated colors of autumn. WRONG. WRONG. WRONG. Life is not linear is it? Yes, earth time is linear and I can chart my 'progress' chronologically, but life is one cha-cha-cha forward and one frantic tango backwards. Here am I, sat on my increasingly chubby backside with my high heels needing a cobbler and my fancy skirt making me appear as mutton dressed as spring lamb.

I want to be a nun. Every night I have the same nightmare, well, variations on a theme. I am a Carmelite nun in York (we are in the dream at the mo.) and there I am in a beautiful brown habit with rosary beads swinging from my cincture and something is not right. I am told that I have to leave and I do not want to leave. I do not know why I am a Carmelite nun instead of a Servidoras but dreams flow where they will. So I am a nun, I do not want to leave; I am told that I have to leave and then I wake up every morning with that sinking feeling of being a rejected woman. You recall that feeling the morning after you have been dumped by the love of your life, or the rejection letter from the university you have longed to call your Alma Mater, or when your faithful dog has had to be put down or when you realize that your dream job is never going to be yours, well I wake up with that horrific feeling every morning.

I don't fit in.

Look at the pretty girls,
with their pretty faces
and pretty manners.
I don't fit in.
Look at the ambitious Cam. students
who want to be the cream
on top of the milk bottle.
Who want to be billionaires
and prime-ministers.
I don't fit in.
Look at the young mammas
with their bawling babes
and swollen breasts.
I don't fit in.
Look at the women with partners
the betters half,
the trouble and strive.
I don't fit in.
Look at the young nuns
with their innocent faces
and willing hearts.
I want to fit in,
I want to fit in more than I want anything.
But, I don't fit in.
Isn't that a giggle?
I don't want to be pretty,
I don't want to be rich,
I don't want to be a mummy,
or a partner,
I want to be a nun
with an innocent face and a willing heart.
But that is the one thing I can never be.
I don't fit in.

Now, I am not kidding myself, I want to be a nun again all for the wrong reasons. I want the security and protection of being a holy, pure and happy sister. I want to wake up to the sound of a bell where I would jump out of bed and instantly kneel to dedicate my day to the Holy of Holies. I want to wash and dress in silence and float to the chapel where the candles are lit and the incense is filling the air with the scent of frankincense. I want my day to be permeated by bells and to KNOW with every fiber of my being that I am doing the will of God and if I just stay on this road it will lead to heaven (via purgatory of course). I want Jesus to be a real presence so that all notions of loneliness are cast aside. I want to walk down the street and have people approach me because I am a nun and they want to talk to this mini saint (if only they knew!). I want to go to bed exhausted in the security that I have filled my day with good acts that actually help me and the world.

I no longer belong to the Catholic community and I simply do not belong full stop. Since I was a girl I wanted to be a nun and now aged thirty eight my heart is rendered because I know that I will never be a nun. My life has been wasted praising a God who does not exist, or if he does then he has no care of me. All those saints I have spent my life invoking do not even know my name; I might as well have watched the clouds for faeries and dragons and teddy-bears and I could have held my one-way conversation with them. It is a mini-death is it not? A desire held for over thirty years has died but I want to go back where I believed in God as much as I believe that chrysalis becomes a butterfly and bees make honey. I want to feel the order of bells and the peace of the chapel, I want to wear a habit so that I know exactly who I am. Who am I now? Haven't got a clue! Of course these are not the correct reasons to be a nun and I have no tardis to take me to 1997 but I have come to a, I am not sure what is the correct word, a sort of brick wall where I cannot move forward, or rather I do not want to move forward. I am a blundering mess.

I am one of those people you see in front of a set of doors and you wonder why they are just stood there when you are required to press a button before you can exit. It is as though I have no corporeal existence, I am not in this world but I am also nowhere else. It can be some time before I am back in the world of bricks, flesh, words and all the rigmarole that goes with life.

I could easily sit down and stare at a blank wall as time passes but without me hearing the tick-tock of the twenty-four hour clock. It is a strange way of passing time pa.s.s.ing.. ti.m.e..p.a.ss..i.ng .t.i.me..t.i....m....e.

Comments that piss me right off:

1.   'You do not look depressed.' I have heard this many times and so far I have managed to restrain myself from replying, 'do you have a fucking idea of what you are talking about? Do you want me to stop showering, walk around with greasy hair and dirty clothes? Shall I fall onto the pavement and weep every time I find life an impossible burden? Shall I walk around ringing a bell crying 'woe is me'? Have you ever been so depressed that the thought of suicide fills your every waking moments? Have you ever been so depressed that your life is lived in a fog where everything is sapped of color and meaning. Fuck off and engage your brain before your gob.' That is what I want to say but I do not. Yet.
2.   'Just try and look on the bright side and you will feel better.' I would feel better if I punched you on your nose. I wonder how you would look then.
3.   'You do not look ill.' Oh, have you developed x-ray vision so that you can see inside my brain? Mental ill health does not show up on a MRI scan.
4.   'You have put on a bit of weight.' Yes, I gathered from the fact that none of my clothes fit me that I have developed a double chin and a size sixteen waist. You stuff yourself with tablets and try and keep slim.

When I was in the convent I would spend many hours a day sitting or kneeling very still. Sitting very still during the hours or study or kneeling in the chapel. Ignore the itch on the back of my neck; ignore the pins and needles; ignore the fly that buzzes around my nose, it all just a matter of will-power. Everything we did was to strengthen our will in the right direction. Now I cannot stay still. I went to the cinema last Saturday with a friend and I felt so sorry for her because I wriggled and jiggled as if I had flees in my pants. I crossed and uncrossed my legs, moved from left to right, my arms moved as if I suddenly turned into Mr. Tickle. Poor Nadia, thank goodness she is such a kind and patient friend so her desire to poke me never materialized. If I were her I would have soon told me to sit still.

My bed is just wonderful. I love it. When I am sad I want to take to my bed and as I turn over towards the wall I find some peace that I cannot find in any other place. I am jealous of tortoises, hedgehogs and all those animals that hibernate. I would give anything if I could lie down and wake up after the winter has passed with the hope that I would feel better. My bed draws me like a bottle of cider draws the alcoholic. When I wake up in the morning (and sometimes the afternoon) I have to collect all the powers of my will to cast aside the duvet and put my feet on the floor and face a new day. I never want to face a new day. All day, even as I chat to the old lady at the bus stop, or sit in math's class, or read a book, or swim, or ride my bike, or buy milk and bread I have a permanent voice in my head calling me to don my nightie and return to my safe place, that is my lovely, welcoming, comforting bed. That is why I have to leave my bedsit in the morning and stay out all day; otherwise I would not be able to resist the call of the mermaid to cast myself on the rocks of my bed.

<u>MY BEDSIT</u>

I sit here alone
no family,
no friends,
no god.
I hate it.
My new home
with a television,
pretty pictures
and depression.
I am lonely
and there is nothing that can fill my blackness.
Sex, alcohol, self-harm
are all pointless.
So I take too much lithium
and take to bed as the stomach cramps start.
Diarrhea, dehydration, deliriousness.
I cannot think as I sweat
the last drop of liquid in my poor ravished body.
What more must I do
to die?

<u>CHAPTER ELEVEN</u>

The Mad House

If you are the sort of person who gets annoyed when people criticize the NHS then please skip the next few pages as I am just about to rant like a curmudgeons old man sat on a park bench.

My experience of the NHS has been two-fold; as an out-patient and an in-patient. As an out-patient I have received truly wonderful treatment; the psychiatrists are easy to talk to, I have seen a number of psychiatrists and they have all been amazing; the psychiatric nurses are compassionate and wise. I really want to emphasis how great has been my treatment, an A+. I cannot thank these doctors, nurses and my incredible social worker enough. All the psychiatrists I have spoken to have listened, offered sagacious advice and gave me hope. The nurses have given me the time and space to talk and talk and talk. My social worker is professional, wise and I wish that all people who need a social worker get one as fab' as mine. As I read once in a card, 'thank-you from the bottom of my stomach, which is a lot lower that my heart.'

As an inpatient it was as if I had stepped back in time and found myself in the original Bedlam; all that it lacked were the spectators who would come and gape at the crazy inmates. I was an inpatient at a center named the Irwell Unit, for me the Irwell Unit is an anagram for hell.

I return to the twenty-third of December when I was taken to A&E. I had taken too much lithium and my body was reacting badly to it. I had diarrhea and a lot of pain in my stomach. I went by ambulance to hospital. The male nurse who came to extract by blood, take my temperature and blood pressure was super friendly and chatted away to me. I have found that male nurses are much better nurses than the majority of females I have encountered. There is a delightful Scottish male nurse in the out-patient department and he helped me so much, I felt that I could chat to him for hours.

Of course it was hours and hours before I saw a doctor, but when he did arrive at my cubicle I could find no fault with him. He gave me some pain relief and basically they just had to keep taking my blood like a legal vampire to see if the lithium had passed through my system. I was very dozy and as it was late in the evening my parent's went home and I fell asleep.

In the early hours of the morning a porter came to whisk me away to a ward. I presumed I would be going to a hospital bed as all I longed for was sleep, but alas it twas not to be. I was taken to an area that was rather strange. There was an area for waiting in, with was a television and about ten chairs. There were three beds, the sort of beds where a person is examined and not for snoozing. The nurse who 'took care of me' (allegedly) was a utter bitch. Bitch, bitch, evil bitch. If this book was just about her it would be called Nurse Bitch.

She took me to a chair and told me to sit in it, I say told, I mean in a very horrid manner. The pain-relief was starting to wear off by this point and I felt so weak and disorientated. I consumed very little liquid in the pass few days and I had lost a lot of fluids by sweating and diarrhea. I had not slept properly for days and I had too much lithium in my system. I asked if I could lie of a bed and she gruffly said no and I had to sit in a chair. I told her that I was in a lot of pain and felt very weak and I needed to lie down. The bitch just shrugged her shoulders and walked off.

I wanted to lie down and die; I had no energy to keep living. All I wanted was to lie down, why did she not understand this desire? So I took off my dressing gown lay it on the floor and I tumbled from the chair to the floor and through the pain, sweat and weakness I tried to find relief. Bitch returned and I am going to write out the dialogue.

Bitch (shouting like a banshee): **'Get off the floor, you are disgusting. People have vomited on that floor, get up now.'**

Me: Silence (I did not have the energy to reply).

Bitch: **'Get up now, I don't have time to be bothered with you.'**

Me: Silence.

At this point the bitch drags my right arm and painfully hauls me back to the chair of torture.

Me: 'You should not do that.'

Bitch: 'Do what?'

Me: 'Drag me by my arm.'

Bitch: 'I did not touch you.'

Bitch, bitch, bitch.

Me: 'Please will you phone my parent's?' (I had a mobile but it had no signal).

Bitch: 'No, you have to wait till your blood results come in.'

Me: 'Please will you check if they have come back?' (My blood tests were sent to Rochdale so the results were being sent by email).

Bitch: 'No, I don't have time to deal with you. Sit there and don't move.'

For me the most horrible swear word in the English language is 'cunt' and I would never say that word. However, I reserve this word for this vile excuse of a nurse; she is a cunt.

I thought about leaving the ward but I did not have the energy to walk that far. I just about managed to walk to the toilet that was only a few meters away. I was trapped. I became hysterical, crying, struggling to control by breath, panicking. I could not sit on the chair so I did more movements than a contortionist. After a while an angel arrived and rescued me. A nurse who was actually worthy of the name. She calmed me down, helped me to one of the beds, gave me a pillow and a blanket and told me to try and get some sleep. She also gave me a jug of water and a glass and encouraged me to drink. I did not want to drink as I did not want to walk to the toilet. It was hard to slumber as this lovely nurse came and took my blood pressure and temperature on a regular basis, but I did not mind. She could have cut of my right ear lobe and I do not think I would have cared, all I wanted was to lie still.

I know a doctor came to see me at some point, as did two women who tried to talk with me, but that was a non-starter as I did not have the life in me to actually answer questions. So they left and I was left in peace for a short time. After a few more hours another porter arrived to move me to another ward. However, this ward was as a ward should be. Two lovely nurses (one female, one male) took care of me when I arrived. I was put in a wheelchair to go to the toilet. I was put on a drip as I was dehydrated and they kept giving me a glasses of water to consume. Best of all I was in a bed where I could doze. I love these compassionate nurse, they deserve a noble prize for nursing. I was in pain and the nurses were unable to give me any medication as that would have to be prescribed by a doctor.

The next morning the pain was getting worse, but again I could not get pain relief as I was a medical patient and I was on a surgical ward; so the surgical doctors could not prescribe medicine for me. Eventually I did get some pain relief, and I presumed that I would soon be discharged. Again, there was a male nurse on the ward who went above and beyond the call of duty. I lay in bed and without any request by me, he came and gave me a pile of magazines to distract myself with. I did not have the strength or inclination to turn the glossy pages, but his thoughtfulness was a ray of sunlight in a very dark period of my life. Christmas Eve.

Various doctors came to see me that day, but as I look back in anger that day is hazy. My psychiatrist came to speak with me and eventually he said that they were going to move me to the Irwell Unit (psychiatric ward) because my mental health was not flourishing. I was sectioned for twenty-eight days under Section Two. When I told my Mother she thought I was joking...sectioned on Christmas Eve was a sick joke.

When my parents came to visit me they bought me a card-thingie so that I could watch the television. This was a wonderful gift as I was unable to sleep that night so rather than lie there and slowly drown in my own misery, I was distracted my night-time television trash. Actually that is not true, because being Christmas Eve there was a very fine production of Charles Dickens's *A Christmas Carol*.

Christmas Day was a very touching experience. The Salvation Army came and played some Christmas carols on the ward and gave each of us a box of chocolates. Lunch was extra special and rather yummy. One of the nurses helped me have a shower (I was really rather stinky by this stage, as you can imagine).

Christmas day evening, my lovely Scottish nurse from outpatients came and took me over to the den of misery, otherwise known as the psychiatric unit. He was so kind and I was such a mess, that even now I am embarrassed when I see him. What a mess...and it was not about to get any better.

The unit itself is rather swanky, with individual en-suite rooms, a nice dining room and a television room with a kitchenette. I was shown my room which was perfectly acceptable, much better than the facilities in Ireland, but that is where the advantage to England ceased. The treatment in England does not hold a candle to the care given in Waterford.

I was so sleep deprived that I had no idea what time it was and my behavior was rather erratic. I was very cold so I requested from one of the sullen, unhelpful nurses an extra blanket. I was duly given one, but I could not stop shaking so I asked if I could have another one and I was informed that I was only permitted one extra. Seriously! Are the resources of the N.H.S. so depleted that a patient who is shaking with the cold is not allowed two blankets? If that is the case then we truly are up the creek without a paddle.

I had no concept of time and I thought it was the morning so I went for a shower. The water from the shower overflowed from the basin and caused a stream in the corridor. The delightful nurse from the blanket fiasco came and shouted at me but I was beyond understanding the situation. Then I remember that I sat in the wardrobe eating some tangerines that my Mother had brought me. Do not ask, I have not a clue what was spewing from my broken mind. At some point in the night a nurse came into my room and she took me to the common room. The television was not on but the lights were lit and so I sat there for the rest of the night. Eventually I returned to bed and there I remained for the majority of my stay in that hell hole.

I did not shower or eat. My parents came twice a week and brought me food, fruit, crisps, chocolate and pop that I consumed in my room. When I had been dwelling there a few days I got out of bed and went to the dining room with the intention of partaking in the evening meal. A nurse saw me on the corridor and he said that unless I had a shower and got dressed I would not be allowed to have any food. I was incredibly depressed at that point so I just turned on my heel and returned to my pit.

On other evenings I did have tea (without showering and in my pj's) and many of us were in our night attire, so the rule about getting dressed was just an arbitrary rule of the pillock mentioned above. Then I would go to the television room to spend time with the other inmates as I found it beneficial to be near those who were in the same situation as me. From them I discovered that it was not just me that was treated appalling by the majority of the staff, it was not personal, they were equally incompetent with all of us.

I spent all day in bed, and I broke out in horrible sores on my face and body because of dirt and lack of fresh air. No-one changed my bed or cleaned my room for the entire time I was on the ward. Only one nurse came into my room to see if I was okay. Again, it was a male nurse and he tried to encourage me out of bed; it did not work but at least he tried which is a hundred percent more than any other nurse did. Thank-you John!

One morning as I lay in bed a nurse opened my door thinking it was another patient's room and she screamed with the tones of a fish wife, 'Nicola, get up. Don't tell me to fuck off, get up.' I turned and pointed out her mistake and she just shut the door. What a lovely way to wake up a mentally ill person!

And so Bury's answer to Disney Land continued to spread joy and magic dust. This was my day, I lay in bed all day until five in the evening when I arose for the evening meal (I did not get up every day). Apart from the John (the nurse I mentioned previously) no one ever came near me. Sometimes a nurse would go around and knock on everyone's door when it was tea time (tea is what we call our evening meal in the north). Sometimes a nurse would stand in the middle of the corridor and shout 'food' as if we were mere animals.

Every time I went for tea they had run out of something. Actually the food was okay. There were a few young nurses who were so snotty, but there was one who was so far up her own backside I am surprised she was able to find her way without a white stick. She was pretty, in her early twenties and completely unsuited to being a nurse. When it comes to sullenness, Vicky Becks has nothing on this little cow.

One evening I went for tea and they had already run out of sausages and I will again resort to dialogue:

Me: 'Why don't you just order more, you are always running out?'
Nurse snotty-nose: 'Well you should come on time.' (Said in her poshest Bury accent).

There are times when I really flip and it is usually a comment that will send me over the edge (please excuse my mixed metaphors). Her comment sent me over the edge of crazy.

Me: 'I came as soon as the nurse knocked on my door.'
Nurse snotty-nose: 'You know tea is at five.'
Me: 'I was asleep and I do not have an alarm clock.'
Nurse snotty-nose: 'That's your problem.'

I was so mad, so I picked up the tureen of green soup and threw it on the floor. It went all over me, in my hair, on my face, and all over the floor. I remember there was a Liverpudlian woman also in the queue and all I heard was her saying 'fucking hell.' Exactly.

I went to my bathroom, stripped off my now green pj's and got into the shower. A nurse came into the bathroom, pulled back the shower curtain and shouted at me to get out. She handed me a towel. I had tablets hidden in my room, previously they had been under the towels, but I had moved them to under the mattress. As no one ever changed my bed or checked my room for anything as they did in Ireland, I knew they would not be found. They were my safety net in case things got to the point where I wanted to end it all). I ignored her and carried on with washing the gunk of my body. She left the bathroom and went away.

Eventually, like the wicked witch of the west, she returned. Apparently she was a staff nurse (or charge nurse?). Boy was she mad. She did not ask me my account of the situation but told me that she could phone the police and have me arrested for assault. I did not reply but inwardly I was screaming at the top of my voice, 'I do not give a shit what you do. I am so miserable that I could not give a fuck if I am here, or in a police cell. I am so far beyond caring you have no idea.' She did not give a shit so I remained silent and she left.

On a Friday I would see a psychiatrist who fitted in perfectly with the ward, that is, he was crap. One morning this delightful charge nurse came to tell me that the doctor was ready to see me. I got straight out of bed and said that I was going to the toilet (ever since I was sick as a child I have had bladder weakness, so I always make sure I go to the toilet before I go to a meeting, travel, exam etcetera). My God, how do these nurses not have laryngitis the amount of screaming that they do? Well the screaming began: think of the cox in the Boat Race.

Couldn't Care Less Nurse: 'You knew you were going to see the doctor today.'
Me: 'I did not know what time.'
Couldn't Care Less Nurse: 'Hurry-up, we are already running late.'
Me: Inwardly – 'fuck off and let me die.'

So after I had emptied my bladder I went off to see Doctor Useless. I did not speak at these consultations, I was spoken at. The Couldn't Care Less nurse said that I should apologize to the snotty-nose nurse but I declined her kind offer. Doctor Useless waffled on about depression but I was beyond understanding or caring. Then I was released back to my cage till the following Friday.

After tea in the evenings I would sit in the television lounge with my fellow survivors. The nurses treated them like crap also. One example of this is that in the evening we had to line up to get our medicine. This was a long convoluted business (why I do not know, because there were more of us in Ireland and they were so efficient). The nurses generally sat on their ample backsides at the nurses' station whilst one nurse would dispense the magic mushrooms. There was an elderly man on the ward who was annoying but harmless. He lived in his own special world consisting of spitfires, cats and coloring books. The nurses just told him to shut up all the time rather than spending time with him. No, it was the other patient's that helped him, never the nurses.

One evening as we were lining up to see the nurse and as Alan Alburge claimed *'and in my opinion there is nothing worse.'* The phone at the nurses station rang and there were nurses sat on their little thrones but they thought it amusing to tell this elderly man to answer the phone. This he did obediently, but he was unable to hold a cohesive conversation. Obviously, this was an important phone call, but the incompetent nurses merely giggled.

Another evening the nurses were again laughing at this man and the strong Liverpudlian lady I mentioned previously, turned on the nurse and asked, 'what is funny? Why are you laughing at him?' This soon wiped the smile of their mucky pussies.

Also, it was so easy to self-harm on the ward. In the kitchenette we had access to boiling water which was my weapon of choice. They never checked our stuff for self-harming aids such as glass or razors. Another patient told me that it was easy to get alcohol or drugs as some people were permitted to leave the ward and they were not checked when they returned. I was told I could whatever I wanted – I just had to ask.

I never spoke to the nurses or asked for any help whatsoever. Although I was not on sleeping tablets permanently, if I was struggling to sleep I had previously (in Ireland) been able to ask for a tablet. One night I felt awful. Not just depressed but hysterical. I had gone to bed at eleven in the evening but I tossed and turned and I felt as if seventy seven demons had sent up camp in my brain. That evening there were three nurses on duty, one female who was in charge, the blanket hording nurse and another male nurse.

At one o'clock I was crying and starting to go really mad, that is I could not cope. So I went to the female nurse and told her (as my eyes cascaded with hysterical tears) that I wanted to kill myself and I needed a tablet to help me sleep. Have a guess what she did and said. If this were a work of fiction I would argue that her comment was too farfetched; but this is not fiction, this is the reality of what is offered to people with mental ill health on the N.H.S in Bury. She coldly looked at me, and said, 'I am busy, go and speak to Jeremy.' He of the blanket restriction. I said that I wanted to talk to a female and she just turned her back and walked away.

I returned to my room and as much as I did not want to talk to Jezza, I was desperate. Depression makes one a desperate creature. I would do anything to be better. I would swallow any pill, partake of any therapy no matter how strange. If I was told that doing a Lady Godiva would loosen the bonds of this straight jacket then I would throw aside my togs in an instant and mount the horse and canter through the cobbled streets of Radcliffe.

After another hour, (this is three hours after I had initially tried to find respite in sleep), I approached Jezza and asked him for a tablet as I felt rather desperate. This man, who did not know me at all, who I doubt even knew my name, replied, 'No, I am not giving you anything as I do not believe you have made any effort to go to sleep.' Honestly, even the most vivid of imaginations could not invent this stuff. I reiterated that I was desperate and that the staff nurse had sent me to him. He was just too fucking lazy to care. At this point I flipped (are you discerning a pattern in this memoir?). He said that he would speak to the staff nurse when he had finished, but his attitude was one of 'bugger off you annoying twerp, I do night shifts so that I do not actually have to deal with ill people and now you are here with your problems disturbing my reading of G.Q.' So I picked up the papers in front of him and ripped them up and I said, 'you are finished now.' He grabbed me by my wrists, and suddenly the other two nurses appeared (not too busy now where they?) They caught my ankles and dragged me to my room, where they threw me on the floor (not even on the bed).

Did any of them come near me for the rest of the night? Did they fuck. I was left alone. Even the next day no one inquired after my well-being. It was never mentioned again. When I eventually left hospital my Dad commented that I was worse than when I went in. Of course I was because in that place there was no care, compassion, or even basic nursing. Why are these people nurses? Is it a power trip? Flo must be turning in her grave. All English nurses should be sent to Ireland to train.

There was an activity room on the ward, but it was never open. I know it was a nice room because we had to go through this room on our Friday jollies to see Doctor Dread. We were not even allowed to take anything from this 'invisible' room to use on the ward. One of the other patients asked if there was a chess set in the activity room, the answer was a yes but as we were not permitted to actually use this hallowed space the patient asked if he and another patient could take the chess board to the dining room to play a game. A reasonable request, but no, the chess board must remain gathering dust in the locked activity room because a piece might get lost! Have you ever heard such a load of crap? So instead of a well used activity room we had a locked museum. Great therapy.

There was also a well equipped gym, including a pool table. We were only permitted to use this room if there was a nurse with us. Occasionally a nurse would open the room for a short period, but the majority of the time Flo Nightingale made use of that large bundle of keys she carried. It would be different if the nurses were stretched but all they did was make endless cups of tea and sit in their coven and plot their spells. The exception was dear, dear John (previously mentioned) who took patients for walks and out to the garden. I kn ow this because he would come and ask me to join them, I always declined but bless him for trying.

So why did I not complain? For two reasons. Firstly, I was so depressed at that time I hardly had the energy to take a shower, I had no fight in me at the time. Secondly, one has to pick one's battles, and who is the N.H.S actually going to listen to; the crazy woman or the N.H.S doctors and nurses? I am not a betting woman, but even I could guess the odds on this one.

So after twenty-eight days in Dante's inferno I was sent back to the land of the living. My Dad came to collect me but no one would bloody open the door for me. I was going ballistic shouting 'let me off this fucking ward, open the fucking door.' The nurses I asked said they were busy, I could see them sat at the nurses' station, they clearly were not busy. Those women are on some weird sadistic power trip. I was ready to punch in a window to get out of there. Poor Papa, he was trying to calm me down but I was so past...everything that he gave up. Eventually I got out but I was a mess.

I went back to my bedsit and I went to bed and there I stayed for about ten days. I wanted to die so much. I have to give a huge thank-you to the wonderful nurses who came to see me at home; without them I do not know what I would have done. After a week I returned to the ward to see the doctor who was as useless as a chocolate tea-pot. One of the home-care team nurses took me back to my bed-sit. I cried. A lot. I felt crap, physically with my attractive body of facial and bodily sores, having spent five weeks with little personal hygiene and no fresh air and a diet of fruit, crisps, chocolate and carbonated pop. Mentally I had no hope and saw that the end of the yellow brick road was just an empty promise of recovery. I still feel like I am never going to get to a point where depression does not push me around like a fat, spotty, greasy school bully.

WHAT IS A NURSE?

You grabbed me by my arm,
is this a nurse?
You pushed me into a chair,
is this a nurse?
You left me to shiver,
without a blanket,
is this a nurse?
You would not listen to my pain,
is this a nurse?
You swore at me,
is this a nurse?
You never bothered to enter my room,

is this a nurse?
You left me without food or drink,
is this a nurse?
You walked away when I asked for help,
is this a nurse?
You grabbed my wrists and ankles and put me on the floor,
is this a nurse?
You made fun of me and spoke to me as if I were a dog,
is this a nurse?
You failed to do you job.
You are not a nurse!

Out-patient	_In-patient_
• A psychiatrist who listens. Thanks Dr. F!	• A psychiatrist who barely looked at me and did not know my name
• My psychiatrist is available	• A psychiatrist who saw me for a few minuets once a week
• Nurses who care (especially Tony)	• Nurses who do not care (apart from John)
• Nurses who are worthy of the name nurse	• Nurses who are not real nurses
• Nurses who were lovely human beings	• Bitches
• A psychologist who is professional, wise and just fab'	• No psychologist
• Therapy that is hard work because it helps	• No therapy
• A social worker who I respect and who actually makes my life just that bit easier	• No social worker
• Places to go for people with mental ill health	• No activities
• Help	• No help

CHAPTER TWELVE

God and the Church

On a Saturday morning I often go to a Buddhist center in Manchester. I have no interest in becoming a member of another religion; I have not studied what is Buddhist teaching but I go there because it is peaceful and most importantly, safe. No one is going to raise their voice, everyone is considerate to others and there is not going to be what we call in the north, agro. There is a class from eleven till one in the afternoon and an ordained minister (I am not sure minister is the correct terminology) leads us in a class called 'Tools for Living'. So every week there is a topic such as kindness, meditation etcetera; today we were invited into the world of doing nothing. An invitation to step off the running machine of life, permission to sit still, not meditating, just being still.

Okay, fads are fads but this one for mindfulness is everywhere at the moment, it pervades the atmosphere like carbon dioxide. It was even in an episode of *The Big Bang Theory* (the one where they go and volunteer at a homeless shelter for Thanksgiving). So, I am willing to give anything a try and the time came to try this panacea for all ills. What a load of shit. Imagine this; following the example of Raj and Howard I did my washing-up 'mindfully'. The reason this miracle cure fails for me is that I do not like my life, I panic, I stress and by constantly remaining 'in the present moment' I am just reminded of how much I hate my present state of being. Escapism may not be the most psychologically healthy to do, but sometimes it is the only way to make it from the morning to the evening...everyone does what they can to cope and sometimes we mess up...che sera, sera.

Today at the Buddhist center we did an activity that I actually found uncomfortable and my initial reaction (and second and third reaction) was to scuttle away home. We worked in pairs and one of us placed our finger tips on the wrist of the other person; the one with the finger tip role had to shut their eyes and relax so as to be able to follow the wrist of the other person as they moved their wrist around. Then we swopped roles. The touch freaked me out. When I was a nipper-nun and first in Carmel my superior told me that tactility is a sign that there is something wrong with a person. How chilling was that?

Now let me put this in context. When I read the autobiography of C.S. Lewis he wrote that when he was at a boy's boarding school, homosexuality was prevalent; not because all those lads desired the flesh of other fellows but because when there is no other choice any flesh will do. It can be the same in a convent. We take a vow of chastity (along with poverty and obedience) so nuns aim to be pure, but flesh is flesh and in a convent that so-called 'fallen' flesh needs to be constantly subdued. In Italy there was also a rule of no-touching. After eleven years of imparting the rule of touch equals bad, I now find any form of touch freakish. This is why I found the simple act of placing my finger tips on the wrist of another person so uncomfortable. I think my attitude is incorrect and unhealthy but I am not sure how to rectify this reaction.

Why do we find the middle ground so difficult to attain? Hollywood lies when it preaches pleasure is derived from the flesh; the intellect produces a pleasure that can result in ecstasy. The Church lies when the flesh is held in suspicion and scorn (especially the female flesh) because if there is a God then pleasures of the flesh, the warmth of the sun on the skin, the feel of soft rain on an upturned face, the gentle breeze on a hot day, the feel of sand beneath unshod feet, the crunch of autumnal leaves, the scrunch of snow as one makes an image of an angel, the sound of an upbeat song on the radio, the rush of endorphins at the end of a run, the wonder of being able to float in water, the smell of an old book, the beauty of a favorite painting hanging on a gallery wall, that first cup of tea in the morning, and so on are good, holy and pure. John the Evangelist claimed that he would need all the books the world could contain to tell the message of Jesus, the same is true of pleasure, because each one of us is unique and my R4 is your Key 103! We are flesh and intellect and both should be cherished as pleasure givers, but in the middle path because all excess leads to a distortion of the truth. Sex is not an invention of humanity, it is natural, for us, for animals, that is just the way it is and we should stop treating it as something dirty but should aim at finding a healthy attitude that will lead to a holistic approach to life and happiness.

I presume most of you have heard about women and men who are canonized by the Church (where people are named saints). Some of the most famous being St. Francis of Assisi (he loved his animals), St. Clare (patron saint of televisions), St. Anthony (the finder of lost things), St. Joan of Arc (fought the English and got burnt at the stake for her trouble) and so on. Well, if you go through the Martyrology, (Martyrologium Romanum where all Catholic saints are listed, each with

114

their particular feast day) there are practically no married saints. How disgraceful. Even Mary, the mother of Jesus is known as the Virgin Mary. Now, when she was pregnant with Jesus she was declared a virgin so that Joseph would have no claim to biological paternity, which makes sense if one wants to argue that Jesus was divine. However, if sex is natural between a wife and husband, and Mary and Joseph were truly married, I fail to understand why she had to remain a virgin after she gave birth to Jesus. Not all Christian Churches teach that she remained a virgin forever, because the gospels refer to the sisters and brothers of Jesus (linguistically there is an argument that the Arabic word for siblings can refer to cousins). The Catholic Church teaches that Mary never had sexual intercourse with Joseph because this fits with their theology of virginity being a prerequisite for sanctity. Strange but true.

Let me continue with my rant. Augustine of Hippo argued that women were created as body, but men were created as mind, that is in the image of God; and he was not the only jerk to write such trash. Really? I live in a European country (well, since Brexit, the land mass of Europe if not the EU itself) in the twenty-first century and these ideas need to be repudiated by the Church as ideas of their time, but in our contemporary society they are erroneous. There is a difference between tradition and old-fashioned, outdated and dangerous. These ideas just keep women subjected to man.

Yesterday was Sunday and my Father picked me up in his car and we had to go round the town because Dad had a few errands to run. So I saw a some people going into various Churches, but all the Christians I spied were old (sixty years old plus) and I thought in twenty years, who will be getting up early on a Sabbath to go to worship?

I have reached the conclusion that religion is a social construct. Not in the same sense as Karl Marx understood it as the opium of the people, a way to keep women and men under control, but in the same sense as football, the Women's Insitute, social media, cycling clubs and other such groups have a role of social cohesion, to be part of a club consisting of like-minded people who support each other. Humans are social beings, not solitary, so it is useful for women and men to come together in a group as an expression of their humanness.

Also, religion can be a great comfort to a soul in pain. I recently asked a friend if she believes in God and she said she has to because she wants to have the hope that she will see her Mum again in heaven. The problem comes when religion claims that we all have to believe the same thing (which are concepts men have created); you have to think the same as me and if you do not, then well my friend, even though I preach a God of love and mercy, salvation is not for the likes of you, hope you have your factor fifty sun-cream ready, because it is frightfully hot where you are headed! It is as though Christianity were a game of snakes and ladders; do what the Church teaches and you constantly land at the bottom of a ladder with the die on six, go against the Church and you will be sliding down those snakes quicker that you can say Amen.

Male and FEMALE He Created Them

I bleed,
it's only natural you know.
It is a sign
my body is functioning
as a woman's body should.
There might be pain.
There might be mess.
But when you tell me

115

I am unclean,
I need to be purified,
I am unworthy to worship,
I need to sit in parda.
Then you are wrong
and you should
get back to biology class.
Idiot.

There is of course a difference between God and the Church. The Roman Catholic Church teaches that Jesus founded the Church, I always found this impossible to accept. If I read the Gospels and the radical message of Jesus, and I look at the Church, there is little correlation. What would Jesus say if he went to the Vatican and saw all the pomp and ceremony, the riches, the fancy clothes and deference shown by Christians to mere men? I do not think he would recognize his message as a living reality. Maybe in shanty towns where the priests and sisters live with the poor one may see the Christian message is embraced in its entirety, but in the hidden wealth of the Vatican in contrast to the homeless of Rome, then I do not see the community that Jesus founded.

I have a dear friend who is an Anglican. I met her husband at university where he was training to become an Anglican priest and through him I met her. After uni when I went to stay with them for the weekend, L would come with me to Mass on the Saturday evening and then I would go to their celebration on the Sunday morning. A very ecumenical relationship. I was so embarrassed when she came to Mass with me because the Church was invariably dull and dingy, with a small congregation who did not make any response during the Mass (I did and I stood out like a sore thumb). The priest was so lacking in life even I was almost asleep during the homily. No hymns or music and at the sign of peace the people turned to cold, marble statues and only L and I exchanged a hand-shake. We were by far the youngest members of the congregation and when Mass concluded and we all moved like ants to the exit, there was no friendly smile or goodby, nice to see you, welcome to our community. I did not mind this so much because I have been to hundreds of Catholic Churches and this pattern was repeated on the majority of cases. However, I wanted L to have a positive experience. On the way home, all she said was, 'you were the only one who made the responses.' Sometimes, words fail and silence must prevail.

The following morning I went to 'their' Church and what a different experience. Not that I think Church gatherings should be all singing and dancing, I personally prefer quite music with periods of silent reflection, but a Church celebration must be ALIVE! Where everyone has a role to perform and the minister leads the congregation in a holistic experience. A community that wants to be with their neighbor in praise of the divine. As Jesus said, *'I have come that you may have life and have it to the full.' (John 10:10)*

At the Anglican celebration we were lead by S. (Lovisa's hubby) in a lively and profound celebration. The words of the hymns were on overhead projectors so there was no excuse for people not to join in the singing (hymn books either remain shut in their appointed places at the end of the pew or the few people who sing have their noses in the spine of the book and very little noise is projected outwards). S. gave a lively sermon that was easy on the ear. Afterward we all went to the back of the building and had a cuppa with each other. There was no instant procession to the exit, people knew each other and wanted to have their weekly catch-up.

Another time when I was at uni. a young woman (about eighteen) came to spend a few weeks in Cambridge over the summer holidays. She stayed at MBIT and was a shy and sweet Baptist. As a college warden I kept an eye on this girl as she seemed rather overwhelmed by being so far from home. She asked me to go to the Baptist Church with her on the Sunday as she did not want to go by herself. So I went to an early Mass at the Catholic Church and then I accompanied her to the Baptist Church. The thing that struck me was the friendliness of the congregation. After the celebration a number of women came over and welcomed us to the parish and one of the women even invited us to her house for lunch. I was overwhelmed. At this point I had been going to the main Catholic parish in Cambridge, on an almost daily basis, and not one person had ever spoken to me or welcomed me to the parish. The difference was very striking. What would Jesus do? I think he would have invited us to his house for lunch!

We are so narrowed minded when we decide that we can learn nothing from other people. A beautiful aspect of Islam is the religious obligation to learn, from cradle to grave. When the Indians in their genius formulated the decimal system, the Christian Europeans not only initially rejected this mathematical development, but they went as far as to consider it a product of the evil eye because Indians were not Christians. Wow. Other cultures enrich our society.

When I returned to England in the summer of 2015, I had not given up on my faith entirely and I had no intention of not continuing as a practicing Catholic, but when I went into to a Catholic Church I panic, feel nauseous and have trouble breathing normally. I physically could not do it; it just reminded me of the convent. I have not been to Mass since I have returned to this green and pleasant land.

I had a plan! I would go to all the Churches in the area and I would try and find a new religious home. Every Sunday I went to another Church, Anglican, Methodist, United Reformed, Baptist and Unitarian. Nope, none of these could be my home. I sat at the back of the Churches and it was though I was at a theater and watching a play. I could not commit intellectual suicide and kneel and stand and sing and pray to a God who was every day more distant and more irrelevant to my life. This was not a case of 'I do not want to go to Church because I do not like the music/priest/building and I want a lie-in.' This was a case of 'I do not want to go to Church because I quite simply no longer believe.' *'To your own self be true'.*

Most of my life I have spent some part of my day in mediation; sometimes I would prayer for hours. When I look back I ask, 'to what was I praying to, what or whom was I raising my heart and mind to?' It seems the answer is 'nothing' and the joke is on me. What a waste of time. I suppose other people waste time watching telly or on face book or chatting or at the pub, I wasted my time trying to communicate with non-existent aliens.

Let's talk about money, money, money, always funny, in a rich man's world. You know that cardinals are known as the 'princes of the Church' and boy do they live palatially. A bishop's residence is known as a palace. It is disgusting and no matter how they try and theologize it, there is no way to justify the money that the Church has. Have you ever seen where a bishop lives? On the way to Manchester I pass the bishop of Manchester's palace, it is humungous. Is that acceptable when people live on the streets? Why should we listen to the princes of the Church when they are so removed from society? I think priests, bishops, cardinals and the pope should live in a council flat and then what they say might actually have the ring of authenticity.

A few years ago the bishop of Lancaster sold his bishop's palace for over a million pounds and he went to live with the priests of the diocese (he takes it in turn to spend time in different parishes). I was so impressed, the bishop living in the parish. However, there was a lot of uneasiness among the other bishops; God forbid that they might also sell their lap of luxuries and live like most normal people. Did Jesus live in luxury? He was born in a stable and spent a few years as a refugee. I had hoped that the new papa might make some real, concrete difference in this respect but he has failed and the status-quo reigns.

The other day there was an item on the news lauding the archbishop of Canterbury who has permitted a refugee family live in a house in the grounds of Lambath Palace (the name Palace is a bit of a give away). Who bloody ray. What difference does that make to him? He is not going to be sitting down for breakfast with them is he? It says how ridiculously large Lambath Palace is if they have houses on the estate. The Senecan excuse springs to mind...It is the same as me giving away one of my coats, or rather not actually giving it away but allowing someone else to borrow my coat, a nice enough act, but it has no real impact on my life.

The rich, greedy men of the Church say that they need a posh estate because they have heads of state visiting them, what a load of shit. It comes down to the fact that Jesus would not live in such an inappropriate lodging. Gandhi did not live in opulence and he message was still heard all over the world. Also, they say that the riches do not belong to them but to the Church, try telling that to a young mother who has to make the choice between food and heating. Do you hear the echo of the message that it is harder for a rich man to enter heaven than for a camel to pass through the eye of a needle? Maybe they just have a selective memory. Then they have the audacity to constantly ask parishioners for more and more and more dosh. You can even donate by direct debit now! Piss off and get a grip on how most people live in this world.

In the Catholic Church only certain people can receive Holy Communion, Catholics who are deemed 'worthy'. Anyone who is in mortal sin is not welcome at the table, those in second marriages, those not married but having sex, practicing homosexuals, in fact there is an incredibly long list and anyone who is not Catholic can go and whistle in the wind. I always struggled with this concept of the Eucharist as a sort of prize for good behavior. My theology of the Eucharist is that it is more a sort of spiritual help for those who are broken and struggling and desperate. If one accepts that the Eucharist communicates the presence of Jesus to the human soul, then one must return to the Gospel to understand who were the sorts of people the big J.C. reached out to, prostitutes, a woman married numerous time, lepers, outcasts, in summation, sinners. Jesus hung out with sinners, and now mere men have decided that sinners may not have access to Jesus; this I cannot agree with.

I believe that Churches should be places of refuge for those who are battered by the storms of life. People make mistakes; rather than condemn them, the Church should welcome them home and help them rise. Who are men to say that a person is not worthy to come to Church and receive Holy Communion? Men are nothing and all women and men should have unlimited access to their God.

Okay, so I take God out of the equation, now I am left in limbo. I have tried to understand some science (which was never my forte), read a few books, listened to programmes on the radio, watch endless episodes of *The Big Bang Theory*. Matter, anti-matter, dark matter, black holes and what-not, but if there is no God then why is there anything at all? What was at the start? We have the concept of infinity, just think of the number pie, but how can anything have no beginning? Why are there so many different plants? If evolution is true, then why have we not evolved so as to eliminate all genetic defects? Why if it is a case of survival of the fittest, do we still care for the weak in our society? Why do we not practice infanticide (well, some countries such as China still do) as they did in Roman times? Why are there mosquitoes that can eat on the eyes of dying children? Why, why, why, why, why, why, why, why, why, why, why, why, why, why, why, why, why, why, why, why, why, why, why, why, why, why, why, why, why, why, why, why, why, oh my God, why, why, why??? I will never settle till I find some answers.

Evil has always been a big issue. We should not underestimate the all pervading concept of original sin in the formation of Christian Western culture. Augustine of Hippo, whose theology was adopted by the Church as its bench mark of orthodoxy, claimed that babies are born with a leaning towards sin. Concupiscence. Our souls are born with original sin, that makes evil attractive and we require sacramental baptism if we are going to avoid hell, limbo and make it to the gates of heaven. I am not stating that I agree with this theology, but it must be acknowledged, that we cannot understand Western culture for the last two thousand years if we do not seriously have a look at Gus's thinking. Even in the Reformation, Luther and his pals adopted the theology of Augustine, Luther was in fact an Augustinian friar. We can only really reject this dark thinking if we accept and understand it in the first place.

Somewhere, at sometime there was a pre-lapsarian paradise and then bang, Eve the temptress was tempted and behold a piece of fruit was the price of original sin just did not intellectually satisfy me. Is it, a la mode Sartre, that freedom is in fact a form of condemnation? When I was a nun, I spent every moment of the day trying to love God to the best of my ability. If I, a miserable sinner would never willing turn against my creator and beloved, then there is no way that the first human being, created without sin would ever be tempted to reject God and believe a lie. The only other person created without original sin was Mary and there is never a question raised that she would reject God. Also Jesus, but he was 'begotten not made.' (Nicean Creed)

Giving a person total freedom and then expecting them to reach from earth to heaven, unharmed, and without harming another person is like taking a wobbly toddler, strapping skates to their pudgy feet, putting them on an icy lake and telling them to get to the other side. Impossiblie! The child will spend most of the time on its behind or banging it's head. They will hurt themselves and possibly hurt others. The ice may be thin in places and if this child happens to venture onto this patch of frozen water then its demise is inevitable. Oh I can hear the theologians now, yes, yes I know, there is grace, God-given grace that will help us on our journey of life. However, I asked for God's grace and it has not saved me...it is a risky venture and the inventor of the game should play with fairer rules.

The story of Adam and Eve has lead to the abuse of women for centuries. Why did God create man and woman physically unequal so that man could hit, beat, batter, abuse, rape, torture, degrade women every moment of every day? When I lived in Italy some of the sisters from certain countries such as Egypt said that it is just 'normal' for husbands to hit their wives. Disgusting. Yet if the story of Eve is perpetuated that idea is somehow 'acceptable'. As Eve is 'bone of my bone and flesh of my flesh' then Adam can break those bones and tear that flesh. It should make us rise up and call for a female revolution, rather than worrying about whether we are size ten or fourteen or making our talons even longer and our tan an ever deep of shade of mahogany.

At university a professor once said in a lecture that evil will never be understood, even in heaven, we will never be able to grasp the meaning of evil and we just have to accept that Jesus is our redeemer. I wanted to jump from my bench and shout 'you have got to be joking'. I want answers. I deserve answers. Humans are made of a body and an intellect and although we often abuse both of them, we are designed (by whom or what I know not) to seek the truth and the idea that we will never reach a conclusion for one of the greatest questions ever posed, that is the role of evil, then I will never give up seeking the answer for anything.

Augustine of Hippo stated that we do not see the world as it is we see it as we are which makes perfect sense. When I was a Christian I would look at the world and be amazed at the intricate design and the breathtaking harmony. Everything was fascinating and the universe was a strange mixture of a joyful playground and an instrument of torture. Now I have depression; actually I do not have depression in the same sense that I have a handbag, or I have a cold, or I have a kidney, and to say I am depressed seems just as superficial, today I am happy, yesterday I was confused, tomorrow I will be angry; rather I AM depression, it permeates my entire being, every organ, every cell, my mind, heart and soul. It is bigger that the black holes Professor Hawking meditates about and it makes me look out at the world and I see nada but utter, stark, withering ugliness.

I look at a tree and instead of thinking 'wow, what an amazing piece of architecture' I think 'so what? It is a meaningless piece of wood with a few leaves stuck on for good luck'. I am miserable and when I look at the world I see misery. I am the sister of Orwell's Winston and my soul and mind have been crushed so that I no longer see beauty, and what is even more, I do not actually care. I feel that I have been trying to make two and two make five but without the thought police I must insist it makes four. I was happier when it made five, and I am miserable that it makes four, but it does and that is that my comrade. I do not believe in a deity, and I do not believe in what the Catholic Church preaches, but I have no idea what I do believe in, but I do know that I cannot go back; the hexagonal peg is just a hexagonal peg.

A quick hop back to the Garden of Eden. Women have, from the beginning, been second-class citizens, the temptress, the whore, the one who must cover her fallen flesh from head to toe so as not to lead men astray. Bastards, you should learn to control your erected member and leave us to act as we choose. There is an incredible unhealthy line of thought that has resulted in many good and holy women falling into anorexia. Look at the effects of eating disorders, the woman becomes thin and her female form disappears and her breasts lie flat and man like. Her periods cease and her bodily hair becomes darker and coarser. More and more man like at every change and less and less like the wicked woman she is portrayed to be because that portrayal suits men, because then men have the excuse to blame women and keep them under the proverbial thumb. There are many canonized women who lived only on the Eucharist; anorexia for a heavenly cause. Just think about the Jewish tradition that a woman is 'unclean' when she menstruates, and yet the women has done nothing unnatural, that is just the way men want to view it. Let's bind women's feet, no matter the agony and deformation of what is natural, because that is the way men like them.

I bought a tee-shirt yesterday with the comment printed on the front 'Eve was framed'. Lets return to the fauna of the Garden of Eden where Adam and Eve were given a choice and they fucked up. The theological argument goes that if humanity was not given a free choice then they would be robots and without freedom of choice we cannot love. God is all about love and so for humanity to have a 'real' relationship with God they must be able to choose to love with the possibility of rejecting God. I think God was the one who fucked up big time. If God is omniscient and omnipotent then surely humanity could have been given a better choice?

If God cannot act against his nature, if God's nature is love then he cannot, logically do anything that is not love. If that is the case, then why do human beings have the ability to act against love because this is the price of freedom? Is God not free? But God cannot lie, love one people more than another, or command murder...oh wait, there are plenty of accounts of God in the Bible of God lying, loving the so-called Chosen People more than other nations and commanding murder, accounts that theologians must theologize away.

Dostoyevsky puts on the lips of Ivan in The Brothers Karamazov the problem that a child suffering is not worth heaven. If you gaze on a toddler who has leukemia, what Alexander Masters sarcastically calls, 'These victims of God's omnipotent love,' and the wee nipper is oh so sick, is this the price of freedom? It is not worth it my friend. On the radio the other day it was stated that there are an estimated thirty million slaves in the world today! The reply to this is not to simply state that suffering now leads us to heaven, as the slogan goes 'we believe in life before death'. Rather the reply to this quandary is to say, why did the all powerful God get it so, so, so wrong.

Years ago I read a philosopher (I cannot recall who) who wrote that we can never be sure that we are not really sat in a nut house. I thought about this a lot; what if I am really crazy and everything I believe is true is really just a figment of my imagination. I concluded that it did not matter, because I was content so if my life is real, great, and if it is not real, great because it makes no difference to my happiness. Now, I might still be sat in that mad house, however, now I am unhappy and I am trapped in this horrible, scary, unfriendly, ugly and hostile world and. I want out, I WANT OUT. I WANT BLOODY OUT OF THIS MAD HOUSE.

Please someone help me out

I am passionate about philosophy. So many people hear the big Greek word and get freaked-out, but philosophy is for everyone, without exception because philosophy is about life, death, morals, education, the benefits system, the disabled, the elderly, abortion, euthanasia, religion, policing, justice, human rights, everything you can think of, but that is the key, you must think about things. Philosophy in the academy often has a ring of irrelevance because those people sometimes never leave their ivory tower and therefore have no right to tell other people what to do. This is why I believe that politicians should not go straight from private school, to Oxbridge, to Westminster....has David Cameron ever actually been on a bus? If politicians worked for at least ten years before entering politics then they might have a clue of how the other half live. *'He who is to be a good ruler must have first been ruled.' (Aristotle)* I also think that politicians should live on a council estate whilst they are in office and their kid's should go to the local state school, but I doubt that will ever happen

Back to philosophy. I have always been a people watcher, that sounds a bit creepy, but I watch people because philosophy grows from our senses, the observation of the world around us. We observe, then we rudiment, then we discuss with other people, rudiment some more, and then philosophize, that is we form opinions about the world. I am scared for the future of philosophy because people are not observing in the way they have in the past. Now people are on their phones all the time, even as they walk down the road.

I go to Manchester a few days in the week and I like the opportunity to sit on the bus and watch the panorama that is on display outside the window. Manchester is an amazing city, it is so cosmopolitan, I go through the Jewish area with their kosher shops, the Polish area, an Asian area with their beautiful saris, it is Fascinating (it deserves that Capital). What I find disturbing are the number of people walking down the road gazing not at their surroundings, but at their phone. Even people, who are pushing perambulators, are not chatting amiably with their toddler, but texting. Bizarre. Even on the bus, many parents ignore their child who is usually prattling away about what they are able to see, because they find something more engrossing in an electronic device. Face book does not lead to outstanding philosophy.

If a person studies classical philosophy then the concept of one truth is paramount. In modern and contemporary philosophy there is a move toward the idea that truth is relative; what is true for you is true for you and what is true for me is true for me...what a load of shit. Fake news, fake philosophy. There can be only one truth and although we may all understand a particular facet of this supreme truth there cannot be six billion truths. Imagine there is a dog sitting in front of me; I say that it is a cake and you say it is a dragon. Well, I understand one thing and you understand something different, but the fact remains that there is one truth and that is that it is a dog.

That is why I disagreed with the claim that the 'fullness of truth' subsists in the Catholic Church.

Other people may have a particle of truth but only Rome inherits all of it. Now that I have come to understand religion as a social construct, I am struggling so much with the meaning of life. Other people are also asking these profound questions of life, death and eternity. We want meaning and so if one can find some comfort and meaning and peace and joy in religion, then okay, just do not impose your truth on others. Live and let live. Seek and accept the truth, but do not punish me if I am coming to the truth from a different direction.

I was speaking with a lovely lady today and she was telling me how precious her faith is to her and how it comforts her in her pain. I have no problem with that, but I can no longer suspend my disbelief.

I want to introduce a little theology here. Sorry if it not your cup of tea, but I think it could possibly be one of the most important changes in the Church. Okay, let us begin. In the early 1990's the Anglican Church permitted women to become priests (about bloody time!). To become a priest there are various stages, but to keep life simple there are three main stages, deacon, priest, bishop. Now these are not three distinct stages, but rather three parts of one intrinsically state of being. If you become a deacon then you have joined the priest club, and there is nothing (theologically speaking) to stop one becoming a bishop. Imagine, being pregnant, giving birth, bringing up a child; three different stages but they are all part of one act. Saying to a person who has become a deacon that they cannot become a priest is like saying to a pregnant woman that she cannot give birth.

So, the Anglican Church questioned whether a female priest could become a bishop which is a theologically flawed question because a bishop is what is called 'the fullness of the priesthood'. So thankfully the Church of England came to their senses and now have women bishops. However, what I am really excited about is a movement that is occurring in the Catholic Church at the moment. Pope Francis has set up a commission, made up of female and male theologians to study the question of whether women can be ordained as deacons. I have high hopes that Pope Francis actually makes some radical changes in the Church. By the time you read these words I am sure the commission has made a judgment. This is the really exciting bit, following the theology of the Church, if a woman can be ordained a deacon, she can be ordained a priest and yes....a bishop. And oh my God, if a woman can be a bishop there is absolutely NOTHING to stop her becoming the Pope. Pope is a term of honor, and the actual title for this role is bishop of Rome...so bishop, to bishop of Rome; viva il papa!

There is evidence from the early Church that women were ordained deacons. Male theologians have conveniently ignored this fact, the elephant in the monastery. If you say 'not true' enough times then it becomes not true? No, eventually people will demand the truth, and the house of cards will come tumbling down. Also, priests were married in the early Church, even St. Peter, the first bishop of Rome, that is the Pope was married (in the Gospel Jesus heals Peter's mother-in-law). Not that I have any desire to become a priest, but the Catholic Church is an incredibly powerful institution and if they allow women to enter this role then that has to be for the good of all humanity, women and men alike because truth and equality are good for everyone.

Ponder on one of my favorite women, Hilda of Whitby. Women were important in a ruling capacity in the early Church; as time has passed, and moved further away from time of Jesus, women were pushed, shoved and jostled to the kitchen and bedroom. At one point there were a number of what are referred to as 'double monasteries' where there was a community of women and a separate community of men (in fact, if we move over the water to the Celtic Church there were communities of nuns and monks who would live together and would often get wed, bear children but remain as religious).

The key point to these large communities is that they were headed by a woman, a strong, intelligent and powerful woman such as Hilda...how did we fall so far from this ideal to where nuns were put behind bars with their faces covered? Men and power. On the radio the other day they introduced some bishop and it was 'the Right, Reverend, Honorable, blah, blah, blah...' why does he want such pomp and ceremony? After all can you imagine Jesus wanting such accolades? The humble man who washed other people's feet? The village carpenter? The naked man who was nailed to a cross?

You do not have to be Sherlock Holmes to have deduced that I am a complete R4 junkie. My brother always rolls his eyes when I tell him something I heard on R4, even when we are communicating by phone I can tell he is rolling his eyes. He claims that middle class people listen to R4 so he thinks teasing me will irritate me as he knows that I am too much of a socialist to ever desire to be 'upwardly mobile', leave me in my working class roots. In fact, I admit, I am an inverted snob; when I encounter someone who is almost a cliché with their detached house on the edge of town, two cars, a cleaner, a gardener and the only underwear to be found in the well ordered drawers are from M&S, then I too roll my eyes. If they happen to read either the Daily Mail or The Telegraph, then do not get me started. This of course is completely unfair and I judge without evidence. I am a woman of many faults and this is one of them.

There are times when I get mad at some interviewer or interviewee on the radio and I often find myself having a one-sided argument at some obnoxious homo-sapien whom I happen to disagree with. I get particularly mad at the weather people who invariably pronounce the weather cloaked in their opinion. For example, 'unfortunately it is going to rain today'. This makes me mad. Tell me the bloody weather and let me form my own opinion of it; what if I want rain because I am Farmer Giles and my crops require a good soaking? This makes me so mad that I actually wrote to R4 and asked them to refrain from treating the weather as part of the nanny state that feels that I must be guided in my opinion. I was telling my friend Nadia this one day and she said that her husband feels exactly the same, so I am not alone. First world problems hey? I bet they do not worry about such crap in Syria.

This is a long winded way of introducing a fascinating piece I heard on the radio about 'perverse impishness'. Now this piece turned my world on an angle. Perverse impishness (a new term to me) is when you want to do something completely out of character that is rather cheeky, for example, you are traveling home on the train and when the ticket conductor goes past you have an overwhelming urge to pinch his bottom. I do not mean when you are drunk or on a hen party, but when you, a nice, respectable, history teacher just has the desire to do something not socially acceptable; we cannot go around pinching conductors derrieres, life is not a *Carry On* film.

This changed my world because I thought that I was alone in having these urges and they were a sign I was predominantly an evil soul. I have to go back about fifteen years. One day I was at a friend's house and we were chatting in her living room. This room had a cream carpet and I had a cup of coffee in my hand and the thought popped into my noggin 'what would happen if I just threw this cup of coffee across the cream carpet?' Now, I was never going to take thought to action because I love and respected my friend and I am not given to wanton destruction.

However, my friend is a committed Christian and when I told her of my thought she did not hesitate to inform me that such thoughts are evil, from the devil and must be combated. I believed her and so for the last fifteen years I have frequently entertained these thoughts which has made me believe that I am so inherently rotten, that there was almost no hope for me. Now here I was, fifteen years later listening to this hilarious piece on the radio, with nice, respectable women and men informing the nation about their perverse impishness; and I realized that I am not alone and there is another word for my condition which is not satanic. Thank-you R4!

So the next time I have the desire to pinch a bum I will not cast myself into hell but realize that I am simply a member of the human race. I just want to be a normal member of the human race.

I am ashamed. No that is not exactly right. It would be more accurate to say that I have shame, in the way I could say, I have a verruca. It is almost tangible. If only I could bazuka that verruca, cut it off with a scalpel, I would not care if I had a scar, but the virus would be eliminated from my being.

So shame. From the moment I get up to the moment I go to sleep I have shame. Shame that I am gluttonous and have sugar on my porridge. Shame that I am lazy and turn over in my bed when the alarm clock rings. Shame that I do not save more so as to give more to the homeless. Shame that I read novels as a form of escapism. Shame that I am not kinder, more loving, more generous, a better person in every way. It is like my shadow, I do not spend my time focusing on it, but it is always there, I can never run away from it.

This shame makes me believe that I am going to hell. Yesterday I was chatting to a very interesting lady who was working in a coffee shop (I chat to everyone because I find people endlessly fascinating, their opinions, and their life story) and we ended up discussing what happens to you when you die. Now I do not usually go up to a stranger and ask them about their views on the afterlife, but I mentioned Christmas and she said that her husband died of cancer last Christmas so she did not want to celebrate it and from there the conversation flowed to life, death, God and hell. I stated that I was an atheist but from my early days I had heard about hell and I cannot get the idea from my mind.

I hear the contradiction. Why would there be a hell if there is no heaven? A devil if there is no God? Well, I consider myself a fundamentally evil, rotten and irredeemable person and therefore if I commit suicide I will go to hell. When I was a nun at least I knew that through my sacrifices, prayers and penances I could access heaven, but outside the convent I have no chance. This lovely woman told me that I have to change my way of thinking, but how does one change a conviction, an idea that one has heard for over thirty years? Being thrown out of the convent was such an horrific trauma that it broke something in my brain that resulted in the rejection of the concept of a divine being. What experience will I have to undergo to escape from the horror of hell?

Despite what I claimed a few paragraphs earlier about my atheistic leanings, one cannot simply eradicate a teaching imparted over a lifetime.

I have reached a conclusion (very good for a theology and philosophy student whose job is more about finding questions than coming to a concrete conclusion) that there are three fundamental propositions about religion.

1.   Believe what you want but never, ever, ever tell other people that they have to agree with you. They will not go to hell because they happen to think differently. If our intellect is one of the aspects that make us divine, then our intellect should be free to explore every possibility, free to roam to every corner of the universe.

2.   The fundamental question about theology is 'what sort of God does this theology portray?' A loving God? A father figure? A maternal being? A judge who sends souls to hell for all eternity? A God who only chooses some people and rejects others? A God who gazes on the world and sees rich men living in fancy houses and calls these his representatives on earth? A being that delights in people ignoring the homeless and destitute because Latin and rules are more important? A God who

ignores the cries of the refugees and the holocausts because somehow this is all for a higher good and it will all be worth it in heaven?

3.   Be kind. If we all followed this rule of life then we would all be a lot happier.

I remember so vividly a moment in Ireland when an uncle, who is by nature not a demonstrative fellow, told me that he was so proud of me. Proud of me, which meant that I was not a failure, not an outsider, not just the strange English cousin who never fitted it, an asset to the family, a place and position that actually meant something. Well, I bet he is not proud of me now. I have returned to my failure status, the outsider, the odd English relation who has never done much with her life, an embarrassment to my family and myself, the mad kin who appears as a shadowy name on the family tree.

Now, the feast of All Souls is an odd fish indeed. It is rather complicated. Not a mere matter of remembering and praying for our dead, but a day to make deals with the gods. You get what is known as an 'indulgence' which is basically time off purgatory and a fast lane to heaven. So, because we are all sinful (we cannot escape sin for long when inquiring about the Catholic faith system) we cannot go straight to heaven because God is pure and we are riddled with badness. However as they say, where there's a will there's a way'. If you say certain prayers then this is time taken off for good behavior, for example go to a cemetery and say a Pater Nostra for the intentions of the Pope and bingo, you hit the jackpot and get fifty days off purgatory.

> *'An indulgence is a partial or plenary according as it removes*
> *either part or all of the temporal punishment due to sin.'*
> *(Catechism of the Catholic Church. 1471)*

I have always had a problem with the concept of indulgences.

1.   Firstly, if there is an afterlife I do not think it will be based on our twenty-four hour clock and therefore to speak of days in reference to what is timeless is just nonsense; I cannot grasp how intelligent folks swallow this clap-trap.

2.   Secondly, why would God listen to my prayers if I am stood in a cemetery rather than say in a chapel? Is it like a divine mobile phone, is there a better signal near the graves? Maybe God needs to switch mobile phone provider. Or is he caught in an eternal contract?

3.   Thirdly, the whole concept of purgatory is strange. Professor Eamon Duffy (who I admire immensely) wrote in one of his books (*Faith of Our Fathers* – damn good read) that purgatory is actually an act of God's mercy. We have to be pure to be in the presence of God and let's be honest, none of us is without blemish. So purgatory is like the poodle parlor for humans, it makes us all clean and fluffy and smelling lush and fit to face the almighty. However, purgatory is painful, a fire that burns our sins away.

The theologians claim that fire is a necessary suffering; for those in hell the fire is eternal (what a nice concept of God is painted with this little nugget of theology); but the fire of purgatory is similar to the pain of childbirth, yes it hurts, but at some point it will cease and you will receive your reward. Back to my fundamental questions; what kind of God is worshiped in this theology? What parent would take a child and place her hand in a fire and claim that it is for her own good? A pity there are no heavenly social workers who could monitor this divine child abuse. It is God who is at fault here; maybe God should only have supervised visitations with us.

Oh my gosh, I can hear all the defenders shouting at me. I do not understand the theology correctly. God has to be just and give just punishment for sins. I am failing to grasp the metaphysical aspect of this teaching. Well, imagine me shouting this response; I DO UNDERSTAND THE THEOLOGY CORRECTLY, I HAPPEN TO BE A RATHER INTELLIGENT LASS AND I DO

GRASP THE METAPHYSICAL ASPECT OF THIS TEACHING, BUT IT IS A LOAD OF SHIT. THIS THEOLOGY HAS BEEN INVENTED BY MEN WHO HAVE TOO MUCH TIME ON THEIR HANDS.

Here is a syllogism for you:

M: People who burn other people are cruel and evil.
m: God burns people.
C: God is cruel and evil!

Justice does not come into the equation.

As you may recall many chapters ago I wrote about my experience of having Gwilem Barre Syndrome. Most people make a full recovery, but I was not one of them. Ask any of my friend's about my constant need to go to the loo, every break in school I was off to the lavatory. If I am going out for a day then I did not have anything to drink until I knew I could locate a toilet when required (and it was required frequently). This often resulted in severe headaches and in hotter climates, heat stroke, but that was an accepted part of my life. I never asked for any dispensation. It is horrid, embarrassing and inconvenient, but life is life.

Also, my legs suffer from pain and weakness. When I was in the convent I often knelt for a long time, but I never asked permission to sit down. I just strapped up my knees and got on with it because I did not want to stand out. I think that the main reason I did not complain was because I had no depression and faced the world with a cheery disposition. I am not writing this so I sound like a good little warrior, but I had those problems since I was twelve so I just accepted all these problems. A small pain and inconvenience is not a big deal. A phrase a once heard which I find inspiring is, do not grow a wishbone where your backbone should be; no point wishing to be a trapeze artist if heights make you dizzy! As Horace advised, Carpe Deim.

The last eighteen months I have found my legs becoming increasingly weaker. It is normal for me to fall once or twice a day, but now I find that I spend more time on my knees (involuntary) than I did when I was a nun. The paving stones that are ever so slightly raised and wham-bam I have ruined another pair of trousers as my knees hit the deck. I now only wear those black plimsolls that children wear for gym class because they are light and cheap. I get through a pair a week as holes appear where I drag my legs. I have tried all sorts of shoes, expensive shoes, taking them to the cobblers to be repaired, all a waste of time, so now I am a pump girl. If I am tired, or have done a lot of exercise then I am practically dragging my right leg, I feel as though I am in shackles. Riding a bike is actually easier than walking, but I do not do hills. I love my bike because it gives me a sense of freedom that walking does not, walking is painful but when I am on my bike I have no limits.

A few months ago the back of my right leg went numb, the sort of numbness when you have been sat in a deck chair for a sleepy afternoon by the sea-side, when the wooden bar has made its home in your thigh and when you get up it is a though you have been hitting cheap cider. It is not painful just a weird sensation.

Let me not forget my friend the bladder. My incontinence has become more pronounced; I even have to go to the loo before I take the recycling out in case I do not make it back on time. So the weakness in my legs has crept its way up to kindly include my bladder in its rampage. Yes, I have done all the pelvic exercises but I think this is going to be my shadow till I rest in the grave.

The last few weeks I have struggled to swallow food and sometimes choke if I put too much grub in my gob at the same time (greed). I thought it was because I had a dry mouth due to lack of liquid but it is new and odd.

Honestly if a benevolent angel appeared now as I sit in the cafe at Waterstones and made me the offer of either cutting off my legs or having depression then in a heartbeat I would willingly sacrifice my legs. In fact I wish someone would make me that offer (grow a backbone Debs). Depression sucks the life out of one, what is the point of being able to walk if everywhere your pins take you is just another path of misery. Without depression and legs life can still be fun.

So I want for the wise-man who knows about these things to tell me the true situation. Waiting puts my life on hold as my aim for employment is put in the balance. Will I be found wanting? Depression makes one's tolerance for pain lower, and I have wondered if it is my mind that is failing to control my body correctly, after all there is an intrinsic connection between the physical and the mental. Notwithstanding, my body is ailing objectively and I wonder were this will end.

CHAPTER THIRTEEN

Women

As a nun, being a woman is of no importance, so now I must ponder the point. I find myself heading for forty without the suit of armour of my habit. One constructive thing about being in a convent is that there were no men, so if something needed doing, changing a light-bulb, transporting a sixty-four chairs to the attic, carrying a pan full of pasta for a hundred people, killing a chicken, getting rid of mice, we rolled up our sleeves and did it ourselves. We were strong women and I that is fab'.

As I return to Radcliffe after such a long time I am amazed (and distressed) at the number of beauty salons where you can get a tan and have your nails elongated to a startling degree. There are such a disproportionate number of them considering that this is just a small town. In order to keep going, the women of Radcliffe must be spending a relatively large proportion of their week in these places.

Now, I was in the monastery by the time the Spice Girls exploded onto the music scene, but I am all for Girl Power so hurrah for Posh and her mates. Now if a woman wants to don a pair of stilettos, a mini skirt and a boob-tube in mid-November then go for it girlfriend, I have no objection, but what I plead to the female of the species, is do not let it stop there. Be strong, independent members of humanity, where the brain is exercised to the maximum. In your manicured hand hold your university degree with pride.

I am ugly and no amount of cosmetics is going to hide that factoid, I do not have the knees for a mini-skirt and I even chop my own locks. However, I defend my right to show my legs and if they offend other people then tough titties. If I want to spend an afternoon having my hair become mysteriously blond then I will, but I will do it as I also work for my Masters. Girls, women, ladies, females, you can have it all; you really can and please do not settle for second best.

What I like about Theresa May (I wait for my computer to explode as I write the name of a tory and like in the same sentence) is that she is a strong woman who is not afraid to show quite a bit of leg. People call her boring but I like that she is single minded and as the merest hint of cleavage shows, she answers questions about the economy. If she wants to spend her Saturday evening out on the town in a pair of hot-pants and bikini top, fine with me, because she is also at her desk early on

Monday morning settling matters of extraordinary importance. She is a woman who does not compromise.

Women, the Church and virginity. Yesterday I was listening to a very funny Irish comedian on the radio. She was performing at the Edinburgh festival and she asked the audience what they call their private parts in Scotland; she went on to say that in Ireland, anything below the waist is just called sinning. Gosh, the Church has a problem with sex.

As nuns we were presumed to be virgins. From an early age I desired to be a nun so I was not about to throw away my virginity in a night of teenage passion (or rather a quick ten minutes of passion in the park). It was not the same for the blokes. There are some famous Catholic male saints, such as Augustine of Hippo, who 'knew' women in the biblical sense and illegitimate children abounded. One rule for the fellas and one rule for the lily white lassies whose farts even smell of roses!

Every day the Church celebrates a different saint, and the prayers would be taken from what is called the 'common'. So, there is the common of martyrs, or the common of doctors of the Church, the common virgins (which is only used for women), and the common of men saints. There are other commons, but I am sure you get my point. Early on in religious life I questioned this format. How did we know that these women were virgins? Yes, if we have their writings such as Teresa of Avila, we can hear it straight from the horse's mouth, but otherwise, should we not use a common of women saints? Also, why is the common of virgins never used for the blokes? Are we erring on the side of corrosion? As the old saying goes, 'saints have pasts and sinners have futures'.

The Church is so screwed up about sex; just look at all the abuse scandals. It is hard to imagine how the Church in Ireland will ever recover. Young men will not want to enter the priesthood with the all the negative connotations that are part of the package. Why, oh, why are priests not permitted to marry? There is nothing in Church teaching that prevents men from marrying, it is just Church discipline. If a Catholic man from Ireland went to the Ukraine, he could marry and still become a priest. Some men, like some women, want to be celibate because that is a state of life that they feel God is asking of them. However, it should be a choice, not imposed.

How healthy it would be if a priest came home at the end of the day and had a partner to discuss things with; someone to share a meal with, someone to laugh and cry with, someone to share a bed with a feel the love of another human being. In the past priests lived in group setting with maybe two or three other priests and a housekeeper ruled the roost. Now, a priest lives alone, often caring for more than one parish and there is no housekeeper. I do not mean that a priest should marry so as to have a housekeeper, but to have a partner, a friend, a lover, a confidant, a helper, an adviser.

We cannot cover up all the abuse cases in Ireland. Why were priests raping young boys and girls? What was missing in their lives that they had recourse to such evil behavior? We cannot go back and change what has happened, but the Church must hold up its hands and claim the guilt. What must change if the crimes of the past do not become the crimes of the future? I am sure you have heard of the Magdalene laundries. Evil places, ruled by wicked nuns, where girls went who were pregnant and unmarried. I refer to them as girls and not women, because most of them were still children.

If you read the truly chilling accounts of what these innocents endured (I swore, sobbed and had to stop reading as I worked my way through the books) then you quickly realize that many of these girls were impregnated by the parish priest. He continued to reign supreme in his parish, with the larder overflowing with food and the decanter of wine always full; and these girls were shipped off to be 'taken care-of' by nuns till the baby was born, given up for adoption, and the girl could return to her family with her honor intact. I recommend strongly reading some of these books, as they give the female version of history. I strongly recommend *'The Light in the Window'*. This book broke my heart.

When I was at uni. I had the wonderful experience of living with nuns from Africa (various countries). These women were ever so interesting. One of them told be a story that makes me want to knock down the walls of the Vatican and scream 'how dare you'. Apparently, many religious sisters are sent from Africa to study in Rome, which is a great idea on paper, as the knowledge these women imbibed could be taken back to their convents and shared with the other sisters. However, these nuns are generally quite poor, and Rome is very expensive and so it is hard for them to survive. The answer? A priest will 'adopt' one of these sisters and he will give her money to pay for her study fees, food, travel and whatever else is required for living. Isn't that wonderful? A priest who has plenty of money (and they do) helping a sister study so as to be able to teach other sisters back home. Yes, but she becomes his prostitute. That is the deal, he pays for her, and he gets her body. In true Church fashion, this evil on its very doorstep is not only ignored, but denied. That is a man's version, and that is why we must seek out the woman's version because they are very different.

Nuns and monks are different because they live in communities which are meant to support them. They are meant to relax together, watch a DVD, go for a walk, play board games, share a box of chocs', laugh. All the things my community in Ireland failed to give me. However, what is to stop a sister who lives alone getting wed? Nothing, all it would take is a nod from the Magisterium the teaching body of the Church – all men) but that is as likely as a cow jumping over the moon. Ever since Eve women has been held in suspicion, but it is time now for us to stand up and tell the men who rule the Church to fuck off because it is not my fault, each person must take responsibility for their action and men cannot simply have recourse to the original argument of 'the women tempted me'.

If you read the writings of Church theologians then you will encounter horror statements about beastly women as the gateway to sin (because Eve was the cause of the so-called original sin and we are daughters of Eve). Women are temptresses and the one I find most insulting, we are deformed men. The reason generally given that we are not permitted to become priests is that we are simply not good enough because...yes, you guessed it, we are not male. Thank goodness, in the twenty-first century women theologians are standing up and having a say; now we just have to get the fellas to listen and take them seriously.

When I was in the library this morning I was perusing the new books when I came across a tome on *St. Augustine of Hippo by Rowan Williams* (the ex-Archbishop of Canterbury) so I decided to have a little snoop of what this renowned theologian had to say. In the waffle on the inside cover, Williams praises 'Gus to the heavens. I then went to the index and went straight to w for women...and nothing. In 2016 a head of an Oxford College can write a book on a major Church Father and mention nothing about women, are you having a laugh? Augustine had plenty to say about half the human race.

Who gets the blame?

How did women get all the blame?
Is it because I bleed and you call me unclean?
Is it because I am physically weak
and you can break my bones?
Is it because your god is male?

Is it because I carry life within me
and you are jealous of my knowledge?
Is it because my eyes hold a secret
you can never comprehend?
Is it because I work for peace
and you play at war?
Well stop it!
What Eve did was her problem.
She made her choice and Adam made his.
I am not responsible.
I did not inherit original sin,
that is just an invention of men
to keep others under the thumb.
Now is the time.
I bleed and I am not unclean.
I am physically weak
but if you bruise me I will revolt.
Spoiler alert! god is not male.
The life within me is mine
and will never be in you.
Even if I told you my secrets
you will not understand.
I will continue to seek peace
and I will be victorious.
We all make our choices in life
and we live with the repercussions.
I am all women.

I am reading an excellent novel, but every five pages the author gives a long, rather boring paragraph describing strange dreams of the female protagonist, incredibly dull. Reading an account of someone's unconscious musings are about as revealing as the ramblings of a drunk man. So I just skip those bits. Well, unless the bloody tory government does not obliterate all the public libraries within the next decade. Yes, you tory twats, save some money on a public service, put education back seventy years. They can all just pop down to the local independent bookshop and buy lots of jolly good books for Jasper and Arabella, but if you happen to be a low-income household, then books costing upwards of eight pounds can be the cost of food for a day. I can read two books a week, and as I am presently on benefits, I have to rely on the local library and I would be devastated if it ceased to exist and the building turned into more offices for government bureaucrats that generate more paper work in our so-called paperless society.

Well, friend, if you want to skip my meanderings about dreams, skip it and make the most of your precious time.

In Italia we slept in dormitories; it was never a case of nothing stirring, not even a mouse, there were plenty of bumps in the form of people snoring, going to the bog, getting up early to study, late to bed because of kitchen service. One of the frequent disturbances was sisters talking in their sleep. I think this was due to three factors, firstly, some people naturally chatter in the time of slumber; secondly, we all had a lot of pent up emotions that were kept under-raps during the day and found an outlet in the dark hours; and thirdly, when a sister was thinking about a certain subject during the day, for example her sins, then they would sometimes burst forth when she was unconscious.

When you heard a sister starting to confess her sins, one of us would jump from our bed and shake her back to consciousness so as to save the poor soul any embarrassment. Well, the other night I was woken by a woman speaking and from what I could gather it was of a rather personal nature, so I jumped up and went towards the sound only to discover it was just the radio. I hate being alone, I hate silence and I hate the dark so I keep the radio on all night. When I wake up during the night, as I frequently do, I panic in the dark and silence. I also have a night-light which makes me feel about five years old. I wonder, when will I ever be rid of the convent? When will I awake in the morning and not experience that panic of being trapped in a place of torture? When will I be normal?

CHAPTER FOURTEEN

From Now Till Eternity...

I would not class myself as a dedicated television watcher. In fact I had to renew my television license last week and I pondered whether to renew it or get rid of the box all together. However, I capitulated and duly renewed; I am legal again. I like a good period drama and when I am awake at one, two, three, four, five and six in the morning, the TV. has passed many unhappy hours with me.

When I look back over stressful periods of my life, I notice that I have turned desperately to the small screen and begged it to help me pass the time. When I was doing my finals at university I watched every episode of *All Creatures Great and Small.* When I was depressed and in the hospital in Ireland I gazed at endless episodes of *The Big Bang Theory.* I can find no rhythm nor reason to these choices, but that's the way it goes big nose.

When I first returned to Manchester I was in such a dark, ugly place that I lay on my parent's settee and watched, (I have no recollection but I know it was brain mush), and watched, did not move and watched. I must have driven my parent's to despair. I would watch whatever colorful picture was on the box because I could not even be arsed to change channel with the remote control. So I have renewed my license as a safety net, in case I need to lie on my couch, sans showering, sans eating, sans hope and watch mindless drivel.

Smells are so evocative. Yesterday it was tipping it down here in Manchester and on the bus the windows were condensed. If you have never been on a public bus you will have no clue what I am talking about. The water runs down and if you have the joy of having a window seat the water will conclude its journey on your clothes. When I was smaller in stature my nose would be near this waterfall and there is such a horrid smell. Now that I have grown (4'11) my nose does not have to endure the window smell, but it got me thinking about the effect of smell.

The Carmelite monastery had a particular smell which is unique to monasteries. It is a clean smell, but the clean that does not use contemporary cleaning products, but the old fashioned stuff of soap flakes and polish. I suppose this is what houses smelt like sixty years ago before all the sprays and fancy cleaning products appeared in our supermarkets. I love that smell. I have stayed in other monasteries and they all have the same smell. I have tried to recreate that lovely smell in my home but I have failed. I wonder what the secret is?

Now the convent in Italy did not have that smell even though it was a monastery because we were not enclosed and quite frankly it was not spotless, it was indeed far from spotless. We did clean every day, but there were so many of us, and we were young and spent a lot of time running around the place that dirt was not eliminated on a daily basis. The convent did not have a particular smell. I suppose this is a beneficial thing so that I cannot enter a building and be reminded of either Italy or Ireland.

CHAPTER FIFTEEN

Friendship – The Eighth Sacrament

Such friends...I am filled with gratitude

The Catholic Church has seven Sacraments, Baptism, First Holy Communion, Confirmation, Confession, Marriage, Priesthood and the Sacrament of the Sick. A gentle priest once said to me that friendship is the eighth sacrament, how beautiful is that? I have the most AMAZING friends and I am constantly overwhelmed that these intelligent, beautiful, kind, funny people want to be friends with such a miss-fit as me.

The friend I have had for longest time is Rosaleen. I am a September babe and she was born in the December and for the first few years of our life we lived just across the road from each other. My Mum was best buddies with her Mum, Auntie Rose (not my blood aunt, but most definitely a real aunt, in fact she was my second Mum). I remember as children Rosaleen was brilliant at impressions but she was too shy to perform to a wide audience and I alone was permitted to a box seat. She was so very quiet, shy and gentle whereas I was not a bit shy and the lead role in plays beckon to me.

My friend who is more a sister

When we were about five Auntie Rose met a new fella whom she wed and moved to Blackburn; I thought my heart would break. Why were the doors of my second home now barred to me? No more would we toast bread on the open fire. No more would we eat oranges and hide the peel down the back of the settee (I have no idea why we did this, but it is a vivid memory). Now, I would only see my second Mum and my best friend on a Sunday. I hated (I know that is a strong word) the step-family; not because they were horrid, but because they had stolen part of my family and moved them a hundred thousand miles away (not really, Radcliffe to Blackburn is not that far, but when you are five the concept of distance is not measured in miles but in heart beats). She now inherited a step-brother who is only slightly older than we are. Looking at him now I see a strong, smart man, a loving husband and father but when we were kids I would not let him play with us because for me he was the enemy. Rosaleen has since told me that she felt sorry that we always left him out of our games, but I was the strong character and so Rosaleen always capitulated. For me, time with her was precious and I was not willing to share it with some lad.

Oh my gosh, we played the silliest games. No tablets or computers or super-Mario for us, we occupied ourselves with cards, we played cards for hours, just the two of us. Often our Mum's would share a bottle of wine and so Rosaleen and I would get two wine glasses and fill them with ginger ale pretending that it was alcohol. Funny that now both of us detest ginger ale, in fact I dislike all things with ginger in. We would also pretend we had husbands and children, Rosaleen had an old phone and we would take calls from our hubbies who worked away.

Another popular game was called Kerby. This involved two teams (or even two people would suffice), one team would stand on one side of the road, and the other team would stand on the opposite side. There was one football and the aim was for a person to throw the ball to the opposite side of the road with the aim of hitting it off the curb (hence the name) and then the person would stand in the middle of the road and try and try and hit it off the curb again, thereby getting points. These were roads with cars, how one of us did not get knocked down is a miracle. Also, the drivers were never angry with us, it was a popular game in built up areas and I suppose drivers just accepted that it was kids played. If only it had become an Olympic game I could have trained to get gold (some of the activities that they have in the Olympics are must stranger than Kerby).

We were a lot freer then than kiddies now, gadding off around the town to entertain ourselves, climbing on things that we should not have not climbed on. Rosaleen was the sensible one and kept her feet on the ground whereas sometimes I followed her elder brother (her blood bro.) and he was somewhat wild.

Roasaleen has the most beautiful hair, thick, red and long. She is one of the kindest people you could ever wish to encounter. I love her so much. 'Friendship is a single soul dwelling in two bodies' (Aristotle). We took very different paths in life. She is married and a mother of two, a boy and a girl. I am single and childless. I traveled and took the academic path, she stayed near home and did not go to university (although she could have if she had wanted to as she is bright enough). One day I told her that part of me was jealous of her because her role in life was secure whereas I was a will-o-the-wisp; she in turn told me that part of her was jealous of me because she had to do all the mundane that make up the day to day life of a Mum whereas I was like the littlest hobo and constantly on the move. The grass is always greener. So from two different mothers were born two different females and yet we are more like sisters than friends. If I were ever stranded on a desert island I would choose her as my companion.

Ah, Margurita. My eldest bro. Andrew went out with Margaret when I was nine years old. She was older than him and had three children. Well, to cut the story short, they split up but we kept Margaret. It is ironic that I now see her far more than I ever see my brother. Now, twenty-eight years later, we only live a two minuets walk from each other so I often pop over to see her for a cuppa and a chat. The relations we make in our formative years can be so emotionally powerful that time does not dull the sensation. This summer Margaret turned sixty and her son Danny who now lives in Australia came over to celebrate his Mum's special birthday. I have not seen Danny for years, but when I walked into the kitchen and saw him standing there my heart leapt and I was filled with joy at seeing my childhood companion. Later in the day her other son arrived and it was exactly the same. I wish we could have all gone down to the pub and sat and caught up on life.

Friends make the world go round

Now I am going to wax eloquent about a buddy of mine I had the privilege of meeting in my first year at secondary school. I have already referred to this beautiful lady previously but she is such a good friend that like New York, she is so good I must name her twice, Nadia, Nadia. One of the things that has aided my recovery is that Nadia endures me turning up on her doorstep every couple of weeks to spend a delightful few hours with her, occasionally her husband and her cutie pie little daughter.

When I was in the convent Nadia wrote to me on a regular basis, even when I was unable to write to her. Nadia is a natural writer and she would write these long epistles that would make me laugh out loud (the only other person who can cause this level of mirth in me is P.G. Woodhouse). I find that she would spend such a lot of time and effort writing to me, an act of generosity, kindness and true friendship. I gaze at Nadia and cannot understand why she wants to be my pal, but I am infinitely grateful that she does, because I definitely got the best part of the friendship cake...yummy!

To Snoop, Nadia, Clare, Sinead and Bryony, Val, Pat, Anne-Marie and Maurice, Andy and Maretta, Renee, Chris, Lovisa, Sylvester and Kate I bow down low in homage and say thank-you, because without you my life would lack all color.

My Riches

I look at you
and I see
a person so good
that no superlative
is good enough.
I look at you
and I see
a generosity
the sultan of Brunei
could not emulate.
I look at you
and I see
a smile
that makes me smile,
a tear
that makes we weep,
an understanding
that ...

134

when you look at me
do you see
my neediness
that would consume
a black hole?
My sadness
that would
rival Pierrot?
My unworthiness
of your friendship
that leaves me
grateful for your gift.

CHAPTER SIXTEEN

Me Sans Faith

'Last scene of all,
That ends this strange eventful history,

Is second childishness and mere oblivion,
Sans teeth, sans eyes, sans taste, sans everything.'
(Willie Shakespeare)

So Wills claims that the second childhood is sans....but what about me, now, here, a life without faith, without life, without meaning, without purpose, without direction, without faith, without God, without the Church, without peace, without faith?

What am I doing with me days? Actually I am a rather busy bee (Deborah is Hebrew for bee). On Friday I go to a maths class. I am passionate about maths, it is all so logical and any morsel of logic is welcome in my illogical world. My tutor S. is one of the finest teachers I had ever had the privilege to encounter. He is smart, I mean Mensa smart and yet he can teach very simple concepts without being patronizing. I have no problem raising my hand and admitting that I do not know what is going on (in the mathematical sense) and he never makes me feel stupid. Also, my world is so topsy-turvey, most of the time I feel that I am holding onto sanity by the finest of threads that constantly threatens to snap and leave me in a dark, ugly place. When I go into maths, I just have to sit there and think about mathematical problems, I do not have to think about self-harming or suicide or what a waste my existence is, just equations and formulas that all have an answer, bliss.

On a Wednesday I help run a work club with the delightful Karen. This is for unemployed women and men who need help with their C.V. or looking for jobs on the internet which for some people who have used a computer before can be rather intimidating. Now, I like my voluntary work immensely. Helping other people makes me feel useful. I truly believe that if the motto 'be kind' was adopted by everyone in our little world then what a beautiful place that would be to inhabit. I do not mean to sound like a goody-two-shoes, but amassing money and material things might satisfy for a short period of time, but ultimately, only being kind to others will make us happy little beings. I am useless most of my time, but this work club gives me a small taste of what it is to be a useful member of society.

On Monday I have therapy for my screwed up mind. On a Thursday I see a psychologist and my wonderful social worker.

Saturday, as I have previously mentioned, I go to the Buddhist center to be with fellow travelers.

On a Sunday I either stay at home and do home-work, clean, catch-up on this and that, write letters, speak on the phone with my brother, or I go to visit my lovely parent's mybest friend Snoop. When I sit on the couch with Snoopy on my knee I am at peace, all my anxiety flows away. I will also go to visit my folks during the week when I can.

Am I getting better? I think the answer is no, I think what happened to me in Ireland broke me into so many pieces that it would take eternity and magic glue to put me back together. I have learnt to cope, I do not wear make-up, but every morning I paint a smile on my lips, good-will in my eyes and laughter in my throat so that I appear as a normal, functioning adult, but you would not have to look too deeply into my soul to see the truth. Will this sorrow ever depart from me? 'The grief that does not age, that does not go away with time.' (Sebastian Barry).

I have started a new treatment, DBT, which will take a year to complete and then, if miracles are real, I will exit as a happy human. The fear persists though, that I will only be happy for a while and then the depression will return to again engulf me and I know that I will never be able to go through this horror again. The first time mental ill health came to pay me a visit I was a whole, fully functioning person. If madness comes again, uninvited, it will find a sick and fragile invalid at home with no power to throw-out this unwelcome house guest.

I read a memoir by *Sally Brampton* entitled *Shoot the Damn Dog*. It is her account of depression. I found the book gave me hope, because here was a woman who went through the dark tunnel and emerged at the other side, where she again noticed the colors in her garden, the laughter of friends and the joy of life. Then I heard on the radio that she had walked into the sea and committed suicide. Her depression had returned, and like Virginia Wolfe, she just could not battle another war. How far does depression ever go? If I finish this treatment and somehow feel better, will I wake up in six months, two years, ten years and find that instead of blood in my veins, the black, grainy, shit has returned? If I were putting a bet on depression leaving me forever, I would not expect good odds.

The other day a man was interviewed on the radio. This man had been a banker and then given up on this soulless career and became a foreign correspondent. Whilst working in a war-torn area he was shot six times and is now paralyzed from the waste down and is in constant pain. The interviewer inquired whether with hindsight he would have remained a banker and would thereby be able to walk today. The man being interviewed pondered this question and replied that we cannot turn time back and what is, is as it is, however, if the option where available to him, then he would have remained as a banker and kept his health.

I concur. Could I rewind to my eighteen year old self, I would have never have taken the path I did, and then in all probability I would not be writing this memoir, I would be happy, healthy and a fully functioning member of society with a job, paying taxes and with a plan. But what a bag of contradictions humans are, because I still want to be a nun, even now, after all the hellish experiences, I want to be a nun in a small parish in the Irish Republic. That is what I had in my grasp and there was nothing I could do to hold onto that precious vocation, it was torn from me because a wicked witch cast her evil spell and threw me into her cauldron to mix with the toads and snails. If there is a God, then why did this happen? Why, when I desired with every fiber of my being to work in his vineyard, was I deemed an illegal immigrant that had to be deported.

As you may have gathered from my little tale I have a preference for idioms, trouble at the mill, no point cryin' over split milk, do not look a gift horse in the mouth and so on. One saying that I do not care for is two sides of one coin due to over use, yet I find this idiom just perfect for this paragraph. My faith was my life and now I gaze on the other side of the tuppence because now there is no place in my present existence for faith. It is odd, how I have gone from short to tall, thin to fat, male to female, white to black, hard to soft, rose to weed, rich to poor, sight to blind, hearing to deaf, walking to cripple, worth to worthless, clever to stupid, married to spinster, fertile to barren, shod to discalced, warm to cold, sane to mad.

Religion fascinated me, any and every aspect of anything to do with God, Mary, the Saints, the Church, every iota was mesmerizing. Now I consider the whole thing rather dull and I see it as a mere social construct on the same level as maths or a crossword puzzle. Truly the other side of the coin.

Having this madness in my brain is like a person who has brittle bones who lives constantly in fear that an unexpected bang will bring disaster. Or a hemophiliac who stays where it is safe, wrapped in cotton wool, no chance of bleeding. I step out of my front door and I shake with fear that I will walk into a situation where I will 'lose it', fall apart, crumble, shout and scream at strangers, run to a toilet and huddle in a ball where the world cannot touch me. This is not an irrational fear, I know it, I have been there too many times to be idiotic enough not to realize that it will happen again. I do not know when, but it will happen. Should I stay at home 24-7? Yes, this will cause me to descend into a place where there is no coming back from, but at least I will not inflict my insanity on others. What a choice.

When I am in a black mood I see nothing of beauty, nothing makes me appreciate life, nothing causes me joy. When the dark mood hovers around my head like an evil halo I try any find pleasure in the small things of daily existence. So here is my list so far (in no particular order):

- Opening a new jar of coffee, the way the tea-spoon breaks through the seal. Pop.
- Pajamas, I appreciate comfy clothes. That feeling that when you come home, take off the day clothes and put on some soft, warm flannelette night attire.
- Finishing a crossword, realizing the old gray matter is still functioning. I particularly enjoy doing a crossword with my Mum.
- Snoop the Jack Russell. He is my best buddy. When I sit on my folk's couch with Snoopy on my knee and me stroking him, then I am at my happiest and most peaceful. If I was allowed a dog here in my bed-sit (it is private rent and it is not permitted) then I think my mental health would be a lot better.
- Receiving letters, an old fashioned paper letter. When I receive a letter I do not open it immediately, I wait till I have time, and I sit down with a cuppa and read in peace. Sometimes I even save the letter for a few days till I know I will not be disturbed.
- Getting undressed in the dark when the sparks. This was a joy I discovered in the convent, when I often had to get undressed in the dark and as I removed the layers the sparks would light up the air like fairy dust.
- A great cup of tea/coffee. Just as it was hard to find a decent cup of tea in Italy, it is just as difficult to find a decent cup of coffee in England, but what makes a decent cuppa great is the company. To sit down with someone I love and over two mugs we catch up on life then it becomes a thing of beauty. Save the champagne, give me a tea bag.
- Mum's home-cooked food. As you are well aware, I am a crap cook, but thankfully my Mum is an amazing woman in the kitchen (she is also amazing outside the kitchen). She feeds me and that is an act of motherly love.

- A book. 'Many people, myself among the feel better at the mere sight of a book.' (Jane Smiley). A good book is worth its weight in emeralds.
- A double-decker bus. The excitement I had as a child to rid on the top deck is still alive as I head for forty. Most buses as single decker so a double-decker is one big happiness fest.
- Dogs, they are uncomplicated and are easier to get on with than many humans. My best buddie is Snoop the Jack Russel.

I tend to go through periods of reading just one author, so when I was ten I devoured the entire corpus of Nancy Drew. When I was in my early twenties I was obsessed with the work of Albert Camus because he tended towards things being black and white, no gray areas and this resonated with my mind-set at the time. This is right, this is wrong, this is sin, this is virtue, this is courage, this is weakness, this is pure, this is unclean, this is good, this is bad, this is beautiful, this is ugly, no middle ground for me, ever. This is the reason I appreciate maths, this is the right answer, this is wrong.

Now I have experienced more of the pain of living, I tend to dwell in the gray areas, but I hope I will always confess that two plus two is four and not capitulate to those who want me to say it equals seven hundred and six.

So what does the future hold? Bo! At the Work Club I help people fill in applications for jobs so I am offey with the sort of questions prospective employers ask. If I was an employer and I received an application from me, with the gap in employment and my medical history I would soon shred my CV. So, will anyone every take a risk and employer this flaky ex-nun? I hope so. I want to be 'normal' with a job, Monday to Friday, nine to five, playing taxes and claiming no benefits, a two week summer holiday, on no medication and with a brain that is not wrapped in cotton wool, oh, and of course, a dog or two.

I am going to conclude with one last cliché,

NOTHING IS SETTLED, TILL IT IS SETTLED RIGHT.

I know what I think the right thing is...but I may have to bide my time to see a just conclusion to this abuse.

25715746R00081

Printed in Great Britain
by Amazon